Ext JS 4 First Look

A practical guide including examples of the new
features in Ext JS 4 and tips to migrate from Ext JS 3

Loiane Groner

PUBLISHING

BIRMINGHAM - MUMBAI

Ext JS 4 First Look

First published: December 2011

Production Reference: 1081211

Published by Packt Publishing Ltd.
Livery Place
35 Livery Street
Birmingham B3 2PB, UK.

ISBN 978-1-84951-666-2

www.packtpub.com

Cover Image by Parag Kadam (paragvkadam@gmail.com)

Credits

Author

Loiane Groner

Reviewers

Neil McCall

Olivier Pons

Paolo Tremadio

Acquisition Editor

Usha Iyer

Development Editor

Hyacintha D'Souza

Technical Editors

Pramila Balan

Merwine Machado

Copy Editor

Brandt D'Mello

Project Coordinator

Shubhanjan Chatterjee

Proofreader

Aaron Nash

Indexer

Rekha Nair

Production Coordinator

Arvindkumar Gupta

Cover Work

Arvindkumar Gupta

About the Author

Loiane Groner, Brazilian-born (and raised), lives in São Paulo and began her IT career developing Java web applications. While at university, she demonstrated great interest in IT. She worked as an assistant teacher for two and a half years, teaching algorithms, data structures, and computing theory. She represented her university at the ACM International Collegiate Programming Contest – Brazilian Finals (South America Regionals) and also worked as a Student Delegate of SBC (Brazilian Computing Society) for two years. She won a merit award in her senior year for being one of the top three students with better GPAs in the Computer Science department and also graduated with honors.

After three years of Java development, she got a job opportunity at IBM Brazil, where she developed Java and Ext JS applications for an American company, for two years. At IBM, she became the Team Leader and was responsible for training new hires in Java, XML, and Ext JS technologies. Nowadays, she works as a Senior Software Engineer at Citibank Brazilian Technology Solutions Center, where she develops overseas solutions. She also works as an independent Ext JS consultant and coach.

Loiane is passionate about Ext JS and Java, and she is the CampinasJUG (Campinas Java Users Group) Leader and ESJUG (Espirito Santo Java Users Group) coordinator; both are Brazilian JUGs.

Loiane also contributes to the software development community through her blogs, `http://loianegroner.com` (English) and `http://loiane.com` (Portuguese-BR), where she writes about careers in IT, Ext JS, Spring Framework, and general development notes.

I would like to thank my parents for giving me education, guidance, and advice, through all these years, and helping me to be a better human being and professional. A very special "thank-you" to my lovely husband, for being patient and supportive and giving me encouragement. Also, thanks to my friends for all the support.

About the Reviewers

Neil McCall graduated from University of Wales, Aberystwyth, with a degree in Software Engineering. Having already based his dissertation on Usability in User Interface Design, he then pursued his interest in GUI development and usability, through projects ranging from e-commerce websites to enterprise applications, employing bleeding-edge technologies over a variety of frameworks. Ext JS is Neil's first choice for client-side coding with JavaScript, which can be read about on his blog, `http://neiliscoding.blogspot.com/`, and also in his contributions to the Sencha site guides and forums.

Olivier Pons is a programmer and web developer who's been building websites since 1997. In 2011, he left a full-time job as a Delphi and PHP developer to concentrate on the development of his own websites. He currently runs a number of web sites, including `http://www.papdevis.fr` and `http://olivierpons.fr`, his own web development blog. He sometimes works as a consultant; he is specialized in website quality overview and is also a teacher at the University of Sciences of Aix-en-Provence, France, where he teaches C++, advanced VIM techniques, and Eclipse environment.

Paolo Tremadio is an Italian web developer and web designer, who is passionate about User Interface and User Experience. He grew up in a family of advertisers, who inspired him to take courses in principles, visual design, enhancing creativity, and understanding web technology. A few years before jQuery came out, he took JavaScript, and he loved JS from the first line of code.

He has the *1000 ideas syndrome*; currently, he works at a startup in London, while being a consultant for various companies in the UK as well as Italy. His passion is to use technology every day in order to enhance the quality of life.

www.PacktPub.com

Support files, eBooks, discount offers and more

You might want to visit www.PacktPub.com for support files and downloads related to your book.

Did you know that Packt offers eBook versions of every book published, with PDF and ePub files available? You can upgrade to the eBook version at www.PacktPub.com and as a print book customer, you are entitled to a discount on the eBook copy. Get in touch with us at service@packtpub.com for more details.

At www.PacktPub.com, you can also read a collection of free technical articles, sign up for a range of free newsletters and receive exclusive discounts and offers on Packt books and eBooks.

http://PacktLib.PacktPub.com

Do you need instant solutions to your IT questions? PacktLib is Packt's online digital book library. Here, you can access, read and search across Packt's entire library of books.

Why Subscribe?

- Fully searchable across every book published by Packt
- Copy and paste, print and bookmark content
- On demand and accessible via web browser

Free Access for Packt account holders

If you have an account with Packt at www.PacktPub.com, you can use this to access PacktLib today and view nine entirely free books. Simply use your login credentials for immediate access.

Table of Contents

Preface

Ext JS 4 introduces major changes compared to Ext JS 3. There is a new data package, new charts, and new, updated layouts. The framework was completely rewritten to boost performance.

This book covers all the major changes and new features of Ext JS 4 using code examples, explanation, and screenshots of the result of the code. This book will help you understand the framework changes and you will be able to easily migrate Ext JS 3 applications and develop new Ext JS 4 applications using the presented examples.

What this book covers

Chapter 1, What's New in Ext JS 4, provides an introduction to all major changes between Ext JS 3 and Ext JS 4. Ext JS 4 presents a vast improvement in all packages; the framework was completely rewritten to boost performance and make learning and configuring easy. This chapter covers all these changes, from class system, to an overview, to the new Sencha platform.

Chapter 2, The New Data Package, covers all the changes in the data package, which is shared with Sencha Touch framework now. This chapter introduces the new Model class, associations, proxies, operations, batches, and the new features of the Store class.

Chapter 3, Upgraded Layouts, covers the changes made to the existing layouts, and the new component layout engines, such as dock, toolbar, field, and trigger field layouts. It also covers the changes made to the container layouts, such as fit, border, table, anchor, card, accordion, and so on.

Chapter 4, *Upgraded Charts*, presents the new JavaScript-powered Ext JS 4 charts. No flash is required anymore. This chapter introduces the new draw package, which is the base package for the new chart package. It also covers how to configure chart axis, legend, customized themes, and Ext JS 4 chart series, such as Bar, Column, Line, Area, Scatter, Pie, Radar, and Gauge.

Chapter 5, *Upgraded Grid, Tree, and Form*, presents and demonstrates the upgraded Ext JS Components. The Components enable faster performance and more developer flexibility. Some new features and plugins for Components covered in this chapter are: grid, tree, and forms.

Chapter 6, *Ext JS 4 Themes*, presents a step-by-step approach on how to customize and create new themes using the new CSS architecture, which uses Sass and Compass.

Chapter 7, *MVC Application Architecture*, provides an overview about the new MVC architecture applied to Ext JS 4 applications. This chapter covers how to structure an application using the MVC pattern and how to create and organize the components and files in an Ext project structure. This chapter demonstrates a step-by-step approach on how to create an MVC Ext JS 4 application.

Appendix A, *Ext JS 4 Versus Ext JS 3 Class Names*, presents a comparison list between Ext JS 3 classes and Ext JS 4 class names. In this new version of Ext JS, the names of some classes have changed, and this list can help you find the new Ext JS 4 class names easily, while migrating an application from Ext JS 3 to Ext JS 4 Beta.

What you need for this book

The source code listed in this book uses the Ext JS 4 SDK, available from the Ext JS website http://www.sencha.com/products/extjs/download. You need to download and install the SDK in order to run the code presented in this book.

Some chapters of this book present some tips and tricks that require Sencha SDK Tools. You can download it at http://www.sencha.com/products/sdk-tools/.

To create new themes, you need to have Ruby installed. Mac OS and some Linux distributions already come installed. If you are using Windows, you need to install it from http://rubyinstaller.org/. This book will also provide more details about how to install and use it.

It is recommended that you use a JavaScript debugger, such as Firebug or Chrome Developer Tools, when running the code.

Who this book is for

This book is written for web developers who are familiar with Ext JS 3 and want to have detailed insights into the new features of Ext JS 4. And even if you are migrating an application from Ext JS 3 to Ext JS 4, this book is for you.

Conventions

In this book, you will find a number of styles of text that distinguish between different kinds of information. Here are some examples of these styles, and an explanation of their meaning.

Code words in text are shown as follows: "For example, in Ext JS 3, classes such as, `PagingToolbar`, `Toolbar`, and `Spacer`, are grouped under the package widgets (along with other classes)."

A block of code is set as follows:

```
MyApp.NewClass = Ext.extend(Object, {
    //class functionalities here
});
```

When we wish to draw your attention to a particular part of a code block, the relevant lines or items are set in bold:

```
Ext.define('MyApp.MyWindow', {
    extend: 'Ext.Window',

    title: 'Welcome!',

    initComponent: function() {

        this.items = [{
            xtype: 'textfield',
            name: 'tfName',
            fieldLabel: 'Enter your name'
        }],

        this.callParent(arguments);
    }
});

var win = Ext.create('MyApp.MyWindow');
win.show();
```

New terms and **important words** are shown in bold. Words that you see on the screen, in menus or dialog boxes for example, appear in the text like this: "If user clicks on the **Next Step** button, we will increase the `active` index because we want to navigate to the next page, and decrease the `active` index otherwise."

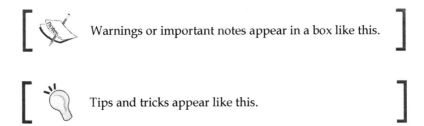

Warnings or important notes appear in a box like this.

Tips and tricks appear like this.

Reader feedback

Feedback from our readers is always welcome. Let us know what you think about this book—what you liked or may have disliked. Reader feedback is important for us to develop titles that you really get the most out of.

To send us general feedback, simply send an e-mail to `feedback@packtpub.com`, and mention the book title via the subject of your message.

If there is a book that you need and would like to see us publish, please send us a note in the **SUGGEST A TITLE** form on `www.packtpub.com` or e-mail `suggest@packtpub.com`.

If there is a topic that you have expertise in and you are interested in either writing or contributing to a book, see our author guide on `www.packtpub.com/authors`.

Customer support

Now that you are the proud owner of a Packt book, we have a number of things to help you to get the most from your purchase.

Downloading the example code

You can download the example code files for all Packt books you have purchased from your account at `http://www.PacktPub.com`. If you purchased this book elsewhere, you can visit `http://www.PacktPub.com/support` and register to have the files e-mailed directly to you.

Errata

Although we have taken every care to ensure the accuracy of our content, mistakes do happen. If you find a mistake in one of our books—maybe a mistake in the text or the code—we would be grateful if you would report this to us. By doing so, you can save other readers from frustration and help us improve subsequent versions of this book. If you find any errata, please report them by visiting http://www.packtpub.com/support, selecting your book, clicking on the **errata submission form** link, and entering the details of your errata. Once your errata are verified, your submission will be accepted and the errata will be uploaded on our website, or added to any list of existing errata, under the Errata section of that title. Any existing errata can be viewed by selecting your title from http://www.packtpub.com/support.

Piracy

Piracy of copyright material on the Internet is an ongoing problem across all media. At Packt, we take the protection of our copyright and licenses very seriously. If you come across any illegal copies of our works, in any form, on the Internet, please provide us with the location address or website name immediately so that we can pursue a remedy.

Please contact us at copyright@packtpub.com with a link to the suspected pirated material.

We appreciate your help in protecting our authors, and our ability to bring you valuable content.

Questions

You can contact us at questions@packtpub.com if you are having a problem with any aspect of the book, and we will do our best to address it.

1
What's New in Ext JS 4?

Ext JS 4 is the biggest overhaul that has been made to the Ext framework. These changes include a new class system, introduction of a new platform, many API changes and enhancements, and new components, such as the new charts and new draw components. Ext JS 4 is faster, more stable, and easy to use.

In this chapter, you will learn the following:

- How to get started with Ext JS 4
- How the Ext JS platform is now organized
- The new Ext JS 4 class system
- Ext JS 4 SDK
- Ext JS 3 versus Ext JS 4 compatibility
- Migrating from Ext JS 3 to Ext JS 4
- A quick overview of new components

Getting started with Ext JS 4

Ext JS is a cross-browser RIA (Rich Internet Application) framework, easy to use with rich UI components, used by one million developers around the world.

The change from Ext JS 1.x to Ext JS 2.x was a major refactoring, including the Component model creation, along with refactoring of many of the existing components. The Ext JS 3.x is backward-compatible with Ext JS 2.x.

Until Ext JS 3, the layout was what expanded most of the time while rendering the application. Ext JS 4 has a vast improvement in this area. The generated HTML was also updated in branch 4.x.

Sencha also created more than 4000 unit tests to provide a more stable framework with 90% code coverage. If a new change is made, they know if anything breaks far before it is released.

Some API improvements include standardized API with name conventions and a simpler configuration (you write fewer lines of code to achieve the same results as with previous versions).

Package and namespace updates

Some API improvements include standardized API with a name convention.

For example, in Ext JS 3, classes such as `PagingToolbar`, `Toolbar`, and `Spacer` are grouped under the package widgets (along with other classes). These classes are also defined directly on the Ext global object, which means you can access them through `Ext.PagingToolbar`, `Ext.Toolbar`, and so on.

In Ext JS 4, every class has been placed into packages and namespaces, based on its functionality. For example, `PagingToolbar`, `Toolbar`, `Spacer` and other toolbar-related classes are now grouped into the new toolbar package and are grouped into a new `Ext.toolbar` namespace. Some of the classes were also renamed based on the new namespaces.

Other packages, such as button, view, picker, slider, tab, window, tip, tab, and menu (along with many others), follow this new package name and namespace update as well. A full list of these changes is provided in *Appendix A, Ext JS 4 Versus Ext JS 3 Class Names*.

All the classes that were reorganized are still available via the new `alternateClassName` property, so Ext JS 3 class names will still work under Ext JS 4. For example, the alternative class name of `Ext.toolbar.PagingToolbar` is `Ext.PagingToolbar`. You can read the list of all Ext JS 4 alternative class names in *Appendix A, Ext JS 4 Versus Ext JS 3 Class Names*.

Although we are using the new alternate class name property, it is recommended that you migrate to the new convention names in your code. For example, in Ext JS 3, we have the Ext.PagingToolbar component. In Ext JS 4, we can create a new instance declaring `Ext.create(Ext.PagingToolbar)`, using `PagingToolbar` (Ext JS 3 name). But, it is highly recommended not to use the alternative class name (Ext JS 3 name), since we have a new name for this class in Ext JS 4 (`Ext.create(Ext.toolbar.PagingToolbar)`).

Upgraded documentation

The Ext JS 4 documentation is one of its most-used resources, because it is easy to use. The Ext documentation has always been good, with a clean and easy to use UI (User Interface). We will learn how to access the documentation offline, but we can also access it online at `http://docs.sencha.com/ext-js/4-0`.

The documentation from previous versions was a little vague, with some examples that sometimes were not very useful. When you first open the documentation, you will see a welcome page. At the top-left corner, we will see the following tabs: **Home**, **API Documentation**, **Guides**, **Videos**, and **Examples**.

When we click on the **API Documentation** tab, we will see the list of all packages on the left side and the center portion. There will be a list of the most relevant classes organized in the following topics: **Base**, **View**, **Components**, **Data**, and **Utilities**.

We can visualize the list of Ext JS classes by package or by inheritance.

When you click on a class, its documentation will get opened in the center portion of the screen. All the content is loaded via AJAX, as we can see in the following screenshot:

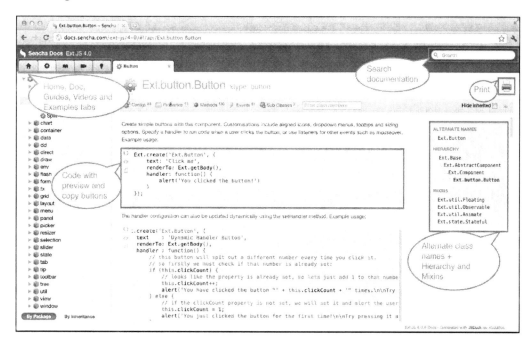

On the top of the page, you will see an icon indicating whether the class you have opened is a singleton class or a component, followed by the class name. If it is a component, the xType (when available) will be displayed as well.

Below the class name, you will see a menu with the following options: **Configs**, **Properties**, **Methods**, **Events**, **Super Classes**, and **Sub Classes** (depending on the class, some of these items will be not available), followed by a search field, where you can easily find a particular property, config, method, and so on.

Then there is a description of what the class does, and, when available, an example showing how to use it. Some of the portions of code available in the documentation have a preview option, so we can see what the code would output if we executed it.

On the right side of the **Document** tab we have opened, we can see the **ALTERNATE NAMES** of the current class, the **HIERARCHY**, and the list of the **MIXINS** of this class. Ext JS 4 documentation also has added support for deprecated members.

There is also a **Print** button we can click on, by which a print version of the class documentation will be presented.

On the top-right corner of the Ext JS 4 API documentation, we can see a **Search** box, where we can search for any Ext JS class name, method, configuration option, property, event, and mixins. This update is very useful for daily work. Ext JS 3 allowed searching for class names only.

The new documentation also includes official Ext JS 4 **guides** to some of the most relevant features of the framework.

As you can see, the Ext JS 4 documentation is improved and is more user-friendly. But is the usage of the API easier to use? Let's take a look at it.

Ext JS 4 SDK quick look

When we download the Ext JS 4 SDK from the Sencha website, we get a zip file. After downloading it, uncompress it to a folder, preferably named *extjs*.

This is how the Ext JS 4 SDK should look:

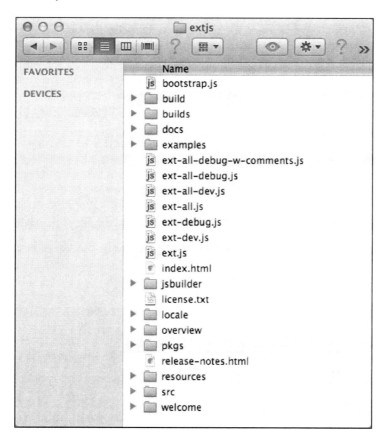

First, let's take a look at the JavaScript files located in the root folder (*extjs*):

- **ext-all.js**: This file contains the entire Ext JS framework, everything we need
- **ext.js**: This file contains the minimum Ext JS code (Ext JS base library)

If we take a closer look at the previous screenshot, we will see there are more than three versions of the `ext-all.js` file and two versions of the `ext.js` file. How and when do we use these files? What is the difference between them?

ext-all.js or **ext.js**: These are minified files; recommended for use in production environments.

*-dev.js: This file is not minified and contains the debug code; recommended for use in development or testing environments.

*-debug.js or ***-debug-w-comments**: These are not minified and do not contain the debug code; recommended for use in testing environments. The file `*-debug-w-comments` is bigger than the `*-debug.js` file and we should avoid using it if the editor is having memory issues.

The SDK also includes the documentation, examples, and the complete source code:

- **docs**: This contains the complete documentation (you need to deploy it on a local server to be able to run it). You can also access it online at `http://docs.sencha.com/ext-js/4-0/`.

- **examples**: This contains examples of how to use Ext JS components.

- **overview**: This contains a quick overview file with the list of new features, a commented release note.

- **pkgs**: This contains the Ext JS modules, packaged up.

- **resources**: This contains the CSS and image files used by the Ext themes.

- **src**: This is the complete Ext JS source code.

- **welcome**: This contains image files used by the `index.html` file, located in the `root` folder.

- **builds**: This contains additional Ext JS files.

- **jsbuilder**: This contains the files for JSBuilder, a project building tool.

For more information about JSBuilder, please go to `http://www.sencha.com/products/jsbuilder`.

Inside the `builds` folder, we will find the following files:

- **ext-all-sandbox.js**: Ext JS 4 is sandboxed and this is the file that replaces **ext-all.js** and **ext-base.js** in sandbox mode
- **ext-core.js**: This is Ext JS core library
- **ext-foundation.js**: This is the foundation library for Ext JS 4
- These files also have the **debug** and **dev** versions.

> Note that the adapter folder is no longer in the Ext JS 4 SDK.

What is the difference between ext.js and ext-all.js?

When we start the development of a new Ext JS project, the first thing we have to do is to add the imports of Ext JS files on the HTML page. If we choose a version of the **ext-all** file, the browser will load the entire Ext JS framework. If we choose a version of the **ext.js** file, the browser will load the minimum code required to execute the application, and we can make use of the new dynamic loading feature.

For development and testing, we can use **ext.js**, because it will use only the required Ext JS code to run the application; but, we cannot forget to add the **src** folder to the application **extjs** directory. For production, we can use the **ext-all.js** file, because it already contains the entire Ext JS framework and has good performance.

> There is also a file named **bootstrap.js**; instead of importing **ext-all.js** into your HTML page, you can import **bootstrap.js**. The only thing that this file does is import **ext-all.js** or **ext-all-debug.js**, depending on the environment you are using. It will load **ext-all-debug.js** in the following cases:
>
> 1. Current hostname is localhost.
> 2. Current hostname is an IP(v4) address.
> 3. Current protocol is a file.
> 4. Otherwise, bootstrap will load the **ext-all.js** file.

Deploying Ext JS locally

Some examples and the documentation use Ajax calls to load their content. If we try to load these examples locally, they will not work. To see them in our local computer, we have to deploy `extjs` on a local server. To do so, we simply need to place the `extjs` folder inside the web root folder of the local web server. Depending on the operating system you are using your web root directory will be located at:

- Windows: `C:\Program Files\Apache Software Foundation\Apache2.2\htdocs`
- Linux: `/var/www/`
- Mac OS X: `/Library/WebServer/Documents/`

After doing that, we can access Ext JS locally at the URL `http://localhost/extjs/index.html`.

In the next topic, we will start showing some code snippets of the new Ext JS 4 features. As we deployed Ext JS 4 locally, we will also create the example code in a web server. To do so, we will create a folder named *ext4firstlook* to host the code presented in this book. And, as we are on *Chapter 1*, we will place the code in *ext4firstlook/chapter01*.

The new Ext JS 4 class system

Ext JS has always provided a class system of its own; this enables developers to write code with a more object-oriented approach, since JavaScript has no classes of its own. Ext JS 4 introduces a new class system to make development easier and more flexible and also introduces some new features. These changes are backward-compatible with the Ext JS 3 class system. The new features are as follows:

- Class definition and creation
- Mixins
- Automatic getters and setters
- Dynamic class loading
- Statics

Class definition and creation

Ext JS 4 introduces the `Ext.define` and `Ext.create` functions to define and create new classes.

In this topic, we will see how to create a new Ext JS class from scratch and how to instantiate it using the new capabilities of Ext JS 4.

Creating a new class

To define a new class using Ext JS 3, we have to extend the `Object` class as follows:

```
MyApp.NewClass = Ext.extend(Object, {
    //class functionalities here
});
```

Downloading the example code

You can download the example code files for all Packt books you have purchased using your account at `http://www.PacktPub.com`. If you purchased this book elsewhere, you can visit `http://www.PacktPub.com/support` and register to have the files e-mailed directly to you.

In Ext JS 4, we define a new class as follows:

```
Ext.define('MyApp.NewClass', {
    //class functionalities here
});
```

The `Ext.extend` is deprecated; it is recommended to use `Ext.define` instead.

Extending a class

Let's compare the code between Ext JS 3 and Ext JS 4 to create the following customized window (extending `Ext.Window`):

This is how we do it in Ext JS 3:

```
Ext.namespace('MyApp');

MyApp.MyWindow = Ext.extend(Ext.Window, {

    title: 'Welcome!',

    initComponent: function() {
        Ext.apply(this, {
            items: [
                {
                    xtype: 'textfield',
                    name: 'tfName',
                    fieldLabel: 'Enter your name'
                }
            ]
        });

        MyApp.MyWindow.superclass.initComponent.apply(this, arguments);
    }
});

var win = new MyApp.MyWindow();
win.show();
```

There is nothing wrong with the code above, right? Correct. But, if you forget to declare the namespace, you will get the error MyApp is not defined; if, when you are loading your application, Ext.Window is not defined as well, you will also get an error and your application will crash.

In Ext JS 4, these problems are resolved with the use of Ext.define:

```
Ext.define('MyApp.MyWindow', {
    extend: 'Ext.Window',

    title: 'Welcome!',

    initComponent: function() {

        this.items = [{
            xtype: 'textfield',
            name: 'tfName',
            fieldLabel: 'Enter your name'
        }],
```

```
        this.callParent(arguments);
    }
});

var win = Ext.create('MyApp.MyWindow');
win.show();
```

We can refer to Ext classes using string, which means we will not get the errors mentioned previously. Ext JS 4 class manager will check if Ext.Window has been defined already, and if not, will defer the creation of MyApp.MyWindow until it is defined. This way, we do not have to maintain a load order in our applications; the Ext framework will manage everything.

Another difference we can see in the code is the simplified call to the superclass to apply the subclass arguments. Instead of calling MyApp.MyWindow. superclass.initComponent.apply(this, arguments), we simply call this. callParent(arguments).

And instead of instantiating the MyApp.MyWindow class using the keyword new, we use the Ext.create function.

We can still use the new keyword to instantiate Ext JS classes instead of Ext.create, but then we will not have all the benefits of Ext JS 4 class system features; we will talk about these features in the next topic.

The Ext.define is an alias of Ext.ClassManager.create, and Ext.create is an alias of Ext.ClassManager.instantiate.

Another benefit of using Ext.define is that it will automatically detect and create new namespaces, as needed.

 Note that we do not have to specify the MyApp namespace in Ext JS 4. The framework will detect that it has not been created and will create it.

Mixins

The mixins configuration is a brand new concept for Ext JS. Mixins define reusable sets of behavior and configuration that can be 'mixed in' to a class. In other words, it allows merging new capabilities (functions or properties) to the class prototype.

 For more information about the mixins concept, please read http://en.wikipedia.org/wiki/Mixin.

It is very similar to the `Ext.override` function, but it does not replace (override) the existing methods.

The mixin can be as simple as follows:

```
Ext.define('MyApp.mixins.Log', {
    startLogging: function() {
        console.log('called funcion startLogging');
    }
});
```

And this is how we configure the mixin in a class:

```
Ext.define('MyApp.MyWindow', {
    extend: 'Ext.Window',

    mixins: {
        console: 'MyApp.mixins.Log'
    },

    ...
});
```

Note that we referenced all class names by string, thus we do not get any errors if the mixins are not loaded on the page yet.

When we instantiate the `MyApp.MyWindow`, we can call the `startLogging` function:

```
var win = Ext.create('MyApp.MyWindow');
win.startLogging();
```

And the following screenshot shows the output (simply writes **called funcion startLogging** on the console):

You can have as many `mixins` in a class as you want; it is a great way to get multiple inheritance.

Config (auto setters and getters)

Ext JS 4 introduces the `config` declaration. There are some classes in Ext JS; you can pass some configuration parameters and you can change these parameters at runtime using getter and setter methods. When you configure properties in the `config` declaration, Ext JS 4 will automatically generate four methods: getter, setter, reset, and apply.

Let's apply the `config` declaration on the `MyApp.MyWindow` class:

```
Ext.define('MyApp.MyWindow', {
    extend: 'Ext.Window',

    config: {
        title: 'Welcome!'
    }

});
```

In the preceding code, the default value for title is `Welcome!`.

Note that now that we have configured the `title` property inside the `config`, the framework will create the following methods automatically for you:

- getTitle: This returns the current title.
- setTitle: This will set a new value for title.
- resetTitle: This will set the title to its default value.
- applyTitle: This method is called every time `setTitle` is called. You can implement a custom code for it.

After we instantiate the `MyApp.MyWindow` class, we can call any of these methods:

```
var win = Ext.create('MyApp.MyWindow');
win.setTitle('I changed the title');
win.show();
```

The following screenshot shows our output:

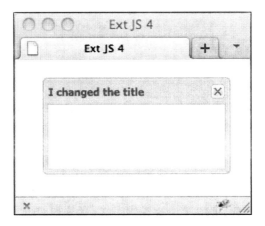

In Ext JS 3.3, we had to manually create it:

```
Ext.namespace('MyApp');

MyApp.MyWindow = Ext.extend(Ext.Window, {

    title: 'Welcome!',

    getTitle: function() {
        return this.title;
    },

    resetTitle: function() {
        this.setTitle('Welcome!');
    },

    setTitle: function(newTitle) {
        this.title = this.applyTitle(newTitle) || newTitle;
    },

    applyTitle: function(newTitle) {
        this.title = newTitle;
    }
});
```

If you need to override any of these methods for any reason, it is very simple. You just need to add the code to your class declaration:

```
Ext.define('MyApp.MyWindow', {
    extend: 'Ext.Window',

    config: {
        title: 'Welcome!'
    },

    applyTitle: function(newTitle) {
        this.title = 'Updated to: '+newTitle;
    }
});
```

This automatic generation of code will save a lot of development time, save some lines of code (and this means your code will be smaller), and add a name convention, resulting in a more consistent API.

Dynamic class loading

The dynamic class loading system is another new feature for Ext JS 4. It also provides an integrated dependency management system.

This new feature is optional and you should avoid using it in production, though it is very useful for the development environment. We are going to learn why it is so useful:

In previous versions of Ext JS, if you wanted to use the following code, you had to wait until the entire framework was loaded, correct? If you tried to use it before the framework was loaded, you would probably get an error:

```
var win = new Ext.Window({
    title : 'Hello!',
    width : 100,
    height: 50
});
win.show();
```

This behavior changes in Ext JS 4. We can ask Ext JS to load the classes that we need to use and then call a function when it is finished loading. For example:

```
Ext.require('Ext.Window', function() {
    var win = new Ext.Window({
        title : 'Hello!',
        width : 100,
```

```
        height: 50
    });
    win.show();
});
```

When we use `Ext.require`, we are telling Ext JS we need `Ext.Window` before calling the function. The framework will also resolve any dependencies that the loaded class has.

To use this feature, you have to use `Ext.define` and define the dependencies in the code using two new class properties:

- Requires: This declares the class dependencies required for a class to work. These classes are going to be loaded before the current class gets instantiated.

- Uses: This declares the optional class dependencies, but is not required. These classes do not have to be available before the current class gets instantiated.

The `Loader` is recursive. If any class has dependencies that are not yet loaded, it will keep loading all the required classes until all of them are ready. All these dependencies are managed internally. This means you do not need to manage all those script tags in the HTML page, because the class loader will do it for you. This kind of flexibility is very useful in the development environment, when this is more important than page speed.

You have to be careful with deadlocks. When you declare your own classes, make sure there is no deadlock; otherwise, your application may crash. For example, let's say we have the following classes: A, B, and C. Class A extends class B, class B extends class C, and class C extends class A, as shown in the following code:

```
Ext.define('deadlock.A', {
    extend: 'deadlock.B'
});

Ext.define('deadlock.B', {
    extend: 'deadlock.C'
});

Ext.define('deadlock.C', {
    extend: 'deadlock.A'
});
```

Now, we are going to try to execute a function that requires class A:

```
Ext.Loader.setConfig({
    enabled: true,
    paths: {'deadlock':'deadlock'}
});

Ext.onReady(function(){

    Ext.require(['deadlock.A'], function() {
        alert("Loaded: " + Ext.Loader.history.join(" => "));
    });

});
```

In the HTML file, we are not going to import the files A, B, and C. That is because we are using the `Ext.Loader`. In this configuration, we can point to a directory where the files we need are located All the three files belong to the deadlock package, so they are located in the deadlock folder, as shown in the following screenshot:

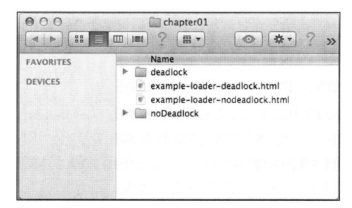

This way, we can configure as many package names as we need. Note that we are only importing the basic Ext JS files in the HTML:

```
<html>
<title>Ext JS 4</title>
</head>

    <link rel="stylesheet" type="text/css" href="../extjs/resources/
css/ext-all.css" />
    <script type="text/javascript" src="../extjs/ext-all-debug.js"></
script>
```

```
      <script type="text/javascript">
       //our code here
      </script>
<body>
</body>
</html>
```

And if you try to execute the preceding code, you will get the following error:

```
Uncaught Error: [Ext.Loader] Deadlock detected! 'deadlock.C' and
'deadlock.A' mutually require each others. Path: deadlock.C ->
deadlock.A -> deadlock.B -> deadlock.C

Uncaught Error: [Ext.Loader] The following classes are not declared
even if their files have been loaded: deadlock.A, deadlock.B,
deadlock.C. Please check the source code of their corresponding files
for possible typos:
deadlock/A.js,
deadlock/B.js,
deadlock/C.js
```

Because of the dependencies, the Ext management system will try to load C
for the first class. But C needs class A, and so on. This will lead us to a loop,
causing a deadlock.

Now let's take a look at another example. We have three classes: A (which extends
B and has a mixin named Mixin), B (which extends C), and C (which uses A).
Remember the keyword uses does a reference to the classes that *are not required* to be
loaded before the class is instantiated. In this case, we will not have a deadlock:

```
Ext.define('noDeadlock.A', {
    extend: 'noDeadlock.B',

    mixins: {
        console: 'noDeadlock.Mixin'
    }
});

Ext.define('noDeadlock.B', {
    extend: 'noDeadlock.C'
});

Ext.define('noDeadlock.C', {
    uses: 'noDeadlock.A'
});
```

```
Ext.define('noDeadlock.Mixin', {
    log: function() {
        console.log('called function log');
    }
});
```

In the HTML page, we are going to import only the necessary files to load our code. We are not going to include the classes A, B, C, and Mixin.

```
<html>
<head>
<title>Ext JS 4</title>
</head>

    <link rel="stylesheet" type="text/css" href="../extjs/resources/
css/ext-all.css" />
        <script type="text/javascript" src="../extjs/ext-all-debug.js"></
script>

    <script type="text/javascript">
        //our code here
    </script>

<body>
</body>
</html>
```

To import the classes which are in the js/myApp folder, we are going to use the Ext. Loader class, which will take care of everything for us:

```
Ext.Loader.setConfig({
    enabled: true,
    paths: {'noDeadlock':'noDeadlock'}
});

Ext.onReady(function(){

    Ext.require(['noDeadlock.A'], function() {
        alert("Loaded: " + Ext.Loader.history.join(" => "));
    });

});
```

And when we execute this code, we have the following output:

```
Loaded: noDeadlock.Mixin => noDeadlock.C => noDeadlock.B =>
noDeadlock.A
```

This new class system is 100% backward-compatible.

Statics

In Ext JS 4, any class can define static methods, which means you do not need to instantiate the class to call the method; you can call `ClassName.methodName()`.

To declare a static method or property, simply define it as `statics` in its class property.

Let's take a look at the following example:

```
Ext.define('MyApp.Math', {

    statics: {
        count: 0,
        appName: 'Math',

        sum: function(number1, number2) {
            return number1 + number2;
        }
    },

    constructor: function() {
        this.statics().count++;
        console.log('You instantiated the class: ' + this.self.
appName);
        console.log('App Name: ' + this.statics().appName);
          console.log('Count is: ' + this.statics().count);
    }

});
```

The class `MyApp.Math` contains two static properties—`count` and `appName`. This means we can access the value of these properties without instantiating the class as follows:

```
MyApp.Math.count;
MyApp.Math.appName;
```

We can also access the method sum:

```
MyApp.Math.sum(1,2); //output is 3
```

Now let's take a closer look at the constructor code to see how we can access these properties outside the statics declaration. When you use `this.statics()` you have access to any static property or method inside the class. When you use `this.self.propertyName`, it depends on which instance you are referring to. It is important if you work with inheritance.

For example, let's declare a class named `MyApp.MoreMath`, extending `MyApp.Math`:

```
Ext.define('MyApp.MoreMath', {
    extend: 'MyApp.Math',

    statics: {
        appName: 'MoreMath',

        multiply: function(number1, number2) {
            return number1 * number2;
        }
    },

    constructor: function() {
        this.callParent();
    }

});
```

Note, we also declared (override) a static property called `appName` with a different value from the super class. Also note that when we instantiate, we call the super class constructor. In this case, `this.statics().appName` does a reference to the `MyApp.Math.appName` (which is `Math`) and the `this.self.appName` does a reference to the current object, which is `MyApp.MoreMath.appName` (with value equals to `MoreMath`).

Execute the following code:

```
var math1 = new MyApp.Math();
var math2 = new MyApp.Math();
var moreMath = new MyApp.MoreMath();
```

We will have the following output:

```
You instantiated the class: Math
App Name: Math
Count is: 1
You instantiated the class: Math
App Name: Math
Count is: 2
You instantiated the class: MoreMath
App Name: Math
Count is: 3
```

If you try to execute `MyApp.MoreMath.sum()`, you will get the error `MyApp.MoreMath.sum is not a function`. The static methods from superclass are not public in the subclass.

Migrating from Ext JS 3 to Ext JS 4

Ext JS 4 introduces major changes in its architecture, core system, and widgets. Most classes were refactored. We already know how the new class system works. We are going to introduce you to the new changes and new widgets. Also, there are some changes that are not compatible with Ext JS 3. To help you to migrate from Ext JS 3 to Ext JS 4, there are some tools that can help you.

Adapters

In previous versions of Ext JS, you were able to use Ext JS along with other third-party frameworks, such as jQuery, Prototype, and YUI, and Ext provided a special adapter so you could use these frameworks.

For example, if you want to use Ext along with jQuery, you have to import jQuery files, then **ext-jquery-adapter.js**, and then **ext-all.js**; only then would you be able to implement Ext code along with jQuery code, on the same page.

The following diagram illustrates how adapters worked until Ext JS 3:

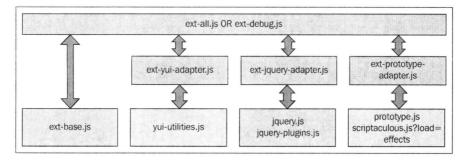

In Ext JS 4, the adapter support has been discontinued. However, this does not mean you cannot use third-party libraries along with Ext JS anymore. They are no longer supported as base library dependencies for Ext JS, but you can still use them in addition to Ext JS files.

The following diagram illustrates how to use third-party libraries with Ext JS 4:

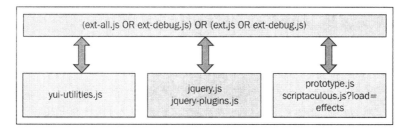

For example, until Ext JS 3, if we wanted to use jQuery along with Ext JS on the same page, this is how we would do it:

```
<script type="text/javascript" src="adapters/jquery.js"></script>
<script type="text/javascript" src="http://extjs.cachefly.net/ext-
3.3.1/adapter/jquery/ext-jquery-adapter-debug.js"></script>
<script type="text/javascript" src="http://extjs.cachefly.net/ext-
3.3.1/ext-all-debug.js"></script>
```

To keep compatibility with your legacy code is very simple; you have to remove the ext-jquery-adapter:

```
<link rel="stylesheet" type="text/css" href="../extjs/resources/css/
ext-all.css" />
<script type="text/javascript" src="../extjs/ext-all-debug.js"></
script>
<script type="text/javascript" src="adapters/jquery.js"></script>
```

JavaScript compatibility file

This JavaScript file contains the aliases and necessary overrides to make most of the Ext JS 3 code run under Ext JS 4.

You can use this file while you migrate all your Ext JS 3 code to Ext JS 4. It is recommended that you do not use this file as a permanent solution; use it only until you finish migrating to Ext JS 4.

 You can read how to properly use the JavaScript compatibility file in *Appendix A, Ext JS 4 Versus Ext JS 3 Class Names*.

Sandbox mode

Ext JS 4 is sandboxed, which means you can run Ext JS 4 alongside with previous versions of Ext JS on the same page.

The distributed release comes with the following sandbox mode files:

- `ext-all-sandbox.js`
- `ext-all-sandbox-debug.js`
- `ext-all-sandbox-dev.js`

To use Ext JS 4 in the sandbox mode, you need to import the `ext-all` sandbox files and the `ext-sandbox.css` file as well. To make the Ext JS 4 code work along with code from previous versions, you need to alias the global `Ext` object to a different name (for example, `Ext4`) and it will be isolated from the previous version's code.

Let's say you have the following page implemented with Ext JS 3:

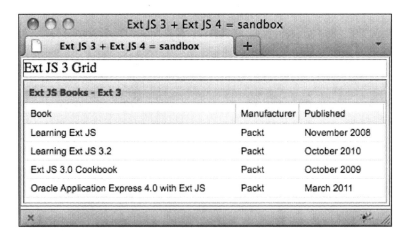

The following is the HTML code used to render the grid. As you can see, we are importing the default Ext JS 3 files `ext-all.css` and `ext-all.js`:

```
<html>
<head>
<title>Ext JS 3 + Ext JS 4 = sandbox</title>

    <link rel="stylesheet" type="text/css" href="http://extjs.cachefly.
net/ext-3.3.1/resources/css/ext-all.css" />
    <script type="text/javascript" src="http://extjs.cachefly.net/ext-
3.3.1/adapter/ext/ext-base-debug.js"></script>
    <script type="text/javascript" src="http://extjs.cachefly.net/ext-
3.3.1/ext-all-debug.js"></script>

    <script type="text/javascript" src="sandbox/grid-ext3.js"></script>

</head>
<body>
    <table border="1">
        <tr>
            <td>Ext JS 3 Grid</td>
        </tr>
        <tr>
            <td><div id="grid3"></div></td>
        </tr>
    </table>
</body>
</html>
```

We are also importing the `grid-ext3.js` file, which contains the Ext JS 3 code to render the grid— a very simple grid:

```
Ext.onReady(function(){

    // static data for the store
    var myData = [
        ['Learning Ext JS',                      'Packt',
'November 2008'],
        ['Learning Ext JS 3.2',                  'Packt',
'October 2010'],
        ['Ext JS 3.0 Cookbook',                  'Packt',
'October 2009'],
        ['Oracle Application Express 4.0 with Ext JS', 'Packt', 'March
2011']
    ];
```

```
// create the data store
var store = new Ext.data.ArrayStore({
    fields: [
        {name: 'book'},
        {name: 'manufacturer'},
        {name: 'published',  type: 'date', dateFormat: 'F Y'},
    ]
});

// manually load local data
store.loadData(myData);

// create the Grid
var grid = new Ext.grid.GridPanel({
    store: store,
    columns: [
        {
            id        :'book',
            header    : 'Book',
            width     : 250,
            sortable : true,
            dataIndex: 'book'
        },
        {
            header    : 'Manufacturer',
            width     : 75,
            sortable : true,
            dataIndex: 'manufacturer'
        },
        {
            header    : 'Published',
            width     : 100,
            sortable : true,
            renderer : Ext.util.Format.dateRenderer('F Y'),
            dataIndex: 'published'
        }
    ],
    stripeRows: true,
    height: 140,
    width: 430,
    title: 'Ext JS Books - Ext 3',
    stateId: 'grid'
});

grid.render('grid3');
});
```

Now, we want to add another grid using Ext JS 4 on the same page, right besides the Ext JS 3 grid, because we want to take advantage of new features such as the Model (new class from the new data package). To make the HTML page support Ext JS 4, we have to add the sandbox mode files, instead of the default Ext JS 4 files (ext-all. css, ext-all.js, and ext-core.js):

```
<html>
<head>
<title>Ext JS 3 + Ext JS 4 = sandbox</title>

    <link rel="stylesheet" type="text/css" href="http://extjs.cachefly.
net/ext-3.3.1/resources/css/ext-all.css" />
    <script type="text/javascript" src="http://extjs.cachefly.net/ext-
3.3.1/adapter/ext/ext-base-debug.js"></script>
    <script type="text/javascript" src="http://extjs.cachefly.net/ext-
3.3.1/ext-all-debug.js"></script>

    <script type="text/javascript" src="sandbox/grid-ext3.js"></script>

    <link rel="stylesheet" type="text/css" href="../extjs/resources/
css/ext-sandbox.css" />
    <script type="text/javascript" src="../extjs/builds/ext-all-
sandbox-debug.js"></script>

    <script type="text/javascript" src="sandbox/grid-ext4.js"></
script>
</head>
<body>
    <table border="1">
       <tr>
          <td>Ext JS 3 Grid</td>
          <td>Ext JS 4 Grid</td>
       </tr>
       <tr>
          <td><div id="grid3"></div></td>
          <td><div id="grid4"></div></td>
       </tr>
    </table>
</body>
</html>
```

The HTML page is now ready to support Ext JS 3 and Ext JS 4 on the same page. Let's take a look on the grid code made with Ext JS 4; we are going to put this code into the `grid-ext4.js` file:

```
Ext4.require([
    'Ext.grid.*',
    'Ext.data.*'
]);

Ext4.onReady(function(){

    Ext4.regModel('Book', {
        fields: [
            {name: 'book'},
            {name: 'manufacturer'},
            {name: 'published', type: 'date', dateFormat: 'F Y'}
        ]
    });

    // Array data for the grids
    Ext4.grid.dummyData = [
        ['Drupal 7 Module Development','Packt', 'December 2010'],
        ['PHP 5 Social Networking','Packt', 'October 2010'],
        ['Object-Oriented Programming with PHP5','Packt','December
2007'],
        ['Expert PHP 5 Tools','Packt','March 2010']
    ];

    var store = new Ext4.data.ArrayStore({
        model: 'Book',
        data: Ext4.grid.dummyData
    });

    var grid2 = new Ext4.grid.GridPanel({
        store: store,
        columns: [
            {text: "Book", width: 250, dataIndex: 'book'},
            {text: "Manufacturer", width: 75, dataIndex:
'manufacturer'},
            {text: "Published", width: 100, dataIndex: 'published',
                renderer: Ext4.util.Format.dateRenderer('F Y')}
        ],
        columnLines: true,
        width: 430,
        height: 140,
        title: 'PHP Books - Ext 4',
        renderTo: 'grid4'
    });
});
```

Note that we are not using `Ext` namespace, as we were in the Ext JS 3 code. Instead, we are using `Ext4` namespace. An alias is required — you cannot use the same namespace (`Ext`); otherwise, your code will not work.

If you try to load the page, the following is the result you will get — Ext JS 3 and Ext JS 4 working together on the same page:

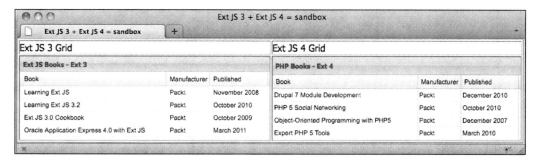

 Remember, it is recommended that you migrate all your code to Ext JS 4. This file can help you to add new Ext JS 4 functionalities into your legacy application, but it is not supposed to be used as a permanent solution.

Sencha platform

Ext JS always provided a class system and architecture of its own — component-oriented, with satellite packages for layout, state, utilities, and data. Ext JS 4 architecture looks much the same as Ext JS 3 architecture:

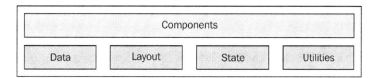

In 2010, Sencha was born and Ext JS got a new brother called Sencha Touch. Sencha Touch is a mobile JavaScript framework. Sencha Touch is to mobile devices, what Ext JS is for desktops. The Sencha Touch architecture is different from Ext JS 3 architecture. For the Ext JS 4 release, they decided to combine Sencha Touch's architecture with Ext JS's. So, the Sencha platform was born, providing some common code shared between Sencha Touch and Ext JS 4. This includes the data package, layouts, most of the utility functions, and the new charting and animation packages. This way, the Sencha team can provide stable code for a product and will be also available for others, creating and maintaining a stable platform. This is also an advantage for developers, because all the knowledge and experience with Ext JS can be easily channeled into developing mobile applications with Sencha Touch, and vice-versa. Plus, a large amount of code can be reused and also increase the community size for platform-based extensions by including web and mobile developers:

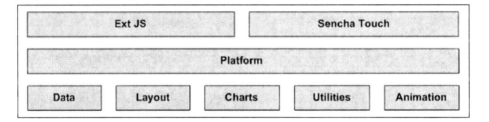

Data package

The data package is one of the packages that Ext JS 4 now shares with Sencha Touch. This package contains the classes that are responsible for loading and saving the data, and it has a large number of changes. Let's briefly discuss some of these changes:

- Store is the class for which you no longer need to set the data format that you are loading on the Store; in other words, you do not need to specify if you are loading JSON or XML (JsonStore or XmlStore), as the Store will automatically detect the data format. The Store API is now capable of sorting and filtering, and the new Reader can read nested data from the server.

- Model is a new class in Ext JS 4, similar to Record, with new capabilities. The new Model class supports associations and validations.

- Proxy is the class responsible for loading and saving the data now, and it receives the Reader and Writer instances. You can attach the proxy to a Store or to a Model, so you don't need to use a Store anymore. There is a new proxy in Ext JS 4: LocalStorageProxy, and it persists the data into an HTML5 local storage. There is also a new proxy that persists the data into session storage.

These changes are not 100% backward-compatible. If you are migrating your code from Ext JS 3 to Ext JS 4, you will need to use the Ext JS 3 compatibility file, but you will still have to change some of your code.

We will take a deeper look at all the data package changes and how to use them in the next chapter.

Draw package and charts

Ext JS 4 introduces the new draw package, which provides custom drawing capabilities, based on HTML5 standards. We can draw basic shapes, such as squares, circles, and also texts. It also provides an engine to draw complex shapes using SVG paths. The new draw package is the base package for the new chart API.

Ext JS 3 introduced charts as newly-available components, but they required Flash to work. In Ext JS 4, you don't need Flash to use charts anymore; now, charts are completely javascript-driven. The charts now use **SVG (Scalable Vector Graphics)**, Canvas, and **VML (Vector Markup Language)**.

With Ext JS 4, you can plot any chart as desired; all charts are customizable. Some of the options are: Bar/Column, Line/Area, Scatter, Radar, or you can also mix any of these charts to create a customized one, according to your needs.

We will dive into the draw and chart packages in *Chapter 4, Upgraded Charts*.

Layouts

Layout is one of the most important and powerful features of Ext JS. In Ext 2, layouts were very fast, but not flexible enough. In Ext JS 3, the flexibility was improved, but it cost some performance. In Ext JS 4, the layout engine was rewritten and now it is faster and more flexible than ever. There are also some new layouts, such as DockLayout, ToolbarLayout, and FieldLayout.

We will take a closer look at the new layout in *Chapter 3, Upgraded Layouts*.

Grids

The grid is the widget that is most used for sure and it is one of the most important components of Ext JS. In Ext JS 4, the grid has been completely rewritten and now it is faster, easier to customize, and has better performance.

In Ext JS 3, when you wanted to display thousands of records in the grid without paging, you had to be very careful, because it was a very heavy rendering. The solution to this issue was to use a plugin to support buffering. In Ext JS 4, the grid natively supports buffering, and now you do not have to worry about this issue anymore.

Ext JS 4 also improved editing capability for grids. In Ext JS 3, if you wanted to use a grid to edit information, you would have to use the EditorGrid, a specialized grid, or a plugin called RowEditor. In Ext JS 4, there is an editing plugin that can be applied to any grid easily, and RowEditor has become a class component supported by the API; it is not an extension anymore.

In Ext JS 3, if you wanted to add any new functionality to a grid you would create a customized grid (create a new class extending the default grid component) or you would create a plugin, correct? Ext JS 4 introduces a new class called Ext.grid. Feature, which provides all the basic features to create new grid features. Now there is a standard way to create new grid functionalities and this makes the grid a more consistent component.

In previous Ext JS versions, when the page rendered the grid, it created an HTML markup to handle all the customizations the grid supported, such as editing, row expansion, and so on, even if you were not using these features. In Ext JS 4, there is a reduction of the HTML markup. Now it renders only what the grid is going to use, only the features you enabled, and this is a great performance boost, making the grid even faster and lighter than the ListView component (in Ext JS 3, the ListView is a lighter version of the grid, used only to visualize the information you display).

We will take a closer look at the Grid component, its new features, and how to use them in *Chapter 5, Upgraded Grid, Tree, and Form*.

Forms

Forms are another very used component in Ext JS. In Ext JS 4, there are some new features that are going to make our lives easier when configuring a form. The first update is that you can use any Layout within a form now. The FormLayout has been removed; it no longer exists.

Ext JS 4 introduces a new class called FieldContainer for managing layouts within forms. Now, you can add any component to a form, such as a grid. There is also a huge improvement in regards to validation.

We will take a closer look at forms, its new features, and how to use them, in *Chapter 5, Upgraded Grid, Tree, and Form*.

Accessibility

Making an application accessible using JavaScript is always difficult. Ext JS 4 introduces three new features that make it easy to do so:

- Ext JS 4 comes with ARIA (Accessible Rich Internet Application) support. All components have attributes to support ARIA.
- Ext JS 4 also supports keyboard navigation on any application.
- There is a new theme with high contrast (dark background and text in a light color).

Theming

If you have already tried to customize a theme for Ext JS 3, you know how painful it can be. Theming in Ext JS 4 is much easier than in previous versions. You can change the color scheme for all components by changing a single variable. That is because Ext JS 4 themes use Sass and Compass, two powerful tools to create CSS easily. Any component can be easily customized now.

We will build and customize a new theme using Sass and Compass in *Chapter 6, Ext JS 4 Themes*.

Summary

In this chapter, we have covered the new Ext JS 4 SDK, learned how to use its new files, the new way to use adapters, and how to use Ext JS 3 (or older versions) along with Ext JS 4. We also covered a very quick overview of the new components and what has changed in the existing ones. We also learned how to use the overhauled documentation and how the packages are organized.

We learned, through examples, how to use the new features from the new class system — for example, how to define a class without using the `new` keyword; how to use `mixins`; the `config` declaration to auto generate methods, getters, and setters; the statics declaration; and how the dynamic class loading works.

In the next chapter, we will learn about the new Ext JS 4 data package — what has changed, what is new, and how to use it.

2
The New Data Package

Ext JS 4 introduces big changes to the data package. There are new classes, and some of the old classes have been refactored to improve performance. With all these changes, the data package is more powerful and easier to use.

In this chapter, you will learn about the following:

- A broad overview of the new features
- Models
- Associations
- Validations
- Store API: sorts and filters
- Proxies (server proxies and client proxies)
- Operations and batches

We will take a look at the new classes of the data package and learn how to use them with real-world examples. In this chapter, you will also learn which features from Ext JS 3 are still compatible with Ext JS 4, so that you can migrate your code easily.

Broad overview

The Ext JS 4 data package introduces some new interesting features, such as the new Model class. There are also some changes related to the Store and Proxy classes. Most of these changes are backward-compatible; the biggest changes are related to the Record, Store, and Proxy classes. The Ext JS 4 data package is also one of the packages that are now shared with Sencha Touch.

The following diagram shows how the data package is organized:

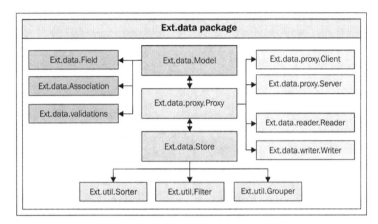

The Model class is one of the most important classes from the data package; it is the new version of the Record class. Now, you can represent your real entities with the Model class, including associations and validations. The following table lists the differences between the Model and Record classes:

Feature	Record (Ext JS 3)	Model (Ext JS 4)
Fields	Yes	Yes
Functions	Yes	Yes
Validations	No	Yes
Associations	No	Yes
Load/Save data directly (Proxy)	No	Yes

The proxy can be directly attached to a Model or to a Store. It receives the Reader and Writer instances, which are responsible for reading/writing and decoding the data from/to a server. Ext JS 4 introduces client- and server-side proxies. The Store also has new capabilities, such as sorting, filtering, and grouping.

The new model class

A `Model` represents an entity, an object; it is a set of functions and fields to operate the data. This new class is very similar to the `Record` class (Ext JS 3 and previous versions), which allowed us to create fields and functions to operate the data. The `Model` class is more powerful; you can create several models and link them through Associations, you can use Validations to validate your data, and you can also load the data directly using a `Proxy` inside a `Model`. The following diagram exemplifies all the capabilities of the `Model` class:

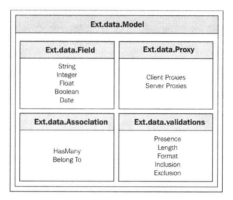

Declaring fields

To create a `Model`, you simply need to use `Ext.define` to define a new class, extend the `Ext.data.Model` class, and declare all the `Model` fields you need, as follows:

```
Ext.define('Patient', {
    extend: 'Ext.data.Model',
    fields: [
        {name: 'name'},
        {name: 'age',      type: 'int'},
        {name: 'phone',    type: 'string'},
        {name: 'gender',   type: 'string'},
        {name: 'birthday', type: 'date', dateFormat: 'd/m/Y'},
        {name: 'alive',    type: 'boolean', defaultValue: true},
        {name: 'weight', type: 'float'},
        {name: 'weightKg', type: 'float',
            convert: function(value, record) {
                var weightPounds = record.get('weight');
                return Math.round(weightPounds * 0.45359237);
            }
        }
    ]
});
```

We are declaring a `Model` for an entity named `Patient` with eight fields. Each field is an instance of the `Ext.data.Field` class. Each field has a `name` and a `type`. The `name` is how you are going to call the attribute. The `type` is used to convert the data to a specific format. The type can be:

- auto (when it is not specified)
- int
- float
- string
- date
- boolean

The first field we declared is called `name`, and we did not specify a `type` for it. In this case, the type is `auto`, which means the data is not going to be converted. Going further in the `Patient` fields declaration, we have a field named `age` with type `int` and two string fields named `phone` and `gender`. Then, we have a field named `birthday` of type `date`. When we declare a `date` field, we can also specify a `dateFormat` to convert the date, but it is optional. This date format has to follow the PHP date format rules.

> Please read `http://docs.sencha.com/ext-js/4-0/#/api/Ext.Date` for further information about Ext JS date format information.

The next field declaration is named `alive` and is of type `boolean`. Another optional field configuration is the `defaultValue`, which is the default value that is going to be used if the item does not exist in the object (that is, `undefined`); when not specified, the default value is ""(empty string). Next, we have a float field named `weight`.

We have explained seven of a total eight fields declared so far. In the last field, named `weightKg`, we are using a function; we did not use this in the previous fields. Sometimes, just declaring the field is not enough—we need to do something else with the data to manipulate it, and, in this case, we can do it using the function `convert`. This function will convert the data from the `Reader` into an object and into the `Model` instance. It receives two parameters: the `data` from the `Record` (if it is `undefined`, it will use the `defaultValue`) and the `Model` instance that is being read. Note that the `Model` is not fully populated yet; the `Reader` populates it in the order the fields are declared. So, if you want to refer to another field, it has to be declared before. In the `Patient` example, we want to convert the `weight` (originally in pounds) to kilo (kg) and store this value in the `weightKg` field. It is ok to make a reference to the `weight`, because it was declared before `weightKg`.

The compatible `Record` declaration in Ext JS 3 (and previous versions) would be as follows:

```
var Patient = Ext.data.Record.create([
    {name: 'name'},
    {name: 'age',       type: 'int'},
    {name: 'phone',     type: 'string'},
    {name: 'gender',    type: 'string'},
    {name: 'birthday', type: 'date', dateFormat: 'd/m/Y'},
    {name: 'alive',     type: 'boolean', defaultValue: true},
    {name: 'weight', type: 'float'},
    {name: 'weightKg', type: 'float',
        convert: function(value, record) {
            var weightPounds = record.get('weight');
            return Math.round(weightPounds * 0.45359237);
        }
    }
]);
```

There are not many differences between the `Model` and `Record` declarations, so far, except for the `Model/Record` declaration itself. The `Ext.data.Field` class from Ext JS 3 is compatible with Ext JS 4, except for the `allowBlank` field configuration, which is no longer present in Ext JS 4. We will show you how to use this validation when we talk about Validations. For now, if you are using this `allowBlank` config in your Ext JS 3 code, you have to remove it from the field declaration when you migrate to Ext JS 4.

 Ext JS 4 no longer supports the `Record` class. Remember to convert your legacy code to the new `Model` class.

Although Ext JS 4 no longer supports the `Record` class, there are some functions on the Ext JS 4 classes that still use `Record` on the method name. So, if you are migrating your code from Ext JS 3 to Ext JS 4, remember to check the documentation to see if the method still exists. For example, on the class `Ext.data.Store`, the following methods still work:

- `findRecord`
- `getNewRccords`
- `getPageFromRecordIndex`
- `getRemovedRecords`
- `getUpdatedRecords`
- `loadRecords`
- `purgeRecords`

For more information about these functions, please go to
`http://docs.sencha.com/ext-js/4-0/#!/api/Ext.data.Store`.

To instantiate a `Model` is very simple. There are two ways you can do it. The first one is to simply instantiate the object (using `Ext.create`) and populate the fields, as follows:

```
var patient = Ext.create('Patient',{
    name: 'Loiane Groner',
    age: 25,
    phone: '9876-5432',
    gender: 'F',
    birthday: '05/26/1986',
    weight: 150
});
```

The second one is to use the `Model Manager` class through the method `create` and pass the parameters. The first parameter is the data, in other words, the `fields`; the second parameter is the `name` of the Model to be created, and the third one is the unique `id` of the `Model` instance, which is optional. The following is an example of how to create a `Patient` instance using the `Ext.ModelMgr` class:

```
var patient = Ext.ModelMgr.create({
    name: 'Loiane Groner',
    age: 25,
    phone: '9876-5432',
    gender: 'F',
    birthday: '05/26/1986',
    weight: 150
}, 'Patient');
```

Now that we have an instance of the `Patient` Model created, we can access its methods:

```
patient.get('name'); //outputs Loiane Groner
patient.get('alive'); //outputs true
patient.get('weightKg'); //outputs 68
```

 Note that we did not specify the `alive` field, but we set a default value to it; when we try to get its value, the output will be true. Another field we did not specify when we instantiated the `Patient` object is the `weightKg` field, but, as we used the convert function, we can get the `weight` value in kilo (kg).

As you can see, there are only six types of `Fields` you can use. There is also another way you can refer to them, that is, by referencing a member of the `Ext.data.Types` class. The following table lists the `Field` types; it is equivalent to the `Ext.data.Types` class and the default value, if none is specified:

Field Type	Ext.data.Types equivalent	Default Value
auto	Ext.data.Types.AUTO	""
string	Ext.data.Types.STRING	""
int	Ext.data.Types.INT or Ext.data.Types.INTEGER	0
float	Ext.data.Types.FLOAT or Ext.data.Types. NUMBER	0
boolean	Ext.data.Types.BOOL or Ext.data.Types. BOOLEAN	null
date	Ext.data.Types.DATE	null

So, if we simply create an empty `Patient` Model, we will get the following output:

```
▼ Ext.Class.newClass
  ▼ data: Object
      age: 0
      alive: true
      birthday: null
      gender: ""
      name: ""
      phone: ""
      weight: 0
      weightKg: 0
```

Here is the `Patient Model` declaration, using the `Ext.data.Types` members:

```
Ext.define('Patient', {
    extend: 'Ext.data.Model',''
fields: [
        {name: 'name'},
        {name: 'age',     type: Ext.data.Types.INT},
        {name: 'phone',   type: Ext.data.Types.STRING},
        {name: 'gender',  type: Ext.data.Types.STRING},
        {name: 'birthday', type: Ext.data.Types.DATE, dateFormat:
'd/m/Y'},
        {name: 'alive',    type: Ext.data.Types.BOOLEAN, defaultValue:
true},
        {name: 'weight', type: Ext.data.Types.FLOAT},
        {name: 'weightKg', type: Ext.data.Types.FLOAT,
            convert: function(value, record) {
                var weightPounds = record.get('weight');
```

```
                     return Math.round(weightPounds * 0.45359237);
              }
          }
       ]
    });
```

In a `Model`, you can declare fields, as you used to do in a `Record`, and you can also declare functions to manipulate the `Model` information, just like you used to do in a `Record`, as well:

```
Ext.define('Patient', {
    extend: 'Ext.data.Model',     ''
     fields: [
         . . .
     ],
     getBasicInfo: function() {
         var info = 'Name: ' + this.get('name');
         info += ' - Gender: '+ this.get('gender');
         info += ' - Age: '+ this.get('age');
         return info;
     }
});
```

The function you created can be accessed by using the following code:

```
patient.getBasicInfo();
```

The output will be the following:

```
Name: Loiane Groner - Gender: F - Age: 25
```

Validating the model

Validations are one of the new `Model` capabilities in Ext JS 4. You can validate the `Model` data against some rules, which you define in the validations declaration inside a `Model`. The `Record` class in Ext JS 3 does not have this feature.

A `validation` declaration (`Ext.data.validations`) follows the same structure as a `field` declaration: you need to specify a `type` (there are five types of validations) and the `name` of the field you want to validate. There are some optional configurations for some validations. You can specify more than one validation for a field. The following is an example of some validation rules for the `Patient` `Model`:

```
Ext.define('Patient', {
    extend: 'Ext.data.Model',''
     fields: [
```

```
        . . .
    ],
    validations: [
        {type: 'presence',  field: 'age'},
        {type: 'presence',  field: 'name'},
        {type: 'length',    field: 'name', min: 2, max: 60},
        {type: 'format',    field: 'name', matcher: /([a-z ]+)/},
        {type: 'inclusion', field: 'gender',  list: ['M', 'F']},
        {type: 'exclusion', field: 'weight', list: [0]}
    ]
});
```

- The `presence` validation verifies if the value is present (0 (zero) is a valid value, but an empty string is not).

- The `length` validation verifies if the length of the given value is between the `min` and the `max` values. The `min` and `max` configurations are optional.

- The `format` validation verifies if the given value matches the given regular expression.

- The `inclusion` validation verifies if the given value matches with one of the given values of the list.

- The `exclusion` validation verifies if the given value does not match with one of the given values of the list.

To validate the `Patient Model`, we need to call the `validate` method. These methods return a `Ext.data.Errors` object:

```
var patient = Ext.create('Patient',{
    name: 'L',
    phone: '9876-5432',
    gender: 'Unknown','',
    birthday: '05/26/1986'
});

var errors = patient.validate();
errors.isValid();
errors.items;
```

The method `isValid` returns `true` or `false`; `true` if the Model is valid, `false` otherwise. In the preceding example, some of the information is not valid, so in this case it will return `false`.

Let's check the Patient validation:

- The field `age` is not present, so we have an invalid value.
- The field `name` is present; it is different from an empty string, so this validation is ok.
- The min length of `name` must be 2 and the max length must be 60. The length of `name` is 1, so the validation will fail.
- The `name` must have only letters (in lowercase); this validation fails.
- The `gender` must be F or M, the model value is `'Unknown'`, `''` (empty string) this validation fails.
- The `weight` can be any value, except zero. It is not zero, so this validation is ok.

The property `items` returns a list of all errors. It will return the following errors:

```
[
    {field: "age"
     message: "must be present"},
    {field: "name"
       message: "is the wrong length"},
    {field: "name"
       message: "is the wrong format"},
    {field: "gender"
       message: "is not included in the list of acceptable values"}
]
```

You can also get the errors for a specific field:

```
errors.getByField('name');
```

And the output will be:

```
[
    {field: "name"
       message: "is the wrong length"},
    {field: "name"
       message: "is the wrong format"},
]
```

Loading/saving data with proxies and stores

Until now, we covered some examples using a `Patient` `Model` and we created some instances to exemplify it. But in real-world applications, you usually load the data from a server. We will take a look at how to set up a proxy inside a `Model` — one of the new features in Ext JS 4.

All the loading and saving data can be done inside a `proxy` in Ext JS 4. Unlike Ext JS 3, in Ext JS 4 you can perform all these actions from the `Model`, with no need to use a `Store`.

```
Ext.define('Blog', {
    extend: 'Ext.data.Model',
''
    fields: [
        {name: 'id', type: 'int'},
        {name: 'name', type: 'string'},
        {name: 'url', type: 'string'}
    ],
    proxy: {
      type: 'rest',
      url : 'data/blogs',
      format: 'json',
      reader: {
          type: 'json',
          root: 'blogs'
      }
    }
});
```

In the preceding example, we have a `Model` called `Blog` with three fields: `id`, `name`, and `url`. We also configured a `proxy`, `RestProxy`, which will load the data using RESTFul URLs (with base `data/blogs/`). We also set up the proxy to use a `JsonReader`.

With a `proxy` configured, we can perform some actions directly from the `Model`. For example:

```
Blog.load(1, {
    success: function(blog) {
        console.log("blog: " + blog.get('url'));
    }
});
```

The preceding code loads (the GET request) the data from the URL js/chapter02/data/blogs/1; 1 is the id we passed as parameter manually to the load method. The response will be a json object, as follows:

```
{
    "blogs": [
        {
            "id": 1,
            "name": 'Loiane Groner',
            "url": 'http://loianegroner.com'
        }
    ]
}
```

Using the same blog reference you loaded the previous code, you can also perform an update on the Model. The following code will make a PUT request to js/chapter02/data/blogs/1:

```
blog.set('name','' 'Loiane');

blog.save({
    success: function() {
        console.log('The blog was updated');
    }
});
```

Another action you can perform is a delete. The following code will make a DELETE request to js/chapter02/data/blogs/1:

```
blog.destroy({
    success: function() {
        console.log('The blog was destroyed!');
    }
});
```

And, if you want to create a new Blog and save it, here is how you can do it:

```
var blog = Ext.ModelMgr.create({
    name: 'Loiane Groner - Pt-BR',
    url: 'http://loiane.com'
}, 'Blog');

blog.save();
```

As we are creating a new `blog`, we do not have an `id` yet. That is why the previous code will make a `POST` request to `data/blogs`. The server should return a `json` object with the blog information plus the `id` created. Let's say the next `id` is 2; the server should return something like the following:

```
{
    "id": 2,
    "name": 'Loiane Groner - PT-BR',
    "url": 'http://loiane.com'
}
```

Setting the proxy to a Model will allow you to reuse the proxy information. This way, you do not need to specify the proxy every time you declare a record. In Ext JS 4, you can also reuse the Model in as many Stores as you want. In Ext JS 3, a `Record` could only belong to one `Store` at a time; if you needed to reuse, you would have to make a copy of it. The following is an example of how to use a `Model` inside a `Store`; we will use the `Blog` `Model` that we declared earlier in this topic:

```
var store = Ext.create('Ext.data.Store',{
    model: 'Blog'
});

store.load(function(records) {
    Ext.MessageBox.alert('Testing Ext JS 4 Models', "Loaded " + store.
getCount() + " records");
});
```

But if you want to declare the `Proxy` inside the `Store`, you can do that as well:

```
Ext.define('Blog', {
    extend: 'Ext.data.Model','',
    fields: [
        {name: 'id', type: 'int'},
        {name: 'name', type: 'string'},
        {name: 'url', type: 'string'}
    ]
});

var store = Ext.create('Ext.data.Store',{
    model: 'Blog',
    proxy: {
        type: 'rest',
        url : 'data/blogs',
        format: 'json',
        reader: {
            type: 'json',
```

```
            root: 'blogs'
        }
    }
});
```

This can be useful when you use the same Model, but will retrieve the data from different URLs.

For now, this is what you need to know. We will take a look at Model Associations in the next topic, and then we will go back and explore proxies and stores in greater detail.

Linking models through associations

When we develop real-world applications, we usually have several Models. Most of the time, these Models are related to each other. Until Ext JS 3, each `Record` was a standalone model; in Ext JS 4, you can express relationships between the Models through Associations (`Ext.data.Association`).

There are two types of Associations between Models:

- `belongsTo`: This represents a many-to-one association with another Model
- `hasMany`: This represents a one-to-many relationship between two Models

To exemplify how to use associations in a `Model`, let's consider the following diagram:

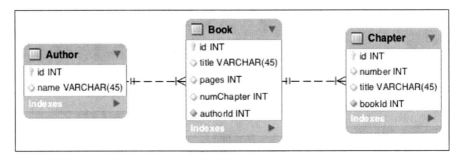

As you can see, we have three tables: **Author**, **Book**, and **Chapter**. An author can write many books and books can have many chapters.

The first step is to create the Models with the `fields` declaration. We will also declare the `association` we described previously:

```
Ext.define('Author', {
    extend: 'Ext.data.Model',
    fields: [
        {name: 'id', type: 'int'},
```

```
            {name: 'name', type: 'string'},
        ],

        hasMany: {model: 'Book', foreignKey: 'authorId'}
});

Ext.define ('Book', {
    extend: 'Ext.data.Model',
    fields: [
        {name: 'id', type: 'int'},
        {name: 'title', type: 'string'},
        {name: 'pages', type: 'int'},
        {name: 'numChapters', type: 'int'},
        {name: 'authorId', type: 'int'}
    ],

    hasMany: {model: 'Chapter', foreignKey: 'bookId'}
});

Ext.define ('Chapter', {



extend: 'Ext.data.Model',
    fields: [
        {name: 'id', type: 'int'},
        {name: 'number', type: 'int'},
        {name: 'title', type: 'string'},
        {name: 'bookId', type: 'int'}
    ]
});
```

Here are some options you can configure when you declare a hasMany association:

- model: This is the name of the model that is being associated with.

- name: This is the name of the function to be created in the owner model; the default is to add an s at the end of the associated model name (in lowercase), as we are going to demonstrate in the next example.

- primaryKey: This is the name of the primary key of the owner model; the default value is id.

- foreignKey: This is the name of the foreign key of the associated model that links to the owner model. Defaults to owner model name plus _id (in lowercase).

- `filterProperty`: This optionally overrides the default filter that is set up on the associated Store. If this is not set, a filter is automatically created and filters the association based on the configured `foreignKey`.

In the previous example, the `Author Model` is declaring a `hasMany` association with the `Book` model. The model is `Book`, the name of the function to be created is `books` (default value), the primary key is also `id` (`Book.id`, is default value), and the foreign key is `authorId` (the default value would be `author_id`). The same rules apply to `Book -> Chapter` association. If we were using the default values for all the options, we could declare the `Author -> Book hasMany` association, as follows:

```
hasMany: 'Book'
```

As we mentioned, when you create an association, a function will be created on the owner model, so you can access the associated data:

```
Author.load(1, {
    success: function(author) {

        var books = author.books();

        console.log("Author "+ author.get('name') + " has written " +
books.getCount() + " books");

        books.each(function(book) {

            var title = book.get('title');
            var chapters = book.chapters();

            console.log("Book " + title + " has " +   chapters.getCount()
+ " chapters");

            chapters.each(function(chapter) {
                console.log(chapter.get('number') + " " + chapter.
get('title'));
            });
        });
    }
});
```

In the preceding example, the functions `author.books()` and `book.chapters()` will be created. The `author.books()` function will return all the books where `authorId` equals the `id` of the `Author` instance (in this case, 1). The function `book.chapters()` will return all the chapters where `bookId` equals the `Book` instance. The `Store` of the associated model will filter the data though the specified primary key (owner model) and foreign key (associated model).

The `filterProperty` object can be useful when we want to filter the associated data. For example, let's say we have declared `filterProperty` as the filter in the `Blog` Model:

```
hasMany: {model: 'Book', foreignKey: 'authorId', filterProperty:
'filter'}
```

And we want to load only the books written by `Loiane Groner`. To do so, we have to execute the following code:

```
var store = Ext.create('Author',{filter: 'Loiane Groner'}).books();
```

The code above is equivalent to the following code:

```
var store = Ext.create('Ext.data.Store', {
    model: 'Book',
    filters: [
        {
            property: 'filter',
            value    : 'Loiane Groner'
        }
    ]
});
```

We will look into filters in further topics. For now, you only need to know that you have this option available in the `hasMany` association.

We can also add a new `book` object to the `author` object through the `add` method; when we call the `sync()` method, it is going to save the new `book` to the `store`:

```
var author = Ext.ModelMgr.create({
    id: 2,
    name: 'Loiane Groner'
}, 'Author');

var books = author.books();

books.add({
    title: 'Ext JS 4: Fisrt Look',
    pages: 250,
    numChapters: 7
});

books.sync();
```

In the preceding example, we first create an Author instance, and then we get the Book Store reference through the books() function. As we have a Store, we can use any function of it, such as the add() function, which we can use to add a new object to the Store. When we call the books.add() function, the Store will automatically set the authorId to 2, before saving it. And, when we call the sync() function, we are asking the Store to save the changes. Similarly, we can add a new chapter to a book.

The Store also can decode nested data. So, we can load an Author and all its associated data at once. It would be something like this:

```
{
    "authors": [
        {
            "id": 1,
            "name": 'Shea Frederick',
            "books": [                       {
                    "id": 11,
                    "title": 'Learning Ext JS 3.2',
                    "pages": 432,
                    "numChapters": 17,
                    "chapters": [
                        {
                            "id": 111,
                            "number": 1,
                            "title": 'Getting Started'
                        },
                        {
                            "id": 112,
                            "number": 2,
                            "title": 'The Staples of Ext JS'
                        }
                    ]
                },
                {
                    "id": 12,
                    "title": 'Learning Ext JS',
                    "pages": 324,
                    "numChapters": 14,
                    "chapters": [
                        {
                            "id": 123,
                            "number": 3,
                            "title": 'Forms'
                        },
```

```
                      {
                          "id": 124,
                          "number": 4,
                          "title": 'Buttons, Menus, and Toolbars'
                      }
                  ]
              }
          ]
      }
  ]
}
```

This way, we can access all the books that belong to an author and all the chapters that belong to a book. What if you want to access the author that the book belongs to? What if you want to have access in both ways, that is, access "books by a specific author" *and* "author of a specific book"? You can access all the books an author has written, and you can find out which author wrote that book. To do so, we will add a `belongsTo` association to the `Book` and `Chapter` models. Let's update our models:

```
Ext.define('Author', {
    extend: 'Ext.data.Model',
    fields: [
        {name: 'id', type: 'int'},
        {name: 'name', type: 'string'},
    ],

    hasMany: {model: 'Book', foreignKey: 'authorId'}
});

Ext.define('Book', {
    extend: 'Ext.data.Model',
    fields: [
        {name: 'id', type: 'int'},
        {name: 'title', type: 'string'},
        {name: 'pages', type: 'int'},
        {name: 'numChapters', type: 'int'},
        {name: 'authorId', type: 'int'}
    ],

    hasMany: {model: 'Chapter', foreignKey: 'bookId'},

    belongsTo: {model: 'Author', foreignKey: 'authorId'}
});

Ext.define('Chapter', {
```

```
    extend: 'Ext.data.Model',
    fields: [
        {name: 'id', type: 'int'},
        {name: 'number', type: 'int'},
        {name: 'title', type: 'string'},
        {name: 'bookId', type: 'int'}
    ],

    belongsTo: {model: 'Book', foreignKey: 'bookId'}
});
```

Another way to declare an association is through the `associations` declaration. It is very helpful when a `Model` has many associations declared. As in the `hasMany` association, the `belongsTo` association also has some configuration options:

- `model`: This is the name of the model that is being associated with.
- `primaryKey`: This is the name of the primary key of the owner model. The default value is `id`.
- `foreignKey`: This is the name of the foreign key of the associated model that links to the owner model. It defaults to the owner model name and `_id` (in lowercase).
- `getterName`: This is the name of the getter function that will be added to the owner model. It defaults to `get` and the name of the associated model.
- `setterName`: This is the name of the setter function that will be added to the owner model. It defaults to `set` and the name of the associated model.

In the previous example, we declared two `belongsTo` associations, one in the `Book` `Model` and another one in the `Chapter` `Model`. In the `Book` `Model`, we specified that the `Book` belongs to an `Author`, so the name of the model is `Author`. The `Book` primary key is `id`, which is the default value, so we do not need to explicitly declare it. The `Author` foreign key is `authorId`, which is not the default value (`author_id`), so we need to declare it. The `belongsTo` association will create two functions in the `Book` model—`getAuthor` and `setAuthor` (default values):

```
Book.load(11, {
    success: function(book) {

        book.getAuthor(function (author){
            console.log("The author of this book is " author.
get('name'));''
        });
    }
});
```

The preceding example shows how to use the getter function created in the Book model. This function will use the Author configured proxy to load its data, and that is why the getter function is asynchronous. There are also success, failure, and callback properties you can configure:

```
book.getAuthor({
    callback: function(author, operation) {},
    success : function(author, operation) {},
    failure : function(author, operation) {},
    scope   : this
});
```

The callback function will always be called. It is the one we used when we called the book.getAuthor() function. The success function will be called if the load was completed successfully. The failure function will be called if the load was not completed successfully. The scope is optional; it is the scope object in which the callbacks are going to get executed.

In each case above, the callbacks are called with two arguments — the associated model instance (in the previous example, it would be author) and the operation object that was executed to load that instance. The Operation object is useful when the instance could not be loaded.

We can also call the setter function:

```
book.setAuthor(1);
```

```
book.set('authorId',1);
```

The functions above are equivalent. As we did for the getter function, we can also use a second argument and get the result from the callback function:

```
book.setAuthor(1, function(book, operation) {
    console.log(book.get('authorId')); //outputs 1
});
```

Like the getter function, there are also some other functions you can configure:

```
book.setAuthor(1, {
    callback: function(book, operation){},
    success : function(book, operation){},
    failure : function(book, operation){},
    scope   : this
});
```

The `callback` function will always be called. It is the one we used when we called the `book.setAuthor()` function. The `success` function will be called if the update was completed successfully. The `failure` function will be called if the update was not completed successfully. The `scope` is optional; it is the `scope` object in which the callbacks are going get executed.

We have learned how to declare the `hasMany` or `belongsTo` config declarations. Another way to declare them is through the `associations` declaration:

```
Ext.define('Author', {
    extend: 'Ext.data.Model',
    fields: [
        {name: 'id', type: 'int'},
        {name: 'name', type: 'string'},
    ],

    associations: [
        {type: 'hasMany', model: 'Book', foreignKey: 'authorId'}
    ]
});

Ext.define('Book', {
    extend: 'Ext.data.Model',
    fields: [
        {name: 'id', type: 'int'},
        {name: 'title', type: 'string'},
        {name: 'pages', type: 'int'},
        {name: 'numChapters', type: 'int'},
        {name: 'authorId', type: 'int'}
    ],

    associations: [
        {type: 'hasMany', model: 'Chapter', foreignKey: 'bookId'},
        {type: 'belongsTo',model: 'Author', foreignKey: 'authorId'}
    ]
});

Ext.define('Chapter', {
    extend: 'Ext.data.Model',
    fields: [
        {name: 'id', type: 'int'},
        {name: 'number', type: 'int'},
        {name: 'title', type: 'string'},
        {name: 'bookId', type: 'int'}
```

```
    ],

    associations: [
        {type: 'belongsTo', model: 'Book', foreignKey: 'bookId'},
    ]
});
```

The preceding code is equivalent to the declaration we made earlier in this topic. The difference is that we can declare more dependencies of the same type at the same time.

Proxies

Proxies are responsible for loading and saving the data in Ext JS. They are used by `Stores` and they can also be used directly in a Model.

In Ext JS 3, we used to load and save data only in a server. Ext JS 4 introduces three new proxies, which can be used to store data locally, at the client side (browser).

Basically, in Ext JS 4, we have two types of proxies—client proxies and server proxies. The client proxies are: **LocalStorageProxy**, **SessionStorageProxy**, and **MemoryProxy**. The server proxies are: **AjaxProxy**, **ScriptTagProxy**, **DirectProxy**, and **RestProxy**.

In the following diagram, you can see the structure of how proxies are organized in Ext JS 4. We will look at each proxy closely in this topic:

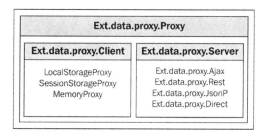

Client proxies

Client proxies are used for local storage (by local, we mean the browser). Client-side storage is one of the new features of HTML5, and unfortunately not all browsers support it, only the newest versions:

- Internet Explorer 8.0+
- Firefox 3.5+
- Safari 4.0+

- Chrome 4.0+
- Opera 10.5+
- IPhone 2.0+
- Android 2.0+

The HTML5 storage is a way for web pages to store named key-value locally, within the client browser. It works like cookies — you can navigate away from the website, exit your browser, and when you open your browser again, the data will be there. The difference between HTML5 storage and cookies is that the data you store locally is never transmitted to the web server (unless you do it manually).

 For further reading on HTML5 and local storage, please read `http://dev.w3.org/html5/webstorage/`.

 The advantage of client-side storage is that you need not make a server request every time you need to load or save some data. The disadvantage is that it does not work on every browser.

The following diagram illustrates the Ext JS 4 client proxies:

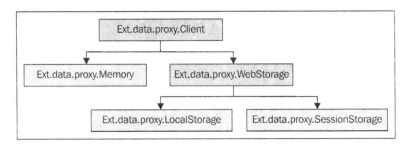

- **Ext.data.proxy.Client** is the base class for every client proxy
- **Ext.data.proxy.Client** is the superclass for **Ext.data.proxy.Memory** and **Ext. data.proxy.WebStorage**, and is not used directly
- **Ext.data.proxy.WebStorage** is the superclass for **Ext.data.proxy.LocalStorage** and **Ext.data.proxy.SessionStorage**, and is also not used directly

  This leaves us with three client proxies that we can instantiate:

- **Ext.data.proxy.LocalStorage**
- **Ext.data.proxy.SessionStorage**
- **Ext.data.proxy.Memory**

LocalStorageProxy

The LocalStorageProxy uses the new HTML5 localStorage API to load and save data into the client browser. The localStorage sets the fields on the domain; this means you can close the browser and reopen it, and the data will be in the localStorage. The localStorage is used for long-term storage; it is also accessible in all browser tabs/windows.

The HTML5 storage is a set of key-value; and you can store any data supported by JavaScript, such as string, integer, float, and boolean. JSON (JavaScript Object Notation) is not supported, but you do not need to worry about it, because LocalStorageProxy does all the work to serialize and deserialize it.

LocalStorageProxy is useful for storing user-specific information without needing to make a server request. For example, consider we want to save some user information, so we are going to create a User Model to represent this information and we will also set the proxy as LocalStorageProxy:

```
Ext.define('UserPreference', {
    extend: 'Ext.data.Model',
    fields: [
        {name: 'id', type: 'int'},
        {name: 'description', type: 'string'}
    ],

    proxy: {
      type: 'localstorage',
      id : 'userpreference'
    }
});
```

Our UserPreference Model contains two fields — id and description. We configured the proxy as LocalStorageProxy and we also used an id. By setting an id to the proxy, we enabled it to mange the saved data, and this is very important.

Now let's set up a Store, add some UserPreferences to it, and save it:

```
var store = Ext.create('Ext.data.Store',{
    model: 'UserPreference'
});

store.load();

store.add({description: 'Blue theme'});
store.add({description: 'Loiane Groner'});

store.sync();
```

And, if we take a look at the localStorage of the browser (Chrome), we will see the saved data— note the id we created for the proxy:

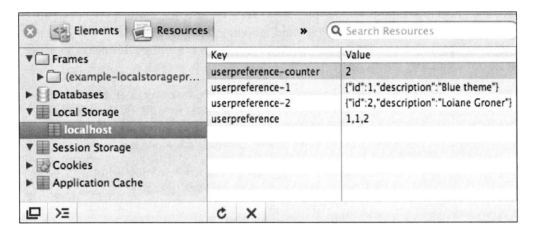

Remember, we can also manage the data directly from the Model:

```
var userPref = Ext.ModelManager.create({
    description: 'Favorite JS Framework: Ext JS'
}, 'UserPreference');

userPref.save();
```

Let's try closing the browser and reopening it. Now, we are going to try retrieving the data:

```
store.load(function(records, operation, success) {

    var userPref,i;

    for (i=0;i<records.length;i++){
        userPref = records[i].data;
        console.log(userPref.id + " " + userPref.description);
    }
});
```

The output will be:

```
1 Blue theme
2 Loiane Groner
3 Favorite JS Framework: Ext JS
```

Works fine! If you try to use the `LocalStorageProxy` in a browser without HTML5 support, such as IE 7, the constructor will throw an error:

SessionStorageProxy

The `SessionStorageProxy` uses the new HTML5 `sessionStorage` API to load and save data into the client browser. `sessionStorage` sets the fields on the window; this means that all the data will be lost when you close the browser, even if the website remains open in another browser window. The `sessionStorage` data is confined to the browser window that it was created in.

Let's modify our `UserPreference Model` to a `SessionStorageProxy`:

```
Ext.define('UserPreference', {
    extend: 'Ext.data.Model',
    fields: [
        {name: 'id', type: 'int'},
        {name: 'description', type: 'string'}
    ],

    proxy: {
        type: 'sessionstorage',
        id : 'userpreference'
    }
});
```

 Remember to always create an `id` to the proxy. If you do not specify any, it will use the store's one. If you do not specify an `id` for the store and the proxy, it will throw an error.

Let's use the same `Store` we used in the previous topic to save some data:

```
var store = Ext.create('Ext.data.Store',{
    model: 'UserPreference'
});

store.load();
```

```
store.add({description: 'Blue theme'});
store.add({description: 'Loiane Groner'});

store.sync();
```

As you can see, the data is stored locally:

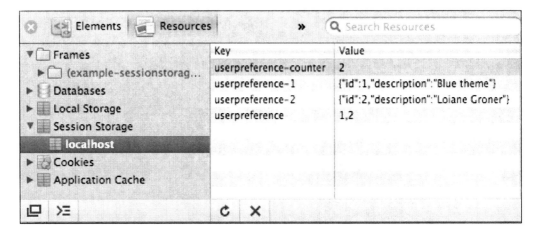

But, if we close the window and try to retrieve the data we saved, we will get nothing, because the data is no longer available.

MemoryProxy

`MemoryProxy` is a helper proxy. Usually, it is used to load some inline data into a store. The `MemoryProxy` contents are lost in every page refresh. It can be useful to load temporary data.

For example, let's say we have to load a `Gender` model to populate a field in a form. A gender can be `female`, `male`, or `unknown`. You can use a `MemoryProxy` to load this data:

```
Ext.define('Gender', {
    extend: 'Ext.data.Model',
    fields: [
        {name: 'id', type: 'int'},
        {name: 'name', type: 'string'}
    ]
});

var data = {
    genders: [
        {
```

```
                id: 1,
                name: 'Female'
        },
        {
                id: 2,
                name: 'Male'
        },
        {
                id: 3,
                name: 'Unknown'
        }
    ]
};

var store = Ext.create('Ext.data.Store',{
    autoLoad: true,
    model: 'Gender',
    data : data,
    proxy: {
        type: 'memory',
        reader: {
            type: 'json',
            root: 'genders'
        }
    }
});

//ComboBox using the data store
var comboBox = Ext.create('Ext.form.field.ComboBox', {
    fieldLabel: 'Gender',
    renderTo: 'genderCombo',
    displayField: 'name',
    width: 200,
    labelWidth: 50,
    store: store,
    queryMode: 'local',
    typeAhead: false
});
```

This will be the output for the preceding code:

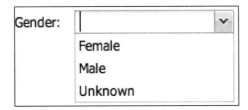

While the page is opened, the data will be stored in the Store and you can manipulate it. The moment you navigate away from the current page, or refresh the page, the data will be lost.

Server proxies

Server proxies are used for loading and saving data from/to a web server through HTTP requests. The diagram below illustrates the Ext JS 4 server proxy structure:

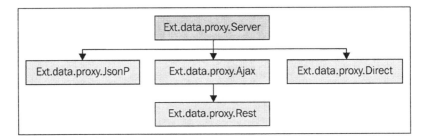

- **Ext.data.proxy.Server** is the base class for every server proxy
- **Ext.data.proxy.Server** is the superclass for **Ext.data.proxy.JsonP**, **Ext.data.proxy.Ajax**, and **Ext.data.proxy.Direct**, and it is not used directly
- **Ext.data.proxy.Rest** is an extension of **Ext.data.proxy.Ajax**

This leaves us with four server proxies we can instantiate:

- **Ext.data.proxy.Ajax**
- **Ext.data.proxy.Rest**
- **Ext.data.proxy.JsonP**
- **Ext.data.proxy.Direct**

AjaxProxy

The `AjaxProxy` is the most-used proxy. It uses Ajax requests to load and save the data from/to a web server. It used to be the `Ext.data.HttpProxy` in Ext JS 3.

To set up an Ajax proxy, you simply need to use `ajax` as the type. For example, let's set up a model with an Ajax proxy:

```
Ext.define('Book', {
    extend: 'Ext.data.Model',
    fields: [
        {name: 'id', type: 'int'},
        {name: 'title', type: 'string'},
        {name: 'pages', type: 'int'}''''''''
    ],

    proxy: {
        type: 'ajax',
        url : 'data/books.json'
    }
});
```

The previous code is equivalent to the following:

```
var ajaxProxy = Ext.create('Ext.data.proxy.Ajax',{
    url: 'data/books.json',
    model: 'Book',
    reader: 'json'
});

Ext.define('Book', {
     extend: 'Ext.data.Model',
    fields: [
        {name: 'id', type: 'int'},
        {name: 'title', type: 'string'},
        {name: 'pages', type: 'int'}
    ],

    proxy: ajaxProxy
});
```

Note that, in the first example, we only specified the type and the URL from where we are going to retrieve the data. In the second example, we are using two extra configurations—`model` and `reader`. When we write the code, as in the first example, these two configurations are default, because the `Store` already knows which `Model` it is going to use and the default `Reader` is `JsonReader`.

When we make a read request to the server, the proxy sends a GET request to the specified URL, and if we make any write request (update, insert, delete), it will send a POST request.

For an example, we will try to load some data; to do so, we will create a store and list all the loaded data:

```
var store = Ext.create(Ext.data.Store', {
    model: 'Book'
});

store.load(function(records) {

    var book,i;

    for (i=0;i<records.length;i++){
        book = records[i].data;
        console.log(book.id + " " + book.title);
    }
});
```

If you open the books.json file, you will find the following JSON object:

```
[
    {
        "id": 11,
        "title": 'Learning Ext JS 3.2',
        "pages": 432,
        "numChapters": 17
    },
    {
        "id": 12,
        "title": 'Learning Ext JS',
        "pages": 324,
        "numChapters": 14
    }
]
```

If you specify any filter, grouping, paging, or sorting options, they will be appended to the request as parameters. The following are the options:

- filterParam: This is the name of the filter parameter that is sent to the server to filter data. The default value is filter.

- groupParam: This is the name of the group parameter that is sent to the server to group data. The default value is group.

- `pageParam`: This is the name of the page parameter that is sent to the server to select a specified page. The default value is `page`.

- `startParam`: This is the name of the start `Model` parameter that is sent to the server (used in paging). The default value is `start`.

- `limitParam`: This is the name of the limit `Model` parameter that is sent to the server (used in paging). The default value is `limit`.

- `sortParam`: This is the name of the `sort` parameter sent to the server for sorting. The default value is `group`.

- `extraParams`: This gives the names of the parameters that are going to be sent in every request to the server. If you send any other parameter with the same name as any of these ones, they will be overridden.

The benefit of using parameters is limiting the number of records to be loaded; this way, the browser memory for JavaScript is not overloaded.

Ext JS 4 introduces the `Ext.data.Operation`, which is every single read or write operation executed by a proxy. The following are some options you can configure in an `Operation`, though you will rarely be using it directly:

- `action`: Any of the actions you want to perform—read, create, update, and destroy (delete)

- `batch`: This operation is part of the `Ext.data.Batch` object (optional config)

- `filters`: This is an array of filters

- `group`: This is for group configuration

- `limit`: This is is the number of `Model` instances you want to load from the server

- `sorters`: This is an array of sorters

- `start`: This is is the number is the initial `Model` to be loaded used by paging

The `filters`, `group`, `limit`, `sorters`, and `start` options can be only used for read requests.

We will create a `proxy` that will be used in the following examples:

```
var proxy = Ext.create(E'xt.data.proxy.Ajax',{
    url : '/books',
    model: 'Book'
});
```

For example, we will create an `Operation` to load five books from the server and, for that, we will use the `start` and `limit` parameters; then, we will use a proxy to load this data from the server:

```
var operation = Ext.create('Ext.data.Operation',{
    action: 'read',
    start : 0,
    limit : 5
});
```

```
proxy.read(operation);
```

When we call the read function, the `proxy` makes a request to the URL `/books?start=0&limit=5`, appending the parameters we set in it.

As mentioned earlier, we can customize the name of these parameters:

```
var operation = Ext.create('Ext.data.Operation',{
    action: 'read',
    startParam: 'firstRecord',
    limitParam: 'limitOfRecords',
    start : 0,
    limit : 5
});
```

```
proxy.read(operation);
```

And when we call the read function again, the URL makes the proxy request: `/books?firstRecord=0&limitOfRecords=5`

We can also create an operation to load a specific page from the server:

```
var operation = Ext.create('Ext.data.Operation',{
    action: 'read',
    page  : 5
});
```

```
proxy.read(operation);
```

And, when we call the read function, the proxy will make the following request: `/books?page=5`

We can also configure a sorter in an operation:

```
var operation = Ext.create('Ext.data.Operation',{
    action: 'read',
    sorters: [
        Ext.create('Ext.util.Sorter',{
            property : 'pages',
            direction: 'DESC'
        }),
        Ext.create('Ext.util.Sorter',{
            property : 'numChapters',
            direction: 'DESC'
        }),
        Ext.create('Ext.util.Sorter',{
            property : 'title',
            direction: 'ASC'
        })
    ]
});

proxy.read(operation);
```

The `sorter` configuration is not a simple value such as the `page`, `start`, or `limit` options; it is a JSON object. When we call the `load` function, the `proxy` will encode it and call the URL `/books?sort=[{"property":"pages","direction":"DESC"},{"property":"numChapters","direction":"DESC"},{"property":"title","direction":"ASC"}]`. Then, on the server side, you will have to decode it.

The filter option works in the same way:

```
var operation = Ext.create('Ext.data.Operation',{
    action: 'read',
    filters: [
        Ext.create('Ext.util.Filter',{
            property: 'pages',
            value    : '250'
        })
    ]
});

proxy.read(operation);
```

And it is going to call the following URL: `/books?filter=[{"property":"pages","value":"250"}]`

If we decide to put it all together in a single `Operation`, this is what we get:

```
var operation = Ext.create('Ext.data.Operation', {
    action: 'read',
    start : 0,
    limit : 5,
    sorters: [
        Ext.create('Ext.util.Sorter', {
            property : 'pages',
            direction: 'DESC'
        }),
        Ext.create('Ext.util.Sorter', {
            property : 'numChapters',
            direction: 'DESC'
        }),
        Ext.create('Ext.util.Sorter', {
            property : 'title',
            direction: 'ASC'
        })
    ],
    filters: [
            Ext.create('Ext.util.Grouper', {
                property: 'pages',
                value    : '250'
            })
        ]
});
```

If we call the `read` function, the `proxy` will append all `config` options at the end of the URL, separated by `&`:

```
/books?start=0&limit=5&sort=[{"property":"pages","direction":"DESC
"},{"property":"numChapters","direction":"DESC"},{"property":"titl
e","direction":"ASC"}]&filter:[{"property":"pages","value":"250"}]
```

The `AjaxProxy` also has two functions that can be used to customize how the sorters and filters are sent to the server; in other words, if you want to encode them in a different format, you can.

The web server accepts the sorters and filters in the format `sort=theme,ASC;title,DESC`, or `filter=theme:extjs`. To do so, we can customize the functions `encodeSorters` and `encodeFilters`. Both will receive an array of objects, `sorters` and `filters`, respectively.

We will apply the changes to our `AjaxProxy` instance:

```
var proxy = Ext.create('Ext.data.proxy.Ajax',{
    url : '/books',
    model : 'Book',

    encodeSorters: function(sorters) {
        var length   = sorters.length;
        var sortStrs = [];
         var sorter, i;

        for (i = 0; i < length; i++) {
            sorter = sorters[i];

            sortStrs[i] = sorter.property + ',' + sorter.direction;
        }

        return sortStrs.join(";");
    },

    encodeFilters: function(filters) {
        var length    = filters.length;
        var filterStrs = [];
         var filter, i;

        for (i = 0; i < length; i++) {
            filter = filters[i];

            filterStrs[i] = filter.property + ',' + filter.value;
        }

        return filterStrs.join(";");
    }
});
```

The following URL will be executed when we call the `read` function. It is much easier to read now:

```
/books?start=0&limit=5&sort=pages,DESC;numChapters,DESC;title,ASC&fil
ter:pages,250
```

The `AjaxProxy` has a limitation: you can only call URLs from the same domain where your application is deployed. For example, if your application is deployed at `http://sencha.com` you can only call URLs from `sencha.com`. This is a browser limitation, which means you cannot make Ajax calls to a different server.

Rest proxy

The `Rest proxy` is a subclass of `AjaxProxy`, but all the CRUD (create, read, update, delete) actions are made to RESTful URLs.

The basic principle of RESTful URLs is to have a base URL to the service, exchange data using JSON, XML, or YAML (YAML Ain't Markup Language); only JSON and XML apply to Ext JS and the CRUD operations are supported by the HTTP methods GET, POST, DELETE, and PUT.

Consider `http://packtpub.com/books` as the base URL. The table below shows the mapping URL and the CRUD operations:

URL	Create	Read	Update	Delete
`http://packtpub.com/books`	POST	GET all books		
`http://packtpub.com/books/26`		GET book with id=26	PUT book with id=26	DELETE book with id=26

> For further information about RESTful URLs, please read `http://microformats.org/wiki/rest/urls`.

To create a `Rest proxy`, you simply need to specify `rest` as the type of proxy:

```
Ext.define('Book', {
    Extend: 'Ext.data.Model',
    fields: [
        {name: 'id', type: 'int'},
        {name: 'name', type: 'string'},
        {name: 'author', type: 'string'}
    ],

    proxy: {
        type: 'rest',
        url : '/books'
    }
});
```

When we create a `book` and call the `save` method, the proxy will make a POST request to the URL `/books`, as we defined in the `proxy`. Consider that the server returned 26 for the `id` when the save was completed.

```
var book = Ext.ModelManager.create({
    name: 'Ext JS 4: First Look',
    author: 'Loiane Groner'
}, 'Book');


book.save(); //POST /books
```

Now, we will try to load the book we created, from the server. The proxy will make a GET request to `/books/26`:

```
Ext.ModelManager.getModel('Book').load(26, {//GET /books/26
    success: function(book) {
        console.log(book.getId()); //outputs 26
    }
});
```

Using the same book reference we created, if we want to update the name of the book, we can call the setter function and then call the `save` method again; but, this time, as we already have a `book id`, it is going to make a PUT request to the URL `/books/26`:

```
book.set('name', 'Ext JS 4');
book.save(); //PUT /books/26
```

Still using the same `book` reference, we can also try to delete it; for that, we can call the method `destroy`. When we do it, the proxy will make a DELETE request to `/books/26`:

```
book.destroy({ //DELETE /books/26
    success: function() {
        console.log('The Book was deleted');
    }
});
```

In the following code, we will try to load the data (all books) from the server. To do so, we will create a store and call the method `load` from the store:

```
var store = Ext.create('Ext.data.Store',{
    model: 'Book'
});


store.load(); //GET /books
```

When we load all the books, the proxy will make a GET request to `/books`.

As the `Rest proxy` is a subclass of `AjaxProxy`, the proxy's call (in the URL) has to be in the same domain, protocol, port, and subdomain as your application. For example, if your application is deployed at `loiane.com`, you can only call URLs that belong to `loiane.com`, not from `loianegroner.com`. If you need to call a URL from a different domain, you have to use `JsonPProxy`.

 For more information about the same origin policy, please go to `http://en.wikipedia.org/wiki/Same_origin_policy`.

JsonP proxy

The `JsonP proxy` is a useful proxy when you need to make requests to a different domain, on which your application is not deployed. It was known in Ext JS 3 as `Ext.data.ScriptTagProxy`. The name is self explanatory; this proxy injects a script tag into the DOM every time the request is made.

For example, your application is deployed on `http://loiane.com`, but you want to retrieve some data (books) that is on `http://loianegroner.com`.

The script tag that would be injected looks like this:

```
<script src="http://loianegroner/books?callback=someCallback"></
script>
```

To set up `JsonP proxy`, you simply need to set the type as `jsonp`, which is as follows:

```
Ext.define('Blog', {
    extend: 'Ext.data.Model',
    fields: [
        {name: 'lang', type: 'string'},
        {name: 'url', type: 'string'},
    ],

    proxy: {
        type: 'jsonp',
        url : 'http://loianegroner.com/extjs/blogs.php'
    }
});
```

The proxy will take care of everything; you do not need to worry about anything else.

Now, we will try to load some data. Let's create a `store`:

```
var store = Ext.create('Ext.data.Store',{
    model: 'Blog'
});

store.load(function(records) {

    var blog,i;
    for (i=0;i<records.length;i++){
        blog = records[i].data;
        console.log(blog.id + " : " + blog.url);
    }
});
```

The output of the preceding code will be as follows:

```
1 : loianegroner.com
```

We loaded the data from `http://loianegroner.com/extjs/blogs.php`. The `blogs.php` file looks like this:

```
<?php
$callback = $_REQUEST['callback'];

// Create the output object.
$output = array('id' => 1, 'url' => 'loianegroner.com');

//start output
if ($callback) {
    header('Content-Type: text/javascript');
    echo $callback . '([' . json_encode($output) . ']);';
} else {
    header('Content-Type: application/x-json');
    echo json_encode($output);
}
```

The preceding code is a php file that processes `JsonP` and `Ajax` proxy calls. If it is a `jsonp` call, the content type of the response will be a JavaScript, and if the request is from an `ajax` proxy, the content type will be JSON.

You cannot simply return a JSON object from the server when the request is made by a `JsonP` proxy. You have to add the callback function in it. If you inspect the return of this file using Chrome developer tools or Firebug (a Firefox add-on) this is what you will see:

```
Ext.data.JsonP.callback1([{"id":1,"url":"loianegroner.com"}]);
```

> Remember that `JsonPProxy` proxy is supposed to be used only when you need to call a URL that is in another domain; if your data is in the same domain where your app ID is deployed, you can use `AjaxProxy`.

Stores

The `Store` is responsible for encapsulating the `Model` and can also configure a `proxy` to load and/or save the data. It is also capable of sorting, filtering, and grouping. The following is the class hierarchy of the Store:

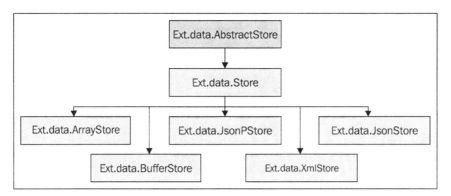

Some changes were made from Ext JS 3 to Ext JS 4 and some classes were added to Ext JS 4. In Ext3, the **Store** class was a subclass of the `Observable` class. In Ext JS 4, there is a new class named **AbstractStore**, which is the super class of all **Store** classes. There is a **TreeStore**, which represents the data for a `Tree` and the `Store` class. The **Store** class is the superclass of several stores: **ArrayStore, BufferStore, JsonStore, XmlStore, DirectStore,** and **JsonPStore**. Each of these stores is automatically associated with its proxy.

Readers

Reader classes are responsible for decoding the raw data from a server that is to be loaded into a `Model` instance or `Store`. The main difference between Ext JS 3 and Ext JS 4 is that, in Ext JS 4, readers are not coupled into a `Store` but are coupled into a `proxy`. Another difference is that, in Ext JS 3, all the reader classes belong to the `Ext.data` package, and in Ext JS 4, the reader classes belong to the `Ext.data.reader` package.

The configuration options are still the same in Ext JS 4; this means the code is backward-compatible. The following diagram illustrates how readers are organized in Ext JS 4:

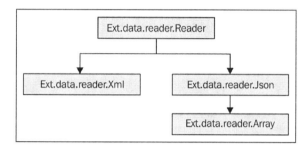

The `Ext.data.reader.Reader` is the superclass of `Ext.data.reader.Json` and `Ext.data.reader.Xml`.

The `Ext.data.reader.Json` is the superclass for `Ext.data.reader.Array`.

Some properties of the `Reader` class (that also extend to other reader classes) are as follows:

- `idProperty` – This is the name of the identifier property of the Model. The default value is the `id` property of the Model.
- `messageProperty`: This is the name of the property that contains a response message.
- `croot`: This is the name of the property that contains the array of objects.
- `successProperty`: This is the name of the property that contains the success attribute. The default value is `success`.
- `totalProperty`: This is the name of the property that contains the total of the records of the dataset. It is used when the whole dataset is not passed at once, as in paging. The default value is `total`.

Consider that we want to load data for a `Blog` model; first, we will declare the `Model`:

```
Ext.define('Blog', {
    extend: 'Ext.data.Model',
    fields: [
        {name: 'id', type: 'string'},
        {name: 'url', type: 'string'},
    ]
});
```

Now we will try to load the data from an array. Each element of the array represents a `blog`. We will also declare an `ArrayStore` and map the data option to the array data we created. For this example, we do not need to declare a `proxy`:

```
var blogData = [
    [1, 'http://loianegroner.com'],
    [2, 'http://loiane.com']
];

var store = Ext.create('Ext.data.ArrayStore', {
    model: 'Blog',

    data: blogData
});

store.load(function(records) {

    var blog,i;
     for (i=0;i<records.length;i++){
        blog = records[i].data;
        console.log(blog.id + " : " + blog.url);
     }
});
```

Now, we will try to load the same data, but from a `JsonReader`:

```
var store = Ext.create('Ext.data.Store',{
    model: 'Blog',
    proxy: {
        type: 'ajax',
        url : 'data/blogs.json',
        reader: {
          type: 'json',
          root: 'blogs',
          messageProperty: 'message'
        }
    }
});
```

We are using a proxy that will load the data from the `blogs.json` file; we also declared a `JsonReader` (reader type = json), and we also specified `blogs` as the root. We have also declared the `messageProperty` config option. We can show this message to the user in an alert box saying that the data was loaded successfully. This means that the `json` file looks like this:

```
{
    "blogs": [
        {
            "id": 1,
            "url": 'http://loianegroner.com'
        },
        {
            "id": 2,
            "url": 'http://loiane.com'
        }
    ],
    "message": 'Data was load successfully!'
}
```

If the data you expect to receive looks like the following (you can remove the root config option from the reader declaration):

```
[
        {
            "id": 1,
            "url": 'http://loianegroner.com'
        },
        {
            "id": 2,
            "url": 'http://loiane.com'
        }
]
```

Next, we will try to load the data from an XML file. We will need to declare a `xml reader` inside a proxy:

```
var store = Ext.create('Ext.data.Store',{
    model: 'Blog',
    proxy: {
        type: 'ajax',
        url : 'data/blogs.xml',
        reader: {
         type: 'xml',
          record: 'blog'
        }
    }
});
```

The XML this store is expecting looks like the following:

```
<blog>
    <id>1</id>
    <url>http://loianegroner.com</url>
</blog>
<blog>
    <id>2</id>
    <url>http://loiane.com</url>
</blog>
```

You can also receive an XML file that looks like this:

```
<blogs>
    <blog>
        <id>1</id>
        <url>http://loianegroner.com</url>
    </blog>
    <blog>
        <id>2</id>
        <url>http://loiane.com</url>
    </blog>
</blogs>
```

To recognize the XML format in the preceding code, you need to make a simple change in the `reader` declaration, which is adding the `root` config option, as follows:

```
reader: {
        type: 'xml',
        record: 'blog',
        root: 'blogs'
    }
```

Ext JS 4 also introduced a new capacity for the reader, which is to load nested data, as we already discussed in a previous topic.

Writers

The writer is responsible for sending data to the server. As with readers, writers are also coupled to a proxy in Ext JS 4. In Ext JS 4, all the writers belong to the `Ext.data.writer` package and not to the `Ext.data` package, as in Ext JS 3.

The following diagram illustrates how writers are organized in Ext JS 4:

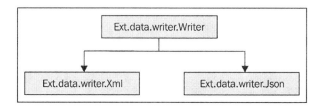

The `Ext.data.writer.Writer` is the superclass of `Ext.data.writer.Json` and `Ext.data.writer.Xml`.

Some `Writer` options you can configure (common for all writers) are as follows:

- `nameProperty` – This property is used to read the key for each value that will be sent to the server.

- `writeAllFields`: The value of this property is set to `true` if you want to send all the fields to the server, or `false` if you want to send only the fields that were modified. The default value is `true`.

JsonWriter

To declare a `JsonWriter` we first need a `proxy`. We will declare an `AjaxProxy`. As we are declaring an `AjaxProxy`, we need to specify a URL for each CRUD Operation: create, read, update, and destroy. To do so, we will use a config option called `api`. As we are also reading data from the server, we also need to declare a `store`. Since we are using a `JsonWriter`, a `JsonStore` makes more sense. Then, we will declare the `JsonWriter`, and we will set two config options: `writeAllFields` as `false` (we want to send only modified fields to the server) and the `root` name, which will be data. There is one config option that we also set in the store, called `autoSync`. If we set it to `true`, it means that every time we make a modification in one of the records of the `Store`, it will automatically synchronize with the `proxy`, saving the data right after we change it. The default value is `false`, which means we have to call the method `sync` of the `store` to save all the modifications at once.

```
var store = Ext.create('Ext.data.Store',{
    model: 'Blog',

    proxy: {
        type: 'ajax',

        api: {
            read:    'data/blogs/read',''
```

```
            create: 'data/blogs/create',
            update: 'data/blogs/update',
            destroy:'data/blogs/delete'
        },

        reader: {
         type: 'json',
         root: 'blogs'
        },

        writer: {
            type: 'json',
            writeAllFields: false,
            root: 'data'
        }
     }
 });
```

If we try to load some data, the proxy will call the read URL, which is /data/blogs/ read.

Next, we will try to create a new record and insert it to the store, at the first position:

```
var blog = Ext.ModelManager.create({
    url: 'http://loiane.com'
}, 'Blog');

store.insert(0, blog);
```

The proxy will make a POST request to the create URL, passing the following as request body—note that it is a JSON object that you will have to decode on the server:

```
{"data":{"id":"","url":"http://loiane.com"}}
```

Consider that when we saved the blog, it was saved with id = 2. Now, we will modify this blog instance. Let's try and change the URL to something else (adding a .br at the end of it):

```
blog.setUrl('http://loiane.com.br');
```

The proxy will make a POST request to the updated URL, passing the following as request body:

```
{"data":{"id":"2","url":"http://loiane.com.br"}}
```

Next, we will try to delete this `blog` instance from the store:

```
store.remove(blog);
```

The proxy will make a POST request to the destroy URL, passing the following request body:

```
{"data":{"id":"2","url":"http://loiane.com.br"}}
```

If you set a `RestProxy`, you will only need to set the default URL config option.

XmlWriter

Now, we will do the same thing that we did in the previous topic, but by using `XmlWriter`. To do so, just change the `reader` and `writer` type to `xml` and add the `record: blog` to the proxy:

```
var store = Ext.create('Ext.data.Store',{
    model: 'Blog',

    proxy: {
        type: 'ajax',

        api: {
            read:   'data/blogs/read',
            create: 'data/blogs/create',
            update: 'data/blogs/update',
            destroy:'data/blogs/delete'
        },

        reader: {
         type: 'xml',
         root: 'blogs'
        },

        writer: {
            type: 'xml',
            writeAllFields: false,
            documentRoot: 'data'
        }
    }
});
```

Now, we will follow the same steps as we did while working with `JsonWriter`. When we try to insert a new record into the `store`, the proxy will make a POST request to the create URL, passing the following parameters:

```
<xmlData><record><id></id><url>http://loiane.com</url></record></
xmlData>
```

Consider, the server returned 2 as the `id`. Now, we will try to change the `blog url`. The `proxy` will make a POST request to the update URL, passing the following as the parameter:

```
<xmlData><record><id>2</id><url>http://loiane.com.br</url></record></
xmlData>
```

If we try to delete this `blog` instance, the `proxy` will make a POST request to the destroy URL, passing the following as the parameter:

```
<xmlData><record><id>2</id><url>http://loiane.com.br</url></record></
xmlData>
```

Remember that you will have to decode the XML or the JSON object in the server.

The writer is only used with server proxies. For local storage, you don't need to use it; the proxy will take care of the reading and writing automatically.

Sorting

Stores are capable of sorting the data. In Ext JS 4, we have the sorter's config option, known as `sortInfo` in Ext JS 3, in the Store class. The sorting can be done locally or remote. Each sort object in Ext JS 4 is an instance of `Ext.util.Sorter`. Even if you declare an initial config in the `store`, you can change it at any time. Let's see some examples to understand how it works.

For the following examples, we will use the following `Model` and `Proxy` as common:

```
Ext.define('Book', {
    extend: 'Ext.data.Model',
    fields: [
        {name: 'id', type: 'int'},
        {name: 'title', type: 'string'},
        {name: 'pages', type: 'int'},
        {name: 'numChapters', type: 'int'},
        {name: 'subject', type: 'string'}
    ],

    proxy: {
        type: 'ajax',
```

```
            url : 'data/books/books.json'
        }
    });
```

The books.json file contains the following JSON object, also common for the examples that follow:

```
[
    {
        "id": 11,
        "title": 'Learning Ext JS 3.2',
        "pages": 432,
        "numChapters": 17,
        "subject": 'Ext JS'
    },
    {
        "id": 12,
        "title": 'Learning Ext JS',
        "pages": 324,
        "numChapters": 14,
        "subject": 'Ext JS'
    },
    {
        "id": 13,
        "title": 'Ext JS 3.0 Cookbook',
        "pages": 376,
        "numChapters": 10,
        "subject": 'Ext JS'
    },
    {
        "id": 14,
        "title": 'Spring Security 3',
        "pages": 396,
        "numChapters": 13,
        "subject": 'Java'
    },
    {
        "id": 15,
        "title": 'WordPress Top Plugins',
        "pages": 252,
        "numChapters": 10,
        "subject": 'PHP'
    },
    {
        "id": 16,
```

The New Data Package

```
        "title": 'PHP Programming with PEAR',
        "pages": 250,
        "numChapters": 5,
        "subject": 'PHP'
    }
]
```

Now, we will declare a store with a couple of Sorters:

```
var store = Ext.create('Ext.data.Store',{
    model: 'Book',

    sorters: [
        {
            property : 'pages',
            direction: 'DESC'
        },
        {
            property : 'numChapters',
            direction: 'ASC'
        }
    ]
});
```

We want to sort the data first by pages (books with more pages first—we like big books!) and then by number of chapters. When we load the data from the store, this will be the output (book id + title):

```
11 : Learning Ext JS 3.2
14 : Spring Security 3
13 : Ext JS 3.0 Cookbook
12 : Learning Ext JS
15 : WordPress Top Plugins
16 : PHP Programming with PEAR
```

We can also change the sort information anytime we want, through the sort function:

```
store.sort('subject','ASC');
```

All the existing sorters will be removed when you change the sorting property of the store.

[92]

You can also pass an array of `sorters` to the `sort` method:

```
store.sort(
    {
        property : 'subject',
        direction: 'ASC'
    },
    {
        property : 'title',
        direction: 'ASC'
    }
);
```

If you prefer to, you can also change the preceding config to the following:

```
Ext.create('Ext.util.Sorter',{
    property : 'subject',
    direction: 'ASC'
}),
Ext.create('Ext.util.Sorter',{
    property : 'title',
    direction: 'ASC'
})
```

These examples show the sorting capability on the client side. But, if you have a large dataset or do not want the sorting to be performed on the client side, you can also configure for the server side. You simply need to set the `remoteSort` store option to `true` (default value is `false`):

```
var store = Ext.create('Ext.data.Store',{
    model: 'Book',
    remotSort: true,
    sorters: [
        {
            property : 'pages',
            direction: 'DESC'
        },
        {
            property : 'numChapters',
            direction: 'ASC'
        }
    ]
});
```

In this case, the `store` will only be a helper, in the `load` request; the proxy will make a GET request to the specified URL and will also send the `sort` object as parameter:

```
sort:[{"property":"pages","direction":"DESC"},{"property":"numChapters
","direction":"ASC"}]
```

The server will be responsible for decoding the `sort` parameter and sort the data as specified.

Filtering

In Ext JS 4, Stores are capable of filtering the data, and are also capable of sorting the data. The filter engine works in a similar way to the sorting. The filtering can be done locally or remote. Each `filter` object in Ext JS 4 is an instance of `Ext.util.Filter`. If you declare an initial config in the `store`, you can change it any time. Let's see some examples to understand how it works.

Consider the same `Model` and data we used for the Sorting examples.

We will declare a `Store` with some filter options:

```
var store = Ext.create('Ext.data.Store',{
    model: 'Book',

    filters: [
        {
            property : 'subject',
            value: 'JAVA'
        },
        {
            property : 'numChapters',
            value: '13'
        }
    ]
});
```

When we `load` the Store, the following is the output we will get:

```
14 : Spring Security 3
```

We can also change the `filter` option anytime through the method `filter`:

```
store.filter('numChapters',10);
```

And, if you need to filter on the server side, you can set the `remoteFilter` to `true` (default value is `false`) and the proxy will pass the filter object as the parameter:

```
filter:[{"property":"subject","value":"JAVA"},{"property":"numChapters
","value":13}]""""""""""""""
```

The server will be responsible for decoding the JSON object and process the filter into the data.

Summary

In this chapter, we have covered the capabilities of the new Ext JS 4 data package through examples. We introduced the new `Model` class with its new capabilities, such as Associations and Validations. We learned there are two model associations— `hasMany` and `belongsTo`. We also learned the validation types.

We covered the three new client proxies— `LocalStorage`, `SessionStorage`, and `Memory`. We also covered the server proxies— `Ajax`, `Rest`, and `JsonP`. We learned how to declare proxies inside Models (and perform CRUD actions directly from the Model) or inside Stores.

We learned new `Store` capabilities, such as Sorting and Filtering, through examples, and we presented how readers and writers are now organized in Ext JS 4 and covered some examples.

In the next chapter, we will dive into the upgraded and new `Component Layouts` and will learn how to use them.

3
Upgraded Layouts

The layout defines how a container sizes its child items. In an application, the layout is one of the most important components, because it defines how your container will be organized. Will it be a single item? Will it have several items organized vertically or horizontally? It is also what takes most time to render in an application. Layouts were improved in Ext JS 4; we will learn what has changed and get acquainted with the new layouts in this chapter.

In this chapter, we will cover:

- Ext JS 4 layouts
- Component layout
- Dock layout
- Toolbar layout
- Field layout
- TriggerField layout
- An overview of the existing layouts

Ext JS 4 layouts

Layouts have been vastly improved in EXT JS 4. The whole layout engine was rewritten, although the API is still the same; in other words, layouts are backward-compatible. The generated HTML was also updated in Ext JS 4.

Layouts were introduced in Ext JS 2, and it was a major feature. It had good performance and speed, but lacked flexibility. Sencha (still called Ext JS at that time) improved the flexibility but lost the speed; in Ext JS 4, the layout engine became slower. They investigated to find what was causing the issue and they finally found a way to improve speed, performance, and flexibility. The Ext JS 4 layout engine is now much faster and flexible than any other previous version of Ext. The following chart compares performance/speed and flexibility between Ext JS versions 2 to 4:

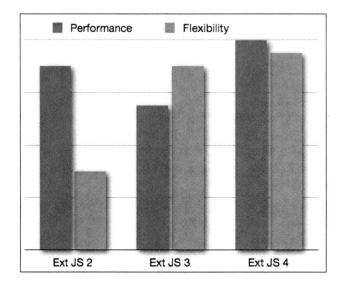

Besides the performance and flexibility improvements, Ext JS 4 also introduces two types of layouts: **Container Layout** and **Component Layout**. The Component Layout is responsible for organizing the HTML elements for a `Component`. The Container Layout is responsible for organizing the elements in their parent Container and managing the size of all Container's children.

Among the Container layouts, we can mention the ones you are probably familiar with—**Border Layout**, **Box Layout**, **Fit Layout**, and so on.

Among the Component layouts, we can mention the **Dock Layout**, **Toolbar Layout**, **Field Layout**, and **TriggerField Layout**.

The `AutoLayout` replaced the `ContainerLayout` from Ext JS 3 onwards. The `ContainerLayout` class in Ext JS 4 is a base class for all layouts that can be applied to containers.

The **Form Layout** is no longer supported in Ext JS 4. It has been replaced by Field Layout, to improve flexibility. We will take a closer look at the new Field Layout in this chapter.

Container layouts

Before we get started with the Component layouts, we will take a quick look at the existing Container layouts—**Auto**, **Anchor**, **Absolute**, **Hbox**, **Vbox**, **Accordion**, **Table**, **Column**, **Fit**, **Card**, and **Border**. The following diagram exemplifies the Container layout's hierarchy. We will take a closer look at each one of these layouts in the following sections:

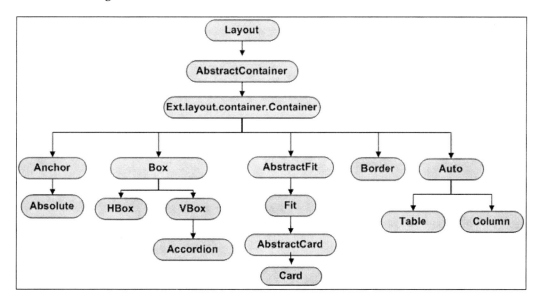

Auto layout

The **Auto Layout** is the default layout manager applied to a Container when no layout is specified.

For example, consider we have four panels and we want to organize these panels into an outer container (for example, a window):

```
var panel1 = Ext.create('Ext.panel.Panel', {
    title: 'Panel 1',
    html: 'Panel 1',
    height: 60,
    width: 100
});

var panel2 = Ext.create('Ext.panel.Panel', {
    title: 'Panel 2',
    html: 'Panel 2',
```

```
      height: 80,
      width: 60
});

var panel3 = Ext.create('Ext.panel.Panel', {
   title: 'Panel 3',
   html: 'Panel 3',
   height: 65,
   width: 100
});

var panel4 = Ext.create('Ext.panel.Panel', {
   title: 'Panel 4',
   html: 'Panel 4',
   height: 70,
   width: '90%'
});

var auto = Ext.create('Ext.window.Window', {
   title: 'Auto Layout',
   width: 100,
   height: 320,
   layout:'auto',
   defaults: {
      bodyStyle: 'padding:15px'
   },
   items: [panel1, panel2, panel3, panel4]
});
```

In the preceding code, we have four simple panels; each one has a `title`, HTML content, `height`, and `width`. Then, we have a `Window` object called `auto`, which has a `title`, `height`, and `width`. We also specified the layout as `auto`, but you do not need to specify a layout at all. We want every child `Panel` (panels we declared before) content to have a `padding` of 15 pixels. The `defaults` option applies all the config settings to all added items: `panel1`, `panel2`, `panel3`, and `panel4` (whether added to the `items` config or via the `add` and `insert` methods). The `auto` panel contains four children (the panels we declared before)—`panel1`, `panel2`, `panel3`, and `panel4`.

If we try to execute the preceding code, the following will be the output:

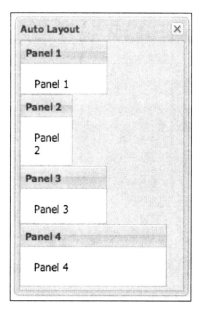

Note that the child panels were added to the main `Window` (auto) in the order as they were declared; in other words, you must append children to the `window` in a specific order to use the `auto` layout correctly. If we try to resize the `Window`, the panel will not change its size, even if we declared the last panel's (panel4) `width` to `90%` of the `Window`'s `width`, because of the properties of Auto Layout.

Anchor layout

The **Anchor Layout** allows anchoring the container's children according to its dimension. If you resize the outer container, all its children will be automatically resized according to the children's anchor rules. Just like the Auto Layout, the Anchor Layout also stacks its children according to the order they were added or declared in, in the `items` config.

For example, we have four panels and we want to add them in a `Window` using the Anchor Layout:

```
var panel1 = Ext.create('Ext.panel.Panel', {
    title: 'Panel 1',
    html: '100% 30%',
    anchor:'100% 30%'
});
```

```
var panel2 = Ext.create('Ext.panel.Panel', {
    title: 'Panel 2',
    html: '80% 25%',
    anchor:'80% 25%'
});

var panel3 = Ext.create('Ext.panel.Panel', {
    title: 'Panel 3',
    html: '-70 20%',
    anchor:'-70 20%'
});

var panel4 = Ext.create('Ext.panel.Panel', {
    title: 'Panel 4',
    html: '-30 25%',
    anchor:'-30 25%'
});

var anchor = Ext.create('Ext.window.Window', {
    title: 'Anchor Layout',
    width: 250,
    height:300,
    layout:'anchor',
    defaults: {
        bodyStyle: 'padding:10px'
    },
    items: [panel1, panel2, panel3, panel4]
});
anchor.show();
```

Let's explain the code starting from the last element declared, which is the `Window` named `anchor`. This `window` has a `title`, `width` (250 pixels), `height` (300 pixels) and is using the Anchor Layout. It also has four children declared in the `items` config.

Going back to the beginning of the code, we declared four panels. Each one has a `title` and HTML content. We also set an `anchor` rule for each one:

- The first panel (`panel1`) has an `anchor` specified as `100%` of the parent's `width` (250 pixels, originally) and `30%` of the parent's `height` (30% of the parent's height = 30% of 300 = 90 pixels)

- The second panel (`panel2`) has an `anchor` specified as `80%` of the parent's `width` (80% of 300 = 200 pixels) and `25%` of the parent's `height` (25% of 300 = 75 pixels)

- The third panel (`panel3`) has an `anchor` specified as -70 pixels of offset — which means this panel will leave 70 pixels of space on the right side of the parent's body — and `20%` of the parent's `height` (20% of 300 = 60 pixels)

- The fourth panel (panel4) has an anchor specified as -30 of offset—which means this panel will leave 30 pixels of space on the right side of the parent's body—and 25% of the parent's height (25% of 300 = 75 pixels)

When we execute the code, the output will be as follows:

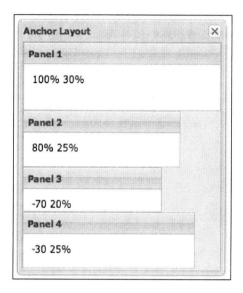

If we try to resize the Window, all its children will be resized according to their anchor rules. Let's try to resize the window to a bigger size to see what happens:

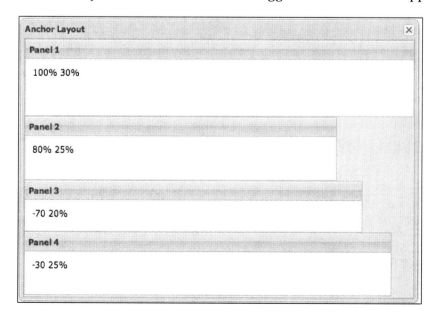

When we compare the two previous screenshots, we see that when we resized the window, it maintained the child panels proportional to their original size.

Absolute layout

The AbsoluteLayout class is a subclass of AnchorLayout, and that is why it inherits the anchoring feature from its mother class. Like the Anchor Layout, the Absolute Layout also allows you to set an x and y configuration, which means the location of the Component will be located in its parent's body.

Let's try to add a Panel in a Window using the Absolute Layout:

```
var panel1 = Ext.create('Ext.panel.Panel', {
    title: 'Panel 1',
    html: 'x: 10; y: 10 - anchor: 80% 80%', /*this config option will
display the given text inside the panel*/
    anchor:'80% 80%',
    x: 10,
    y: 10
});

var absolute = Ext.create('Ext.window.Window', {
    title: 'Absolute Layout',
    width: 300,
    height: 200,
    layout:'absolute',
    defaults: {
        bodyStyle: 'padding:10px'
    },
    items: [panel1]
});
absolute.show();
```

In the preceding code, we have a Window with a title, width (300 pixels), height (200 pixels), using the Absolute Layout. This Window contains only one Panel as the child item.

The panel we declared as the Window item is panel1. This panel has a title and HTML content. We set the anchor as 80% of the parent's width and 80% of the parent's height. We also set the position of panel1 in its parent's body, which is *x=10* and *y =10*.

The upper-left corner of the Window will be *x=0* and *y=0*.

The code output will be as follows:

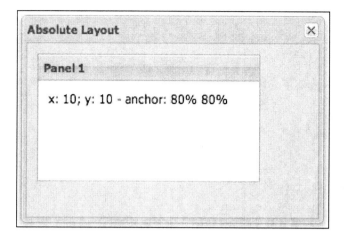

If you resize the outer container (Window), its child is going to be resized according to its anchor rule. The position of the child items will not change with the resizing.

HBox layout

The **HBox layout** organizes its children horizontally across the container.

You can set two optional configurations to organize the child's width and height across the parent's body.

The flex configuration will tell the parent Component how to organize the child Components horizontally, based on the relative flex configuration. The align configuration will tell the child Components how to use the height across the parent.

Let's consider that we have two panels and we want to display these panels inside a Window:

```
var panel1 = Ext.create('Ext.panel.Panel', {
    title: 'Panel 1',
    html: 'Panel 1', //this text will be displayed on the panel body
    flex: 1
});

var panel2 = Ext.create('Ext.panel.Panel', {
    title: 'Panel 2',
    html: 'Panel 2', //this text will be displayed on the panel body
    flex: 3
});
```

```
var hbox = Ext.create('Ext.window.Window', {
    title: 'HBox Layout',
    width: 300,
    height:100,
    layout: {
        type: 'hbox',
        align: 'stretch'
    },
    defaults: {
        bodyStyle: 'padding:10px'
    },
    items: [panel1, panel2]
});
hbox.show();
```

In the preceding code, we have two panels. Each panel has its `title` and HTML content. Each one also has a `flex` configuration. The first `panel` configured `flex` as `1` and the second `panel` configured the `flex` config as `3`. The `Window` will sum these `flex` configs (in this example, the total will be `4`) and will distribute the horizontal space relative to each child. The first `panel` will get one-fourth (25%) of the window's horizontal space and the second panel will get three-fourths (75%) of the window's horizontal space.

In the `Window` declaration, we have the `layout` config. It tells the `Window` that we are going to use the `hbox` layout and `align` of the child Components will be `stretch`, meaning that we can use the full height of the window's vertical space.

When we execute the code, the following will be the output:

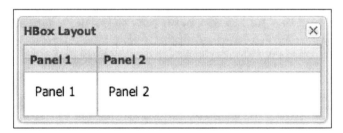

If we try to resize the `Window`, children will be resized as well, according to their configuration.

VBox layout

The **VBox Layout** is very similar to the HBox Layout, but instead of arranging the Components horizontally across the Container, it arranges child Components vertically.

We will change the HBox example to use the VBox Layout:

```
var panel1 = Ext.create('Ext.panel.Panel', {
    title: 'Panel 1',
    html: 'Panel 1',
    flex: 2
});

var panel2 = Ext.create('Ext.panel.Panel', {
    title: 'Panel 2',
    html: 'Panel 2',
    flex: 1
});

var vbox = Ext.create('Ext.window.Window', {
    title: 'VBox Layout',
    width: 82,
    height: 300,
    layout: {
        type: 'vbox',
        align: 'stretch'
    },
    defaults: {
        bodyStyle: 'padding:15px'
    },
    items: [panel1, panel2]
});
vbox.show();
```

Similar to the HBox example, we set `flex` properties for each panel. The first panel has a `flex` config equal to `1` and the second panel has `flex` equal to `2`. This means `panel1` gets one-third (33%) of the `Window` vertical space and `panel2` gets two-thirds (66%) of the `Window` vertical space.

When we execute the code, the following will be the output:

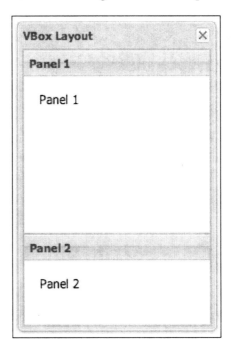

If we try to resize the `Window` all its child Components will be resized according to their configuration as well.

Accordion layout

The `AccordionLayout` is a subclass of `VBoxLayout`. This already tells us that the Components will be organized vertically in the container. The difference between `AccordionLayout` and `VBoxLayout` is that the `AccordionLayout` only displays a Component at a time; we can collapse or expand the items.

In the following example, we have five panels being displayed inside a `Window`:

```
var panel1 = Ext.create('Ext.panel.Panel', {
    title: 'Panel 1',
    html: '<b>Panel 1</b>'
});

var panel2 = Ext.create('Ext.panel.Panel', {
    title: 'Panel 2',
    html: '<b>Panel 2</b>'
});
```

```
var panel3 = Ext.create('Ext.panel.Panel', {
    title: 'Panel 3',
    html: '<b>Panel 3</b>'
});

var panel4 = Ext.create('Ext.panel.Panel', {
    title: 'Panel 4',
    html: '<b>Panel 4</b>'
});

var panel5 = Ext.create('Ext.panel.Panel', {
    title: 'Panel 5',
    html: '<b>Panel 5</b>'
});

var accordion = Ext.create('Ext.window.Window', {
    title: 'Accordion Layout',
    margins:'5 0 5 5',
    split:true,
    width: 210,
    height:250,
    layout:'accordion',
    defaults: {
        bodyStyle: 'padding:35 15 0 50'
    },
    items: [panel1, panel2, panel3, panel4, panel5]
accordion.show();
```

When we execute the code, the output will be as follows:

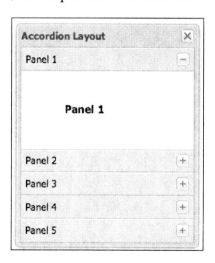

To expand a Panel, simply click on the plus (**+**) icon; to collapse the panel that is being currently displayed, click on the minus (**-**) icon. If we try to resize the `Window`, all the child panels will be resized as well.

Table layout

The `TableLayout` class converts the Components into an HTML `table` and it is a subclass of `AutoLayout`.

For example, let's consider we have nine Components and we want to display these Components in a `Window` using Table Layout:

```
var table = Ext.create('Ext.window.Window', {
    title: 'Table Layout',
    width: 250,
    height: 200,
    layout: {
        type: 'table',
        columns: 3,
        tableAttrs: {
            style: {
                width: '100%',
                height: '100%'
            }
        }
    },
    defaults: {
        bodyStyle: 'padding:10px'
    },
    items:[{
        html:'Cell 1',
        rowspan: 3 //this cell will span 3 rows
    },{
        html:'Cell 2'
    },{
        html:'Cell 3'
    },{
        html:'Cell 4'
    },{
        html:'Cell 5'
    },{
        html:'Cell 6',
        colspan: 2 //this cell will span 2 columns
    },{
```

```
        html:'Cell 7'
    },{
        html:'Cell 8'
    },{
        html:'Cell 9'
    }]
});
table.show();
```

In the preceding code, we set the `Window` layout to `table`. Inside the `layout` config, we set the number of `columns` to create in the table (container). We also set the `tableAttrs` config, where we can set properties to be applied to the HTML table, such as `width` and `height`. We set the `width` and `height` of the table as `100%`, which means the Components will use all the available space horizontally and vertically.

The code outputs the following `Window`:

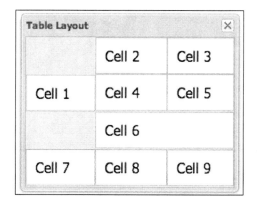

Column layout

The `ColumnLayout` class manages the `width` of its children and, like the `TableLayout`, it is also a subclass of `AutoLayout`.

It does not provide any configuration in the Container. The child Component has support for a `columnWidth` configuration, where you can specify how much of horizontal space the Component will get from its parent.

We will declare a `Window` with Column Layout containing three child panels:

```
var panel1 = Ext.create('Ext.panel.Panel', {
    title: 'Panel 1',
    html: '.25',
    columnWidth: .25 //means 25%
```

```
});

var panel2 = Ext.create('Ext.panel.Panel', {
    title: 'Panel 2',
    html: '.25',
    columnWidth: .25 //means 25%
});

var panel3 = Ext.create('Ext.panel.Panel', {
    title: 'Panel 3',
    html: '1/2',
    columnWidth: 1/2 //means 50%
});

var column = Ext.create('Ext.window.Window', {
    title: 'Column Layout',
    width: 400,
    layout:'column',
    defaults: {
        height: 60,
        bodyStyle: 'padding:10px'
    },
    items: [panel1, panel2, panel3]
});
column.show();
```

In the code, we have a `Window` using the Column Layout with three panels configured as its child `items`. Each panel has a `title` and HTML content. We also configured a `columnWidth` for each one. In the first panel, we set a `columnWidth` equal to `.25`, which means this panel will get `25%` of the `Window` horizontal space. It will be the same for the second `Panel`. The third panel has a `columnWidth` equal to half, which means this panel will get `50%` of the `Window` horizontal space. Note that you can set the `columnWidth` in two different ways.

When we execute the code, we will get the following output:

When we resize the `Window`, the child panels will be resized horizontally. The `height` of the child panels will not change.

Fit layout

The **Fit layout** only displays a single Component in the Container. The Component will fill all the space in the Container's body.

For example, we want to display a single panel inside a window:

```
var panel1 = Ext.create('Ext.panel.Panel', {
   title: 'Panel 1',
   bodyStyle: 'padding:15px',
   html: 'Fit Content'
});

var fit = Ext.create('Ext.window.Window', {
   title: 'Fit Layout',
   width: 100,
   height: 150,
   layout:'fit',
   items: [panel1]
});
fit.show();
```

In the code, we have a window with a panel as an item with `fit` layout. When we execute the code, the following will be the output:

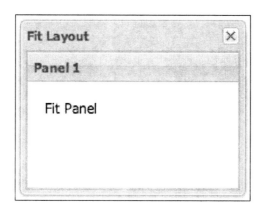

And if we try to resize the window, the panel inside it will be resized as well.

Card layout

The CardLayout is a subclass of FitLayout. Like its superclass, it also renders only one Component in the Container, In the CardLayout, the Container can have multiple items, but it will only display one at time.

This layout manager works well for wizard setup; we are going to demonstrate this in the following example:

```
var card = Ext.create('Ext.window.Window', {
    title: 'Card Layout',
    width: 400,
    height: 200,
    layout: 'card',
    activeItem: 0,
    bodyStyle: 'padding:70 50 0 150',
    defaults: {
        border:false
    },
    bbar: [{
        id: 'prevButton',
        text: 'Preivous Step',
        handler: navHandler,
        disabled: true
    },
    '->',
    {
        id: 'nextButton',
        text: 'Next Step',
        handler: navHandler
    }],

    items: [{
        html: '<p>Step 1 of 3</p>'
    },{
        html: '<p>Step 2 of 3</p>'
    },{
        html: '<p>Step 3 of 3</p>'
    }]
});
card.show();
```

In the code, we have a window using the `Card Layout`. This window contains three Components with HTML content declared in the `items` config. Since only one Component can be displayed at a time, the window manages which Component will be displayed first, using the `activeItem` configuration. In this example, when we show the window, the first item will be displayed in the container body (`index` is 0-based).

We also added two buttons to control the wizard setup—`nextButton` and `previousButton`—so the user can navigate through the screens. When we display the first step, only the next button will be enabled. And when the user clicks on the next or previous buttons, the `navHandler` function will be executed. Let's take a look at this function:

```
var navHandler = function(btn) {

    var activeItem = card.layout.activeItem;
    var active = card.items.indexOf(activeItem);

    if (btn.id == 'nextButton') {
        active += 1;
    }
    else if (btn.id == 'prevButton') {
        active -= 1;
    }

    card.layout.setActiveItem(active);

    var prev = card.dockedItems.items[1].items.items[0];
    var next = card.dockedItems.items[1].items.items[2];

    if (active == 0){
        prev.setDisabled(true);
    } else if (active == 1){
        prev.setDisabled(false);
        next.setDisabled(false);
    } else if (active == 2){
        next.setDisabled(true);
    }
};
```

In this function, first we get which item is the active one. Then we analyze which button the user pressed, either **Next Step** or **Previous Step**. If user clicks on the **Next Step** button, we will increase the active index because we want to navigate to the next page and decrease the active index, if we want otherwise. Then we get a reference for both buttons, so we can control when we need to disable or enable the buttons. We will disable the **Previous Step** button when we display the first step and we will disable the **Next Step** button when we display the third (and last) step; otherwise, the buttons will be enabled.

It is simple logic to exemplify how we can manage a wizard using the card layout.

When we execute the preceding code, the following will be the output (all three steps):

If we try to resize the Window, its content will be also resized.

Border layout

The **Border Layout** divides the Container into five regions: north, south, east, west, and center, as we can see in the following diagram:

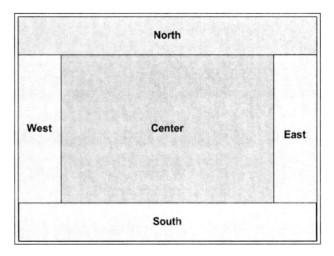

The north and south regions can be resized and the west and east regions can be collapsed. These four regions are optional in a Border Layout. The center is the only region required by a Container while using the Border Layout. You do not need to specify width and height for the center region. It is going to be rendered in the remaining space of the Container's body.

Let's take a look at the following example:

```
var border = Ext.create('Ext.window.Window', {
    width: 700,
    height: 500,
    title: 'Border Layout',
    layout: 'border',
    defaults:{
        xtype: 'panel'
    },
    items: [{
        title: 'North Region is resizable',
        region: 'north',
        height: 100,
        split: true
    },{
        title: 'South Region is resizable',
        region: 'south',
        height: 100,
        split: true
    },{
        title: 'West Region is collapsible',
        region:'west',
        width: 200,
        collapsible: true,
        layout: 'fit'
    },{
        title: 'East Region is collapsible',
        region:'east',
        width: 200,
        collapsible: true,
        layout: 'fit'
    },{
        title: 'Center Region',
        region: 'center',
        layout: 'fit'
    }]
});
border.show();
```

In the preceding code, we have a window using the Border Layout. This window also contains five items (panel) distributed in different regions of the panel.

The first panel is located in the north. The north panel will occupy the full width of the Window and will have a height of 100.

The second panel is located in the south. Like the north panel, it will also occupy the full width of the Window and height equal to 100.

You need to specify height for the north and south panels. When you scroll your mouse over the central border, you will see we can resize the panels. This is because we set the split config to true.

Then we have the east and west panels. We need to specify the width for these panels. If there is a south or north panel (as in this example), the west and east panels will occupy the remaining full height of the Container. We also set the collapse config as true; this means we can collapse the west and east panels.

At last, we have the center panel. The center Component is the only mandatory Component that we have to declare while using the Border Layout (the south, north, west, and east regions are optional). We do not need to set a height or width because this Component will occupy the remaining space left in the Container's body.

If we execute the preceding code, the following will be the output:

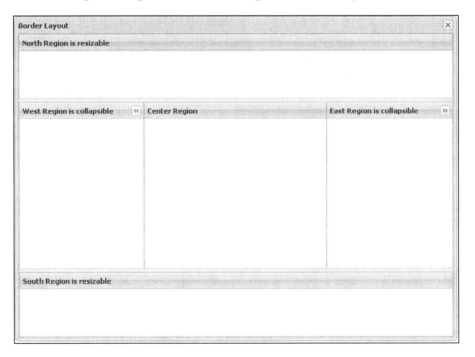

When we resize the window, the north and south panels will resize their `width` (if needed) and the `west` and `east` panels will resize their `height` (if needed). The only panel that will be fully resized, occupying the remaining area, is the `center` panel.

Component layouts

The **Component Layout** is responsible for organizing the HTML elements for a `Component`. In Ext JS 4, there are some new features applied to Toolbars, Headers, and Form Fields. Let's take a look at them.

Dock layout

To improve flexibility, Ext JS 4 now has a new layout engine called `DockLayout`, mostly applied to panel Components. This layout is set internally and it is used for panel Headers and Toolbars.

We will compare the differences between Ext JS 3 Panel and Ext JS 4 Panel. First, we will take a look at the following code implemented using Ext JS 3:

```
var html = '<div style="padding:10px;"><h1><center><span>Body</
center></h1></div>';

var panel1 = new Ext.Panel({
    collapsible:true,
    width:400,
    renderTo: 'ext3-panel',

    title: 'Ext 3 Panel - Header',

    html: html,

    tbar: new Ext.Toolbar({
        items: [{
            type: 'button',
            text:'Button - Top Toolbar'
        }]
    }),

    bbar: new Ext.Toolbar({
        items: [{
            type: 'button',
            text:'Button - Bottom Toolbar'
        }]
```

```
        }),

    fbar: new Ext.Toolbar({
        items: [{
            type: 'button',
            text:'Button - Footer Toolbar'
        }]
    })
});
```

In the preceding code, we are creating an `Ext.Panel` that contains a header named `Ext 3 Panel - Header` and three Toolbars, one located at the top (`tbar`), another one located at the bottom of the panel (`bbar`), and the third one located in the footer of the panel (`fbar`); each Toolbar has a button. This code will generate the following Ext Component:

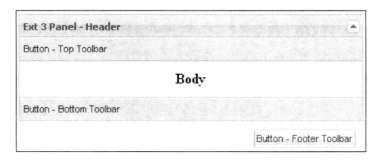

When we analyze the generated code for Ext JS 4 Panel, we have an outer wrapper element (**El**), the panel itself with the **Header**, and a **body wrapper**. Inside the body wrapper, it has the three **Toolbars** and the **panel body**, as demonstrated in the following picture:

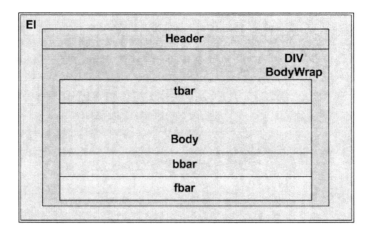

As you can see, the Ext JS 4 `Panel` has almost no flexibility, which means we cannot make many changes. This means we can have a Header on the top, *only one* Toolbar on the top, and *two* Toolbars on the footer of the panel.

Now, let's take a look at the Ext JS 4 `Panel` Component. We will simply migrate the code that we implemented in Ext JS 3 to Ext JS 4:

```
var panel1 = Ext.create('Ext.panel.Panel', {
    collapsible:true,
    width:400,
    renderTo: 'ext4-panel',

    title: 'Ext 4 Panel - Header',

    html: html,

    tbar: Ext.create('Ext.toolbar.Toolbar',{
        items: [{
            type: 'button',
            text:'Button - Top Toolbar'
        }]
    }),

    bbar: Ext.create('Ext.toolbar.Toolbar',{
        items: [{
            type: 'button',
            text:'Button - Bottom Toolbar'
        }]
    }),

    fbar: Ext.create('Ext.toolbar.Toolbar',{
        items: [{
            type: 'button',
            text:'Button - Footer Toolbar'
        }]
    })
});
```

The only thing that changed from Ext JS 3 to Ext JS 4 in both codes is how we instantiate the classes. In Ext JS 3, we used the keyword **new** and in Ext JS 4 we use the **Ext.create** to instantiate a class. Another thing that changed is the name of the classes—`Ext.Panel` is now `Ext.panel.Panel`, and `Ext.Toolbar` is now `Ext.toolbar.Toolbar`.

There is something new in Ext JS 4 about the `Panel`—the Header is now a Component, an instance of the class `Ext.panel.Header`. We can set the Header's position to `top` (default value), `bottom`, `left` or `right`, which means the Header is now very flexible.

The **Toolbar** is also a flexible Component in Ext JS 4. You can set a Toolbar on the `top`, `bottom`, `left`, or `right`. This Component is now a *docked* item.

Let's see how we can write the preceding code in Ext JS 4 using the new features (the following code is equivalent to the preceding code):

```
var panel2 = Ext.create('Ext.panel.Panel', {
    collapsible:true,
    width:400,
    border:true,
    renderTo: 'ext4-panel2',

    title: 'Ext 4 Panel - Header',
    headerPosition: 'top',

    html: html,

    dockedItems: [{
        xtype: 'toolbar',
        dock: 'top',
        items: [{
            xtype: 'button',
            text: 'Button - Top Toolbar'
        }]
    },{
        xtype: 'toolbar',
        dock: 'bottom',
        items: [{
            xtype: 'button',
            text: 'Button - Bottom Toolbar'
        }]
    },{
        xtype: 'toolbar',
```

```
        dock: 'bottom',
        items: [{
            xtype: 'component',
            flex: 1 //will occupy 100% of the width of the panel
        },{
            xtype: 'button',
            text: 'Button - Footer Toolbar'
        }]
    }]
});
```

We added the `headerPosition` configuration to the default value (`top`). And, instead of the toolbar declarations (`tbar`, `bbar`, and `fbar`), we now have three **docked items** of type `toolbar:`—one at the `top` and two at the `bottom`.

When we analyze the generated code for Ext JS 4 Panel, we have an outer wrapper element (**El**), the **panel** itself with the **Header** as a *docked item*, and a **body wrapper**. Inside the body wrapper, it has three **toolbars** and the **panel body**, as demonstrated in the following picture:

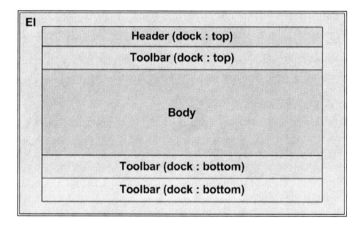

As Header is a new Component in Ext JS 4 and it is a **docked item**, we can set the location of the Header as `top`, `bottom`, `right`, and `left`, as demonstrated by the following screenshot:

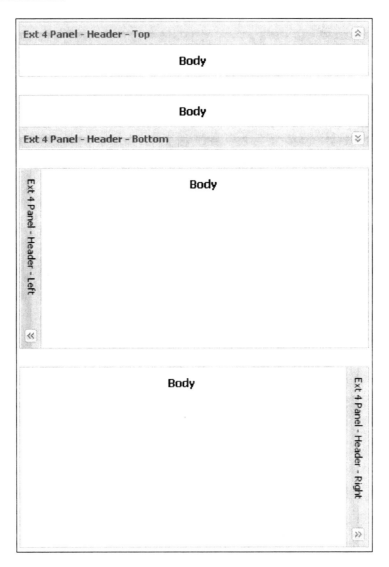

The code to generate the panels above is very simple—you only need to change the headerPosition to one of the four possible values. If the collapse configuration is set to true, the panel will collapse to the header direction, as shown in the following code:

```
var panel1 = Ext.create('Ext.panel.Panel', {
    collapsible:true,
    width:400,
    border:true,
    renderTo: 'ext4-panel-header-top',
    html: html,

    title: 'Ext 4 Panel - Header - Top'
});

var panel2 = Ext.create('Ext.panel.Panel', {
    collapsible:true,
    width:400,
    border:true,
    renderTo: 'ext4-panel-header-bottom',
    html: html,

    title: 'Ext 4 Panel - Header - Bottom',
    headerPosition: 'bottom'
});

var panel3 = Ext.create('Ext.panel.Panel', {
    collapsible:true,
    width:400,
    height:200,
    border:true,
    renderTo: 'ext4-panel-header-left',
    html: html,

    title: 'Ext 4 Panel - Header - Left',
    headerPosition: 'left'
});

var panel4 = Ext.create('Ext.panel.Panel', {
    collapsible:true,
    width:400,
    height:200,
    border:true,
    renderTo: 'ext4-panel-header-right',
```

```
    html: html,

    title: 'Ext 4 Panel - Header - Right',
    headerPosition: 'right'
});
```

Like Header, the Toolbar is also a docked Component in Ext JS 4. It works the same way as the Header does—you can set the position (dock) to top, bottom, left, or right:

```
var panel2 = Ext.create('Ext.panel.Panel', {
    collapsible:true,
    width:400,
    height:200,
    border:true,
    renderTo: 'ext4-panel-toolbars',

    title: 'Ext 4 Panel - Header',

    html: html,

    dockedItems: [{
        xtype: 'toolbar',
        dock: 'top',
        items: [{
            xtype: 'button',
            text: 'Button - Top Toolbar'
        }]
    },{
        xtype: 'toolbar',
        dock: 'bottom',
        items: [{
            xtype: 'button',
            text: 'Button - Bottom Toolbar'
        }]
    },{
        xtype: 'toolbar',
        dock: 'left',
        items: [{
            xtype: 'button',
            text: 'Button - Left Toolbar'
        }]
    },{
        xtype: 'toolbar',
        dock: 'right',
```

```
   items: [{
       xtype: 'button',
       text: 'Button - Right Toolbar'
     }]
   }]
 });
```

You will have a panel like the following one:

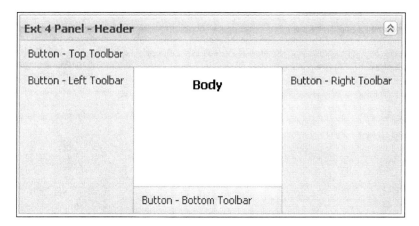

To keep compatibility, you can still use the old configuration—`tbar` (top bar), `bbar` (bottom bar), and `fbar` (footer bar). In Ext JS 4, there are also two new toolbar configurations, `rbar` (right bar) and `lbar` (left bar), equivalent to a toolbar with `dock:'right'` and `dock:'left'`, respectively:

```
var panel1 = Ext.create('Ext.panel.Panel', {
    collapsible:true,
    width:400,
    height:200,
    renderTo: 'ext4-panel-bars',

    title: 'Ext 4 Panel - Header',

    html: html,

    tbar: Ext.create('Ext.toolbar.Toolbar',{
        items: [{
            type: 'button',
            text:'Button - Top Toolbar'
        }]
    }),

    bbar: Ext.create('Ext.toolbar.Toolbar',{
        items: [{
```

```
            type: 'button',
            text:'Button - Bottom Toolbar'
        }]
    }),

    fbar: Ext.create('Ext.toolbar.Toolbar',{
        items: [{
            type: 'button',
            text:'Button - Footer Toolbar'
        }]
    }),

    lbar: Ext.create('Ext.toolbar.Toolbar',{
        items: [{
            type: 'button',
            text:'Button - Left Toolbar'
        }]
    }),

    rbar: Ext.create('Ext.toolbar.Toolbar',{
        items: [{
            type: 'button',
            text:'Button - Right Toolbar'
        }]
    })
});
```

As **Header** and **Toolbar** are **docked items**, you can mix them the way you want. If you want **three toolbars** on the **top**, **two toolbars** on the **bottom**, **one toolbar** on the **right**, **one toolbar header** on the **left**, as demonstrated in the following picture, it is possible:

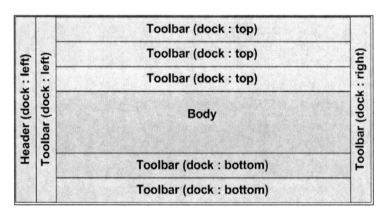

The following code implements the panel shown in the previous image:

```
var panel3 = Ext.create('Ext.panel.Panel', {
    collapsible:true,
    width:430,
    height:200,
    border:true,
    renderTo: 'ext4-panel-mix-toolbars',
    html: html,

    title: 'Ext 4 Panel - Header',
    headerPosition: 'left',

    dockedItems: [{
        xtype: 'toolbar',
        dock: 'top',
        items: [{
            xtype: 'button',
            text: 'Button - Top Toolbar 1'
        }]
    },{
        xtype: 'toolbar',
        dock: 'top',
        items: [{
            xtype: 'button',
            text: 'Button - Top Toolbar 2'
        }]
    },{
        xtype: 'toolbar',
        dock: 'top',
        items: [{
            xtype: 'button',
            text: 'Button - Top Toolbar 3'
        }]
    },{
        xtype: 'toolbar',
        dock: 'bottom',
        items: [{
            xtype: 'button',
            text: 'Button - Bottom Toolbar 1'
        }]
    },{
        xtype: 'toolbar',
        dock: 'bottom',
```

```
            items: [{
                xtype: 'button',
                text: 'Button - Bottom Toolbar 2'
            }]
        },{
            xtype: 'toolbar',
            dock: 'right',
            items: [{
                xtype: 'button',
                text: 'Button - Right Toolbar 1'
            }]
        },{
            xtype: 'toolbar',
            dock: 'left',
            items: [{
                xtype: 'button',
                text: 'Button - Left Toolbar 1'
            }]
        }]
    });
```

We simply need to set the `dock` to a position, and you can have as many toolbars as you want on each side. This new `Panel` configuration is extremely flexible; you no longer need to use any plugin to achieve the above configuration.

When we try to execute the previous code, the following is going to be the panel output:

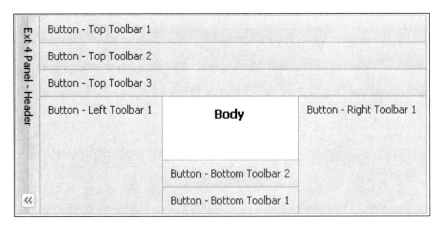

Tool layout

Header Tools are also Components in Ext JS 4. You can configure them in the `tools` configuration. One important thing to know about `tools` — Ext JS 4 will only display the icon; you will have to implement its behavior. For example, if you add the search tool, you will have to implement the function that will be run when a user clicks on it. There are some **tools** that Ext adds to the Header automatically. For example, the `collapse` tool; when we set the collapsed panel config as `true`, Ext will add the collapse button (according to the header position) and will also add a behavior to the `handler` function.

The following are some `tools` that you can configure. You simply need to set the type and implement the `handler` function:

```
var panel1 = Ext.create('Ext.panel.Panel', {
    width:500,
    renderTo: 'ext4-panel-tools',
    html: html,
    title: 'Tools - Header',

    tools: [{
        type: 'close',
        handler: function(){} //some logic inside handler
    },{
        type: 'collapse',
        handler: function(){} //some logic inside handler
    },{
        type: 'down',
        handler: function(){} //some logic inside handler
    },{
        type: 'expand',
        handler: function(){} //some logic inside handler
    },{
        type: 'gear',
        handler: function(){} //some logic inside handler
    },{
        type: 'help',
        handler: function(){} //some logic inside handler
    },{
        type: 'left',
        handler: function(){} //some logic inside handler
    },{
        type: 'maximize',
        handler: function(){} //some logic inside handler
    },{
```

```
        type: 'minimize',
        handler: function(){} //some logic inside handler
    },{
        type: 'minus',
        handler: function(){} //some logic inside handler
    },{
        type: 'next',
        handler: function(){} //some logic inside handler
    },{
        type: 'pin',
        handler: function(){} //some logic inside handler
    },{
        type: 'plus',
        handler: function(){} //some logic inside handler
    },{
        type: 'prev',
        handler: function(){} //some logic inside handler
    },{
        type: 'print',
        handler: function(){} //some logic inside handler
    },{
        type: 'refresh',
        handler: function(){} //some logic inside handler
    },{
        type: 'restore',
        handler: function(){} //some logic inside handler
    },{
        type: 'right',
        handler: function(){} //some logic inside handler
    },{
        type: 'save',
        handler: function(){} //some logic inside handler
    },{
        type: 'search',
        handler: function(){} //some logic inside handler
    },{
        type: 'toggle',
        handler: function(){} //some logic inside handler
    },{
        type: 'unpin',
        handler: function(){} //some logic inside handler
    },{
        type: 'up',
        handler: function(){} //some logic inside handler
    }]
});
```

If we try to execute the previous code, the following is going to be the output:

If you click on any `tool`, it will not work. Remember you have to implement the `handler` function.

Field layout

Ext JS 4 no longer supports `FormLayout`, which was used on `FormPanels` in Ext JS 3. So how are we going to organize the form fields in Ext JS 4? The new version of Ext JS introduces a new layout called `FieldLayout`, which replaces the old `FormLayout`.

First, we will take a look at how a form with two fields was implemented in Ext JS 4:

```
Ext.form.Field.prototype.msgTarget = 'side';

var simple = new Ext.FormPanel({
    labelWidth: 75,
    url:'save-form.php',
    frame:true,
    title: 'Form - Ext 3',
    bodyStyle:'padding:5px 5px 0',
    width: 350,
    renderTo:'ext3-form',
    defaults: {width: 230},
    defaultType: 'textfield',

    items: [{
        fieldLabel: 'First Name',
        name: 'first',
        allowBlank:false
    },{
        fieldLabel: 'Last Name',
        name: 'last',
        allowBlank:false
    }
    ],

    buttons: [{
```

```
        text: 'Save'
    },{
        text: 'Cancel'
    }]
});
```

In the preceding code, we have a form with a `width` value of 350 pixels, a label with a `width` value of 75 pixels, and two fields (text fields) with `width` values of 230 pixels each. The text fields cannot be left blank—they have to contain a value—otherwise, the form will display an error message.

If we execute the code, we will have the following output:

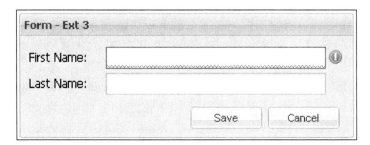

 Note that we left the last name blank and the form displayed an error.

In Ext JS 4, when we are working on form validation, we have to leave at least 20 pixels of space so that the form can display the error message, otherwise we will not be able to see the error icon.

Now, let's take a look at how we implement the same form in Ext JS 4:

```
var simple = Ext.create('Ext.form.Panel', {

    frame:true,
    title: 'Form - Ext 4',
    bodyStyle:'padding:5px 5px 0',
    width: 350,
    renderTo:'ext4-form',

    fieldDefaults: {
        msgTarget: 'side',
        labelWidth: 75
    },
    defaultType: 'textfield',
```

```
    defaults: {
        anchor: '100%'
    },

    items: [{
        fieldLabel: 'First Name',
        name: 'first',
        allowBlank:false
    },{
        fieldLabel: 'Last Name',
        name: 'last',
        allowBlank:false
    }],

    buttons: [{
        text: 'Save'
    },{
        text: 'Cancel'
    }]
});
```

The Ext JS 4 form that we implemented is very similar to the Ext JS 3 form. It has two fields (both required—they cannot be blank) with the same `width` and the same `labelWidth`. The only difference is that we did not set a fixed field `width`. We set both fields to be rendered in 100% of the space they have; in other words, we did not leave 20 pixels of offset for the error icon.

Let's execute the preceding code to see what happens:

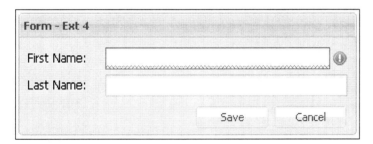

This means we do not have to leave the blank space for the error icon; we can display the field using all the space it can get. If an error occurs, Ext JS 4 will automatically resize the field so the form can display the error.

Since `FormLayout` is no longer supported, we can use any layout we want inside a form.

For example, if you want to use the **Hbox Layout** in a form, you simply need to specify the layout as `hbox`:

```
var hboxForm = Ext.create('Ext.form.Panel', {

    frame:true,
    title: 'Form - Ext 4',
    bodyStyle:'padding:5px 5px 0',
    width: 600,
    renderTo:'ext4-form',
    fieldDefaults: {
        labelAlign: 'top',
        msgTarget: 'side'
    },
    defaults: {
        border: false,
        xtype: 'panel',
        flex: 1,
        layout: 'anchor'
    },

    layout: 'hbox',
    items: [{
        items: [{
            xtype:'textfield',
            fieldLabel: 'First Name',
            anchor: '-10',
            name: 'first',
            allowBlank:false
        }, {
            xtype:'textfield',
            fieldLabel: 'Phone Number',
            anchor: '-10',
            name: 'phone',
            allowBlank:false
        }]
    }, {
        items: [{
            xtype:'textfield',
            fieldLabel: 'Last Name',
            anchor: '100%',
            name: 'last',
            allowBlank:false
        },{
```

```
                xtype:'textfield',
                fieldLabel: 'Email',
                anchor: '100%',
                name: 'email',
                vtype:'email'
            }]
    }],

    buttons: [{
        text: 'Save'
    },{
        text: 'Cancel'
    }]
});
```

In the preceding form, we have four fields: **First Name**, **Last Name**, **Phone Number**, and **Email** (the first three are required and cannot be left blank). The layout used in the form is the hbox with two items, and each item contains two sub-items (which are the fields themselves). The Hbox Layout will organize the items horizontally; as we have two items, we will have two columns in the form, and each column will have two fields. The first column (left side of the form) will contain **First Name** (at the top) and **Phone Number** (at the bottom). The second column (right side of the form) will contain **Last Name** (at the top) and **Email** (at the bottom).

You can configure FormLayout like you were configuring any other Component with an Hbox Layout.

The output for the previous code will be as follows:

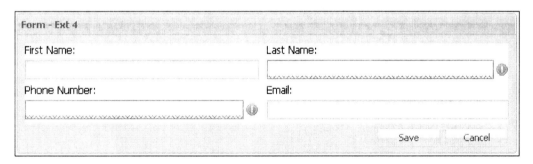

Let's take a look at another example. We will change the above form to use a **VBox Layout**:

```
var vboxForm = Ext.create('Ext.form.Panel', {

    frame:true,
```

```
        title: 'Form - Ext 4',
        bodyStyle:'padding:5px 5px 0',
        width: 300,
        height: 175,
        renderTo:'ext4-form',

        fieldDefaults: {
            anchor: '100%',
            msgTarget: 'side'
        },

        layout: {
            type: 'vbox',
            align: 'stretch'
        },

        items: [{
            xtype:'textfield',
            fieldLabel: 'First Name',
            name: 'first',
            allowBlank:false
        },{
            xtype:'textfield',
            fieldLabel: 'Last Name',
            name: 'last',
            allowBlank:false
        },{
            xtype:'textfield',
            fieldLabel: 'Phone Number',
            name: 'phone',
            allowBlank:false
        },{
            xtype:'textfield',
            fieldLabel: 'Email',
            name: 'email',
            vtype:'email'
        }],

        buttons: [{
            text: 'Save'
        },{
            text: 'Cancel'
        }]
    });
```

We changed the `layout` to `vbox`. The VBox Layout will organize the Components vertically, in a single column. As we will not have more then one column, we can set all the fields to `stretch` (full width of the form), and we can declare all the fields in the `items` configuration of the form.

The previous code will output the following form:

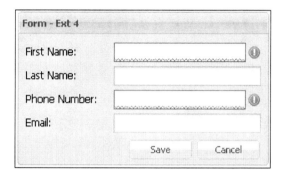

If you do not specify any layout, the form will use the **Anchor Layout**, which is the default layout for forms.

As you can see, the new layout engine for the Form Component is very flexible.

TriggerField layout

The **TriggerField Layout** is an extension of the `FieldLayout`. In Ext JS 4, we do not need to worry about leaving a space (offset) for the error icon. The same applies to the TriggerField Layout.

A `trigger` field can be the arrow of a combo box, a calendar icon from the `DatePicker` Component, and so on. When you worked with Ext JS 3, do you remember that we left a space for the `trigger` field?

Let's take a look how the TriggerField works on Ext JS 3:

```
var simple = new Ext.FormPanel({
  labelWidth: 75,
    frame:true,
    title: 'Form - Ext 3',
    bodyStyle:'padding:5px 5px 0',
    width: 350,
    renderTo:'ext3-form',
    defaults: {width: 230},

    items: [
```

```
    new Ext.form.ComboBox({
        store: new Ext.data.ArrayStore({
            fields: ['id','lang'],
            data: [[1, 'PHP'], [2, 'Java'], [3, 'Ruby']]
        }),
        fieldLabel: 'Favorite Programming Language',
        valueField: 'id',
        displayField:'lang',
        typeAhead: false,
        mode: 'local',
        forceSelection: true,
        triggerAction: 'all',
        emptyText:'Select a language...',
        selectOnFocus:true,
        allowBlank: false
    })
  ]
});
```

In the form above, we have a single item that is a combo box. The combo box contains a `trigger` field; this is the down arrow the user can click to choose an option from a list. Note that we left some space for the trigger field and the error icon:

Now, let's take a look at how the same form is implemented using Ext JS 4:

```
Ext.createWidget('form', {
    renderTo: 'ext4-form',
    labelWidth: 75,
    frame:true,
    title: 'Form - Ext 4',
    bodyStyle:'padding:5px 5px 0',
    width: 350,

    fieldDefaults: {
        anchor: '100%',
        msgTarget: 'side'
    },
```

```
items: [
    Ext.create('Ext.form.field.ComboBox', {
        store: Ext.create('Ext.data.ArrayStore', {
            fields: ['id','lang'],
            data: [[1, 'PHP'], [2, 'Java'], [3, 'Ruby']]
        }),
        fieldLabel: 'Favorite Programming Language',
        valueField: 'id',            displayField:'lang',
        typeAhead: false,
        mode: 'local',
        forceSelection: true,
        triggerAction: 'all',
        emptyText:'Select a language...',
        selectOnFocus:true,
        allowBlank: false
    })
]
});
```

We changed the way we instantiated the Components (instead of the keyword **new**, we used **Ext.create**) and we also removed the fixed `width` for the combo box, so that the Component can use the full width of the form through the config `anchor: '100%'`.

If we execute the preceding code, the output will be as follows:

Note that the Component was rendered using all the horizontal space of the form. When we did not select an option from the combo box (the field does not allow blank values), the form displayed an error and it resized the combo box automatically.

Summary

In this chapter, we covered a quick overview and code samples on the basic concepts of the known Container layouts, such as, Auto (old Container Layout), Table, Column, HBox, VBox, Anchor, Absolute, Accordion, Fit, Card, and Border layouts.

We also covered the features of some of the new Component layouts, such as Dock, Toolbar, Field, and TriggerField layouts. We learned these new features through code examples.

In the next chapter, we will dive into the new draw and chart package, and we will learn how to implement the available chart types in the Ext JS 4 framework.

4
Upgraded Charts

Ext JS 4 has vastly improved on charts and drawing packages. Ext JS 3 introduced some charts, but they still had many features to improve on, starting with the fact that Ext JS 3 used Flash to render the charts. As Ext JS is a JavaScript framework, the chart package has been rewritten, and now, the charts no longer need Flash to be rendered. Ext JS 4 also introduces some new chart series, such as, Radar, Scatter, and Gauge.

In this chapter, we will cover:

- The difference between Ext JS 3 and Ext JS 4 charts
- Ext draw package features
- An Ext chart package overview
- How to configure Legends
- How to use Axis
- Chart Series
- Customize a Chart Theme

We will also learn how to implement:

- Pie Charts
- Area Charts
- Column/Bar Charts
- Line Charts
- Radar Charts
- Scatter Charts
- Gauge Charts
- Mixed Series (Mix more than two Chart series just mentioned)

Ext JS 4 chart upgrades

Ext JS 3 introduced chart components. Although it was a great improvement for Ext JS 3, the Chart component was not entirely implemented with JavaScript; it required a Flash file to run. This Flash file is supported by the YUI Chart Flash file (http://developer.yahoo.com/yui/charts/).

The use of a Flash file to render charts was an issue, because the client had to have Flash player installed to run the charts, and not every device supports flash. Ext JS 3 only supported six types of charts: Pie, Bar, Line, Column, Stacked Bar, and Stacked Column.

Ext JS 4 improved the chart components in a big way. You no longer need the Flash file. All charts are implemented with JavaScript, and now you can run them on any device. Ext JS 4 also supports more chart types than Ext JS 3 — Bar, Column, Stacked Bar, Stacked Column, Line, Area, Scatter, Pie, Radar, and Gauge charts. Plus, you can combine different series in a single chart, and it is much easier to customize them.

Ext JS 4 also introduces the draw package, which provides classes you can use to create graphics and custom animations you can run cross-browser.

Ext draw package

The draw package contains 7 classes to help you create graphics in Ext JS 4, which are: Surface, engine.Svg, engine.Vml, Component, CompositeSprite, Color, and Sprite.

The Surface class contains methods to render Sprite objects or Sprite groups (CompositeSprite) and contains listeners to respond to mouse interactions; it also provides methods to animate. A **Sprite** is a two-dimensional image or animation that is integrated into a larger scene.

The Surface class has two concrete implementations — Svg and Vml. The Svg class provides methods to draw with a SVG engine (**Scalable Vector Graphics**), for SVG-capable browsers. The Vml class provides methods to draw with a **VML** engine (**Vector Markup Language**), for the Internet Explorer browser family.

 For further reading about SVG, please go to http://www.w3.org/Graphics/SVG/, and for further reading about VML, please go to http://www.w3.org/TR/NOTE-VML.html.

The Component class is the superclass for the Chart class. Besides the fact that the Chart class is inherited from the Component class, it also provides a surface where Sprite objects can be rendered. You can create graphics without instantiating a class from the chart package.

To create a drawing surface, you simply need to instantiate the Ext.draw. Component class, as follows:

```
var drawComponent = Ext.create('Ext.draw.Component', {
    viewBox: false,
    items: [{
        type: 'circle',
        fill: '#9966FF',
        radius: 100,
        x: 110,
        y: 110
    }]
});
```

And you can add the drawing to any container class, such as a Window, and use layouts:

```
Ext.create('Ext.Window', {
    width: 240,
    height: 250,
    layout: 'fit',
    items: [drawComponent]
}).show();
```

When we try to execute the previous code snippet, we will have the following output:

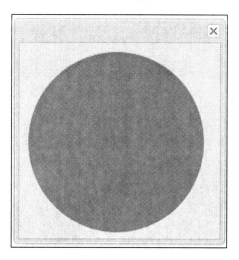

Let's dig into the code of the draw Component we instantiated:

We have the viewBox property we set to false, which means that when we try to resize Window, the draw Component inside will not be resized. The default value is true, which means the drawing will be resized when you resize Window.

Then we have the items declaration. Inside this property, you can add a list of sprites. In the previous example we have a Sprite of type circle, which means we are going to draw a circle; we chose a color to fill the circle and defined the radius size of the circle and the position along the x and y axes that the centre of the circle will be located at.

The following code is equivalent to the drawComponent variable we just declared:

```
var drawComponent = Ext.create('Ext.draw.Component', {
    viewBox: false,
    items: [ Ext.create('Ext.draw.Sprite', {
        type: 'circle',
        fill: '#9966FF',
        radius: 100,
        x: 110,
        y: 110
    })]
});
```

 Every item declared inside the items config option in Ext.draw.Component is an instance of Ext.draw.Sprite.

We can draw some types of Sprite object. Some of them are listed as follows:

- Circle: Used to draw circles
- Rect: Used to draw rectangles
- text: Used to render a text
- square: Used to draw a square
- path: Used to draw complex shapes using the SVG path syntax

We can also set other option properties to render a Sprite. Some of them are listed as follows:

- type: The type of the Sprite (circle, rect, square, text, path) – string
- width: Used to set the rectangle width – number
- height: Used to set the rectangle height – number
- size: Used to set the size of a square – number

- radius: Used to set the size of the radius of a circle – number
- x: The position along the x-axis – number
- y: The position along the y-axis – number
- fill: The color used to fill the sprite – string
- opacity: The opacity of a sprite – number
- stroke: The stroke color – string
- stroke-width: The width of the stroke – number
- path: The path of the sprite written in SVG path syntax – array
- text: The text desired to be rendered – string
- font: Used to set the font of text sprites written as a CSS font parameter – string

Now that we know some components we can draw, let's play with each one to see how to set and use the options we discussed just now.

We already know how to draw a circle. We need to set a radius and we can also set the position of the x and y axes. The next Sprite we are going to draw is a rectangle:

```
var drawComponent = Ext.create('Ext.draw.Component', {
    viewBox: false,
    items: [{
        type: 'rect',
        fill: '#9966FF',
        width: 350,
        height: 200,
        x: 20,
        y: 20
    }]

});
```

To draw a rectangle, we need to set the Sprite type as 'rect'; we are going to set a purplish color as the fill color and we will set the width and the height of the rectangle. We also are going to set the positions on the x and y axes. When the rectangle is rendered on the Window, the upper-left corner will be located at x = 20 and y = 20.

When we execute the preceding code (also add it to a window 400x230 pixels), the output will be as follows:

The next Sprite we are going to work on is text:

```
var drawComponent = Ext.create('Ext.draw.Component', {
    viewBox: false,
    items: [{
        type: 'text',
        text: 'Hello, World!',
        fill: '#000',
        font: '20px "Lucida Grande", "Lucida Sans Unicode", Verdana,
Arial, Helvetica, sans-serif',
        x: 30,
        y: 30
    }]
});
```

To draw a text we need to set the Sprite type as 'text', and we set a text we want to display. We can also set a fill color to fill the text—in this example, we used black; we can also set font, to set a font for the text. The font is written as in CSS. We also set a location (on the x and y axes) to display the text.

If we try to execute the preceding code, we will have the following output:

The next Sprite we are going to draw is a spiral, but we do not have any Sprite type that draws a spiral for us. So, to draw it, we are going to use a Sprite of type path. We are going to use an SVG path:

```
var drawComponent = Ext.create('Ext.draw.Component', {
    viewBox: true,
    items: [{
        type: 'path',
        path: ['M153 334',
                'C153 334 151 334 151 334',
                'C151 339 153 344 156 344',
                'C164 344 171 339 171 334',
                'C171 322 164 314 156 314',
                'C142 314 131 322 131 334',
                'C131 350 142 364 156 364',
                'C175 364 191 350 191 334',
                'C191 311 175 294 156 294',
                'C131 294 111 311 111 334',
                'C111 361 131 384 156 384',
                'C186 384 211 361 211 334',
                'C211 300 186 274 156 274'],
        fill: 'white',
        stroke: 'red',
        "stroke-width": "2"
    }]

});
```

When we use a Sprite of type path, we also need to set parameters for path itself. path is an array of path locations. We also set the fill color for the spiral to white and the stroke to red, with stroke-width as 2. It will draw a white spiral, and the line that defines the spiral will be red, as shown in the following screenshot:

Drawing a path can be very complex. For further reading, please go to http://www.w3schools.com/svg/svg_path.asp.

Applying transformations to a draw

You can also apply transformations to a draw. For example, we will use the text `Hello,World` and we will apply some transformations to it.

The first transformation is the `rotation`. You can rotate a Sprite. Let's rotate the text by 45 degrees:

```
var drawComponent = Ext.create('Ext.draw.Component', {
    viewBox: false,
    autoSize: true,
    padding: 20,
    items: [{
        type: 'text',
        text: 'Hello, World!',
        fill: '#000',
        font: '20px "Lucida Grande", "Lucida Sans Unicode"',
        rotate: {
            degrees: 45
        }
    }]
});
```

In the previous code snippet, we set the `rotate` property, and we also set how many `degrees` the text is going to be rotated. In the example, we chose to rotate the text by 45 degrees. If we execute the previous code snippet, the following will be the output:

Another transformation we can perform is the `scale` transformation:

```
var drawComponent = Ext.create('Ext.draw.Component', {
    viewBox: false,
    autoSize: true,
    padding: 20,
    items: [{
        type: 'text',
        text: 'Hello, World!',
        fill: '#000',
        font: '20px "Lucida Grande", "Lucida Sans Unicode"',
        scale: {
            x: 1,
            y: 3
        }
    }]

});
```

We need to set the x and y attributes for scaling on the x and y axes.

The previous code snippet will produce the following output:

Putting it all together

We learned how to draw the available Ext JS 4 Sprite objects and how to apply some transformation into them. Now, let's implement an example of how to use some of these Sprites together to draw a more complex drawing.

We will draw an MVC diagram using the Sprites mentioned previously, as displayed by the following screenshot:

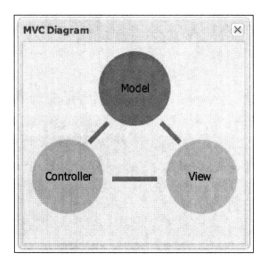

To draw the previous diagram, we will use three circles, three texts, and three rectangles (for the linking lines). We will add all these sprites into a single Ext. draw. Component and will set x and y values for each of them:

```
var drawComponent = Ext.create('Ext.draw.Component', {
    viewBox: false,
        items: [{
        type: 'circle',
        fill: '#0066CC', //blue
        radius: 40,
        x: 125,
        y: 50
    },{
        type: 'circle',
        fill: '#00CC66', //green
        radius: 40,
        x: 50,
        y: 145
    },{
        type: 'circle',
        fill: '#FF9933', //orange
        radius: 40,
        x: 200,
        y: 145
    },{
```

```
        type: 'text',
      text: 'Model',
      fill: '#000', //black
       font: '12px "Arial"',
       x: 110,
       y: 50
},{
        type: 'text',
      text: 'View',
       fill: '#000',
       font: '12px "Arial"',
       x: 185,
       y: 145
 },{
        type: 'text',
       text: 'Controller',
       fill: '#000',
       font: '12px "Arial"',
       x: 25,
       y: 145
 },{
        type: 'rect',
       fill: '#CC0000', //red
       width: 50,
       height: 5,
       x: 100,
       y: 145
 },{
        type: 'rect',
       fill: '#CC0000',
       width: 30,
       height: 5,
       x: 150,
       y: 95,
       rotate: {
           degrees: 45 // line in diagonal \
       }
 },{
        type: 'rect',
       fill: '#CC0000',
       width: 30,
       height: 5,
       x: 70,
       y: 95,
```

```
            rotate: {
                degrees: 135 // line in diagonal /
            }
        }]
});

Ext.create('Ext.Window', {
    title: 'MVC Diagram',
    width: 260,
    height: 250,
    layout: 'fit',
    items: [drawComponent]
}).show();
```

We also used two `rotate` transformations to rotate the two upper rectangles. Now you can use your creativity and create very nice drawings with Ext JS 4.

The draw package provides basic functions to render charts. And, all the examples before and the examples we will see in the following topics are cross-browser, which is very important, and run on any device that has a browser.

Ext chart package

First, we will see an example of how to implement an Ext JS 3 chart:

```
Ext.chart.Chart.CHART_URL = '../extjs3/resources/charts.swf';

var store = new Ext.data.JsonStore({
    fields:['name', 'age'],
    data: [
            {name:'Loiane', age: 25},
            {name:'Peter', age: 24},
            {name:'Claudia', age: 30},
            {name:'John', age: 28},
            {name:'Steve', age: 32}
    ]
});

var chart = new Ext.Window({
    title: 'Friends x Age',
    width:500,
    height:300,
    layout:'fit',
```

```
    items: {
        xtype: 'columnchart',
        store: store,
        xField: 'name',
        yField: 'age',
        xAxis: new Ext.chart.CategoryAxis({
            title: 'Friend Name'
        }),
        yAxis: new Ext.chart.NumericAxis({
            displayName: 'Age'
        })
    }
});
chart.show();
```

As you can see, we can declare the chart type directly in the xtype property. We are saying that the preceding chart is a Column Chart. We also declared a store, the xField and yField, and the xAxis and yAxis. But, an important detail we have to pay attention to is the Ext.chart.Chart.CHART_URL constant declaration, for which we set the path to the charts.swf file.

If we execute the preceding code snippet, we will have the following output:

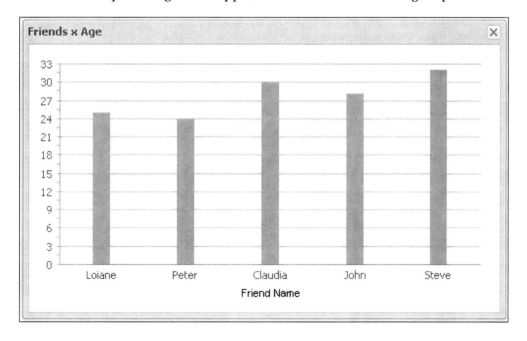

The Ext JS 4 chart package is independent of the draw package, except for the fact that the Chart class is a subclass of the Ext.draw.Component class. A **Chart** contains several parts, as shown in the next diagram:

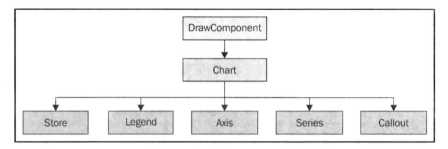

A **Chart** consists of a **Legend**, **Axis**, **Series**, and **Callout**, and can load data from a **Store**.

A **Chart** has access to:

- **Axis** class through the chart.axes property, which defines the axes for a particular chart/series.

- **Legend** class through the legend property, which is the legend box and its legend item.

- It has access to the **Series** through the series property. A series can be a Pie, Line, Bar, Column, and so on.

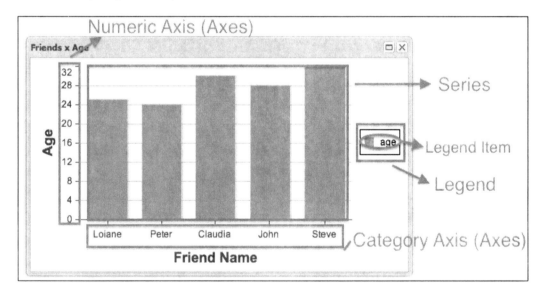

The following code snippet will output the preceding chart:

```
var store = Ext.create('Ext.data.JsonStore', {
    fields:['name', 'age'],
    data: [
            {name:'Loiane', age: 25},
            {name:'Peter', age: 24},
            {name:'Claudia', age: 30},
            {name:'John', age: 28},
            {name:'Steve', age: 32}
    ]
});

Ext.create('Ext.window.Window', {
    title: 'Friends x Age',
    width:500,
    height:300,
    layout:'fit',
    maximizable: true,

    items: {
        xtype: 'chart',
        style: 'background:#fff',
        animate: true,
        shadow: true,
        store: store,
        axes: [{
            type: 'Numeric',
            position: 'left',
            fields: ['age'],
            title: 'Age',
            grid: true,
            minimum: 0
        }, {
            type: 'Category',
            position: 'bottom',
            fields: ['name'],
            title: 'Friend Name'
        }],
        legend:{
        position: 'right'
        },
        series: [{
            type: 'column',
            axis: 'left',
            highlight: true,
            tips: {
                trackMouse: true,
                width: 140,
                height: 28,
```

```
                renderer: function(storeItem, item) {
                    this.setTitle(storeItem.get('name') + ': ' + storeItem.
    get('age'));
                }
            },
            xField: 'name',
            yField: 'age',
            showInLegend: true
        }]
    }
}).show();
```

As in Ext JS 3, the Ext JS 4 chart contains a `store`, to load the data from it.

> The chart structure is more organized in Ext JS 4: we have a `chart` declaration, we set a `style` for it, declared the axis in the `axes` declaration, declared a `legend`, and finally, declared the `series`, which is a `Column` series.

If you compare the Ext JS 3 and Ext JS 4 screenshots, you will note that even the style is very different.

The structure in Ext JS 4 is easier to understand. Using the `series` property, it is easier to use different series and create a chart with mixed series. And you can also customize how the chart looks, using a style or a theme, and customize the legend, as we will learn in the *Customizing a Chart* section of this chapter.

Legend

The `Legend` class is used to configure a `legend` for a chart series. The `Legend` class displays a list of `LegendItems` related to the chart series.

The following is an example of how to configure and customize a legend for a chart:

```
legend: {
    position: 'right',
    padding: 20,
    itemSpacing: 15,
    boxFill: '#CCFFCC',
    labelFont : '16px Helvetica'
}
```

Some configuration options are listed as follows:

- `position`: The position of the legend box. Possible values are `bottom`, `top`, `left`, `right`, or `float`. If you use `float`, the legend box will be rendered at the x,y position.

- `x`: The x position of the legend box, if the position is set to `'float'`.

- `y`: The y position of the legend box, if the position is set to `'float'`.

- `padding`: The padding between the legend border and its items.

- `itemSpacing`: The amount of space between the legend items.

- `boxFill`: The style to be applied to the legend box.

- `labelFont`: The font to be applied on the legend items labels.

If you do not want to display a legend box, simply omit the `legend` configuration. If you want to display the legend for specified series only, use the configuration `displayInLegend: false` (or `true`) in the series declaration.

The following screenshot exemplifies the legend configuration we just declared:

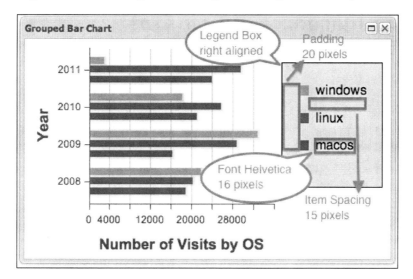

Axis

The **Axis** package contains seven classes:

- There is the `Abstract` class, which is the superclass of all `Axis` package classes. As direct subclasses of `Abstract`, there is the `Gauge` class, the `Radial` class, and the `Axis` class.

- The Gauge axis is used with the Gauge series.
- The Radial class is used with the Pie and Radar series, because it uses polar coordinates.
- The Axis class is the superclass of Category, Numeric, and Time axes.

The Axis class uses cartesian coordinates, and its subclasses are used with Bar, Column, Area, Scatter, and Line charts.

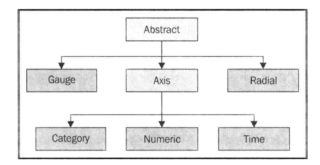

Category, Numeric, and Time axes

The Category, Numeric and Time axes are subclasses of the Axis class. This means they have some configuration options in common:

- position: The position of the axis—it can use the following values: bottom, top, left or right. The default value is bottom.
- minorTickSteps: The number of small ticks between two major ticks. The default value is 0.
- majorTickSteps: The properties minimum and maximum are set; you need to specify a number for the majorTickSteps.
- grid: This can be a Boolean value or an object configuration. If specified, it adds a background grid for an axis. If set to true on vertical axis, it will draw vertical lines; if set to true on horizontal axis, it will draw horizontal lines.
- length: The offset of the axis position. The default value is 0.
- width: The offset of the axis width. The default value is 0.

 Tickmarks (Ticks) divide an axis into equal sections by a step whose value is determined by the special options of an axis. Tickmarks are used to improve comprehension of a chart's data. In addition, axis labels may accompany them. There are two types of tickmarks and grid lines: major and minor, as described in the preceding items.

The following is an example of how to configure the `axes` chart property:

```
axes: [{
            type: 'Numeric',
            position: 'left',
            fields: ['visits'],
            title: 'Number of Visits',
            grid: true,
            minimum: 0,
            minorTickSteps:3
        }, {
            type: 'Category',
            position: 'bottom',
            fields: ['os'],
            title: 'Operational System'
    }],
```

The preceding code outputs the following chart:

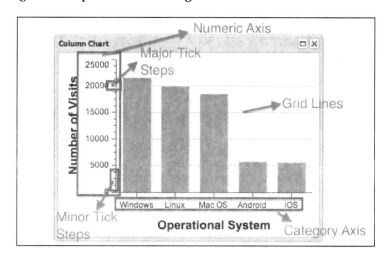

In the preceding example, we have a `Numeric` and a `Category` axis.

The `Numeric` axis handles numeric and quantitative values. You can set `minimum` and `maximum` values, which are going to limit the values of the axis; if you do not set any, Ext JS 4 will use the `minimum` and `maximum` values from the data set.

The `Category` axis handles names of items, such as names, months, and so on. When you have many category items and there is no space to render all of them along the axis, you can set the `calculateCategoryCount` property; if set to `true`, Ext JS 4 will calculate the number of items that will be rendered along the axis; if set to `false`, it will plot all the category items.

If you have to work with time values, you can use the `Time` axis. But, use it only when the dates are dynamic or change very often. If you want to display month names or dates as a category, use the `Category` axis.

Some options you can use to configure a `Time` axis are:

- `aggregateOpt`: The operator used when grouping. Its value can be `sum`, `avg`, `max`, or `min`. The default value is `sum`.

- `groupBy`: The array of fields to group.

- `fromDate`: The starting date. Similar to minimum value.

- `toDate`: The ending date. Similar to maximum value.

- `constrain`: If set to true, the chart will be rendered only if the values belong to `fromDate` and `toDate`. If set to `false`, it will adapt the axis to the values.

- `dateFormat`: The format of the date that will be rendered. Ext JS uses the same date format PHP uses. For further reading about date format, please go to `http://php.net/function.date.php`.

- `timeUnit`: The unit of time used for each step. Its value can be `day`, `month`, or `year`. The default value is `year,month,day`.

Gauge axis

The `Gauge` axis is used with the `Gauge` series. This axis is used to display numeric or quantitative values.

The following is an example of how to configure a `Gauge` axis:

```
axes: [{
    type: 'gauge',
    position: 'gauge',
    minimum: 0,
    maximum: 7,
    steps: 7,
    margin: -10
}]
```

The possible configuration options are:

- `minimum`: The minimum value to be displayed on the axis
- `maximum`: The maximum value to be displayed on the axis
- `steps`: The number of steps and tick marks
- `margin`: Offset of the ticks and labels; the default value is `10`

The `position` of a `Gauge` axis is always set to `'gauge'`.

Radial axis

The `Radial` axis is used with the `Radar` and `Pie` series. This axis is used to display numeric values.

The following is an example of how to configure a `Radial` axis:

```
axes: [{
    type: 'Radial',
    position: 'radial',
    label: {
        display: true
    }
}]
```

The `position` of a `Radial` axis is always set to `'radial'`.

Series

A `Series` is the key to showing data in a chart; with the `Series`, you define how the chart will display the data through x and y axes (or using a single axis).

In Ext JS 4, there is a package named `Ext.chart.series`, which contains all the `chart.series` classes:

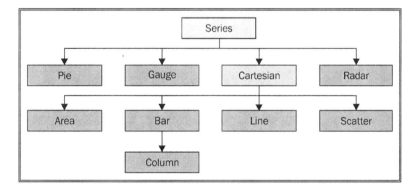

The `Series` class is the super class (abstract class), which contains some basic properties and behaviors applied to all chart series. As direct subclasses, there are the `Pie`, `Gauge`, and `Radar` series classes. There is also a series class named `Cartesian`, which is an abstract series classc ontaining common properties and methods to render a chart through the `x` and `y` axes. The subclasses of the `Cartesian` class are the `Area`, `Bar`, `Line`, and `Scatter` series. The `Bar` class also has a subclass, the `Column` class.

Before starting with each series, we will take a look at some common properties that can be applied to all chart series:

- `type`: The type of the series. It can be `column`, `bar`, `line`, `area`, `scatter`, `pie`, `radar`, or `gauge`.
- `highlight`: This highlights the markers or the series when hovering over them with the mouse, if the value is `true`.
- `showInLegend`: A Boolean value that indicates if the legend will display the series.
- `field`: The name of the field to be displayed in the label. The default value is `'name'`.
- `tips`: Shows a tooltip when hovering over the markers. It is the same configuration used for `Ext.tip.Tooltip`.

Bar chart

A `Bar Chart` is a chart with horizontal rectangular bars proportional to the value they represent. The `Bar Chart` class is a subclass of the `Cartesian` class, which is a subclass of `Series`.

First, we will generate some data to display in the chart. Let's suppose we want to display how many visits your blog has per operating system. If we organize the data in a table, we will have something like the following:

Operating system	Visits
Windows	21548
Linux	19864
Mac OS	18459
Android	5762
iOS	5635

Let's transform the preceding table into a `Store`:

```
var store = Ext.create('Ext.data.ArrayStore', {
    fields: [
        {name: 'os'},
        {name: 'visits', type: 'int'}
    ],
    data: [
        ['Windows','21548'],
        ['Linux', '19864'],
        ['Mac OS', '18459'],
        ['Android','5762'],
        ['iOS', '5635']
    ]
});
```

We will use the previous store in some examples in this chapter, including in the following example:

```
var barChart = Ext.create('Ext.chart.Chart', {
    animate: true,
    shadow: true,
    store: store,
    style: 'background:#fff',

    axes: [{
        type: 'Numeric',
        position: 'bottom',
        fields: ['visits'],
        title: 'Number of Visits',
        grid: true,
        minimum: 0
    }, {
        type: 'Category',
        position: 'left',
        fields: ['os'],
        title: 'Operational System'
    }],

    series: [{
        type: 'bar',
        axis: 'bottom',
        highlight: true,
        tips: {
            trackMouse: true,
```

```
            width: 140,
            height: 28,
            renderer: function(storeItem, item) {
                this.setTitle(storeItem.get('os') + ': ' + storeItem.
get('visits') + ' visits');
            }
        },
        xField: 'os',
        yField: 'visits'
    }]
});
```

In the preceding chart, we have set some chart properties, such as, `animate`, `shadow`, `sytle` (white background), and `store`. We also set the `axes` declaration. We have two axes: a horizontal one, at the bottom, which is going to display the number of `visits` (starting from `0` and ranging to `minimum`); and a vertical one, at the left, which is going to display the operating systems. In this example, we are using a `Numeric` axis to display the quantitative data and a `Category` axis to display the OS names.

Then, we have the `series` declaration. We have a single `Series`, which is a `Bar` chart (represented by `type:'bar'`). We have set the `axis` to `bottom`, meaning the `visits` value will be displayed on the bottom. We also set the `highlight` value as `true`, so when we hover the mouse over the rectangular bars, they will be highlighted. We also set a `tooltip` to be displayed when we hover over the rectangular bars; the `tooltip` will display the name of the operating system and its number of visits. And finally, we declared the `xField` and `yField`.

The following are some common properties used for all `Cartesian` charts:

- `axis`: Which axis the series will be blinded to
- `xField`: Which field is going to be used to access the x axis value from the store
- `yField`: Which field is going to be used to access the y axis value from the store

Let's add the previous chart to a `Window` and display it:

```
Ext.create('Ext.window.Window', {
    width: 400,
    height: 300,
    hidden: false,
    maximizable: true,
    title: 'Bar Chart',
    renderTo: Ext.getBody(),
    layout: 'fit',
    items: [barChart]
});
```

When we execute the preceding code, it will output the following:

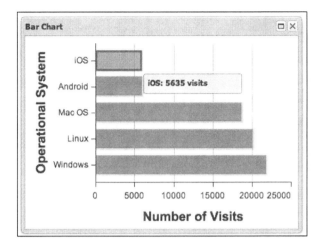

Grouped bar chart

Sometimes we need to display more than one set of data in a single chart to compare the results. In Ext JS 4, you can simply create a grouped Bar Chart.

Let's consider the following data:

Year	Number of Visits by OS		
	Windows	Linux	Mac OS
2008	21548	19864	18459
2009	32458	28475	15874
2010	17856	25418	20673
2011	2635	29183	23584

In the preceding table, we can compare the number of visits, by operating system, to a blog, through the years of 2008, 2009, 2010, and 2011. Let's transform the preceding table in an `Ext Store`:

```
var store = Ext.create('Ext.data.ArrayStore', {
    fields: [
        {name: 'year'},
        {name: 'windows', type: 'int'},
        {name: 'linux', type: 'int'},
        {name: 'macos', type: 'int'}
    ],
    data: [
```

```
                ['2008','21548','19864','18459'],
                ['2009', '32458','28475','15874'],
                ['2010', '17856','25418','20673'],
                ['2011','2635','29183','23584']
        ]
    });
```

Now, we will declare the Grouped Bar Chart:

```
    var groupedBarChart = Ext.create('Ext.chart.Chart', {
        animate: true,
        shadow: true,
        store: store,
        style: 'background:#fff',

        axes: [{
            type: 'Category',
            position: 'left',
            fields: ['year'],
            title: 'Year'
        }, {
            type: 'Numeric',
            position: 'bottom',
            fields: ['windows','linux','macos'],
            title: 'Number of Visits by OS',
            grid: true,
            minimum: 0
        }],

        series: [{
            type: 'bar',
            axis: 'bottom',
            highlight: true,
            tips: {
                trackMouse: true,
                width: 140,
                height: 28,
                renderer: function(storeItem, item) {
                    this.setTitle(String(item.value[1]) + ' Visits');
                }
            },
            xField: 'year',
            yField: ['windows','linux','macos']
        }],

        legend: {
            position: 'right'
        }
    });
```

There some few important changes we need to note in the preceding code snippet. The first one is the `fields` declaration in the `Numeric` axis. We grouped the `fields` that represent the number of visits for each OS. The other important change is we also grouped the `yFields` in the bar series declaration. We also added a `legend` declaration, so we can note the difference between the bars' colors and map them with an OS. Everything else we declared as a simple bar chart.

If we execute the preceding code, we will have the following output:

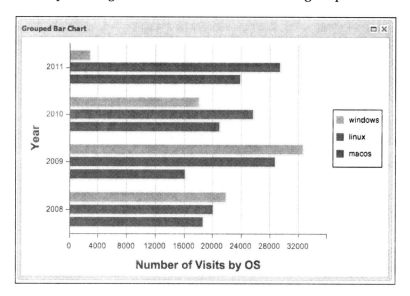

Stacked bar chart

A stacked bar chart is a grouped bar chart, but with one difference: a property. The `Series Bar Chart` class has a property called `stacked`. If we set this property as `true`, the chart will be stacked instead of grouped.

Let's get the code for a grouped bar chart and transform it into a stacked bar chart:

```
var stackeBarChart = Ext.create('Ext.chart.Chart', {
    animate: true,
    shadow: true,
    store: store,
    style: 'background:#fff',

    axes: [{
        type: 'Category',
        position: 'left',
        fields: ['year'],
```

```
            title: 'Year'
      }, {
            type: 'Numeric',
            position: 'bottom',
            fields: ['windows','linux','macos'],
            title: 'Number of Visits by OS',
            grid: true,
            minimum: 0
      }],

      series: [{
            type: 'bar',
            axis: 'bottom',
            highlight: true,
            tips: {
                  trackMouse: true,
                  width: 140,
                  height: 28,
                  renderer: function(storeItem, item) {
                        this.setTitle(String(item.value[1]) + ' Visits');
                  }
            },
            xField: 'year',
            yField: ['windows','linux','macos'],
            stacked: true
      }],

      legend: {
            position: 'right'
      }
});
```

The difference between the grouped bar chart and the stacked bar chart is the last line of code of the series declaration, which is stacked: true.

If we execute the preceding code, we will have the following output:

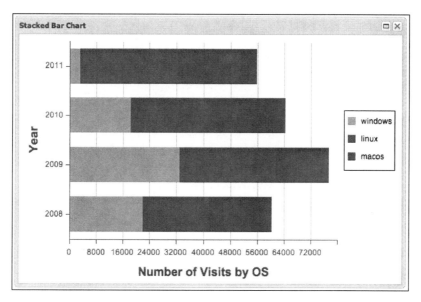

Column chart

A `Column Chart` has vertical, rectangular bars proportional to the value they represent. It is a `Bar` chart, but in the vertical position. The `Column Chart` class is a subclass of the `Bar` chart class.

For the next example, we will consider the store we used for the `Bar` chart example:

```
var columnChart = Ext.create('Ext.chart.Chart', {
    animate: true,
    shadow: true,
    store: store,
    style: 'background:#fff',

    axes: [{
        type: 'Numeric',
        position: 'left',
        fields: ['visits'],
        title: 'Number of Visits',
        grid: true,
        minimum: 0
    }, {
        type: 'Category',
        position: 'bottom',
```

```
        fields: ['os'],
        title: 'Operational System'
    }],

    series: [{
    type: 'column',
        axis: 'left',
        highlight: true,
        tips: {
            trackMouse: true,
            width: 140,
            height: 28,
            renderer: function(storeItem, item) {
                this.setTitle(storeItem.get('os') + ': ' + storeItem.
get('visits') + ' visits');
            }
        },
        xField: 'os',
        yField: ['visits']
    }]
});
```

As the Column Chart is a Bar Chart, let's compare the differences. The differences are in the axes and axis positions. If you notice, the Numeric axis is not on the bottom, it is on the left in the Column Chart. Same for the Category axis; it is not on the left anymore—it is positioned on the bottom. And in the series declaration, the axis is on the left, not on the bottom.

The preceding code snippet will output the following chart:

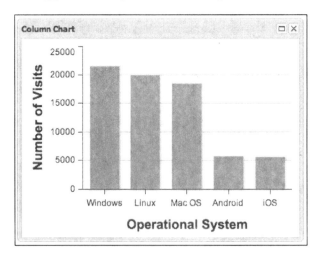

You can also have a `grouped` or `stacked Column chart`. The principle is the same that is applied to the `grouped` and `stacked Bar chart`.

Line Chart

A `Line chart` is a chart with a set of data points connected by a straight line of segments. The `LineChart` class is a subclass of the `Cartesian` class, which is a subclass of `Series`.

Before we start implementing a `Line` chart, we have to generate some data to display on it. Let us suppose that we want to display how many visits a blog had during each month of a year; consider the following table:

Month	Visits
January	4875
February	3854
March	2358
April	5693
May	6751
June	5231
July	8721
August	8642
September	7231
October	5642
November	8642
December	6154

Now, we will transform the preceding table into a `Store`:

```
var store = Ext.create('Ext.data.ArrayStore', {
    fields: [
        {name: 'month'},
        {name: 'visits', type: 'int'}
    ],
    data: [
        ['January','4875'],
        ['February', '3854'],
        ['March', '2358'],
        ['April','5693'],
        ['May', '6751'],
        ['June', '5231'],
```

```
                ['July', '8721'],
                ['August', '8642'],
                ['September', '7231'],
                ['October', '5642'],
                ['November', '8642'],
                ['December', '6154']
        ]
    });
```

Let's get to the `Line` chart implementation example:

```
    var lineChart = Ext.create('Ext.chart.Chart', {
        style: 'background:#fff',
        animate: true,
        store: store,
        shadow: true,
        axes: [{
            type: 'Numeric',
            minimum: 0,
            position: 'left',
            fields: ['visits'],
            title: 'Number of Visits',
            minorTickSteps: 1
        }, {
            type: 'Category',
            position: 'bottom',
            fields: ['month'],
            title: 'Month of the Year'
        }],
        series: [{
            type: 'line',
            highlight: {
                size: 7,
                radius: 7
            },
            tips: {
                trackMouse: true,
                width: 140,
                height: 28,
                renderer: function(storeItem, item) {
                    this.setTitle(storeItem.get('month') + ': ' + storeItem.
    get('visits') + ' visits');
                }
            },
            axis: 'left',
            xField: 'month',
            yField: 'visits'
        }]
    });
```

In the preceding code, we have a `Numeric` Axis representing the number of `visits`, and a `Category` axis representing each `month` of the year. Then, we have the `series` declaration, which we declared of `type 'line'`. We also have the `xField` and `yField`, `tips`, `highlight` and `axis` declarations, as we also had in previous chart examples.

If we execute the preceding code, we will get the following output:

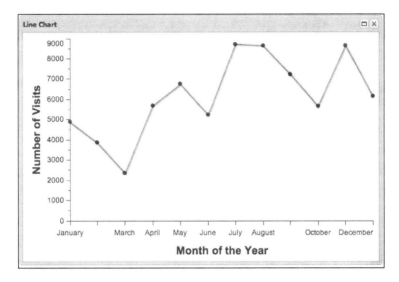

Customizing a Line Chart

The `Line Chart Series` class contains some properties you can use to customize the chart.

Let's get the `series` declaration from the previous `Line` chart example and add some properties:

```
series: [{
    type: 'line',
    highlight: {
        size: 7,
        radius: 7
        },
    tips: {
    trackMouse: true,
    width: 140,
    height: 28,
    renderer: function(storeItem, item) {
        this.setTitle(storeItem.get('month') + ': ' + storeItem.
get('visits') + ' visits');
```

```
        }
    },
    axis: 'left',
    xField: 'month',
    yField: 'visits',
    smooth: true,
    markerConfig: {
        type: 'cross',
        radius: 5,
        'fill': '#f00'
    },
    showMarkers: true,
    fill: true
}]
```

If we execute the preceding code, we will have the following output:

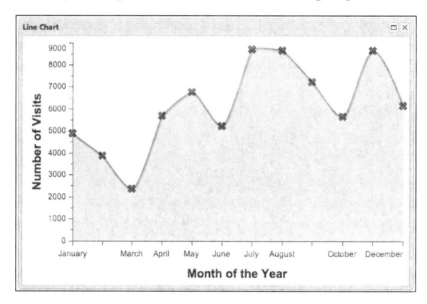

What is different in the code? We have added the following properties:

- smooth: If set to true or a non-zero number, the line will be smoothed/
  rounded. If you compare the previous example with this one, you will note
  the lines are straight in the previous example; in this one, they are rounded
  around the chart points.

- `markerConfig`: You can set a style for the markers (the points in the chart). The configuration is the same for a `Sprite` class. In this example, we set the type of the marker as `'cross'`; you can also set it as `'circle'`. We also set a radius value for the marker and a fill color (red). The marker will be displayed only if the property `showMarkers` is set as `true`.

- `showMarkers`: A Boolean property. If is set as `true`, will display the marker configured in the `markerConfig` property.

- `fill`: Is set as `true`, will fill the area under the line. The default value is `false`.

Grouped Line Chart

We saw that it is very simple to implement a grouped `Bar Chart` or `Column Chart`, we simply needed to group the fields. The `Grouped Line chart` works a little bit differently. We will see how it works.

But first, let's generate some data to be displayed in the chart. We want to display how many visits a blog had in each month of the year, but we are going to compare two years:

Month	Visits in 2009	Visits in 2010
January	4875	3587
February	3854	2489
March	2358	4965
April	5693	1684
May	6751	2943
June	5231	1846
July	8721	4662
August	8642	9712
September	7231	6847
October	5642	5222
November	8642	7304
December	6154	5651

Let's transform the preceding table into a `Store`:

```
var store = Ext.create('Ext.data.ArrayStore', {
    fields: [
        {name: 'month'},
        {name: 'visits2009', type: 'int'},
        {name: 'visits2010', type: 'int'}
    ],
```

```
    data: [
          ['January','4875','3587'],
          ['February', '3854','2489'],
          ['March', '2358','4965'],
          ['April','5693','1684'],
          ['May', '6751','2943'],
          ['June', '5231','1846'],
          ['July', '8721','4662'],
          ['August', '8642','9712'],
          ['September', '7231','6847'],
          ['October', '5642','5222'],
          ['November', '8642','7304'],
          ['December', '6154','5651']
    ]
});
```

Now, we will implement a Grouped Line Chart:

```
var groupedLineChart = Ext.create('Ext.chart.Chart', {
    style: 'background:#fff',
    animate: true,
    store: store,
    shadow: true,
    legend: {
        position: 'right'
    },
    axes: [{
        type: 'Numeric',
        minimum: 0,
        position: 'left',
        fields: ['visits2009','visits2010'],
        title: 'Number of Visits',
        minorTickSteps: 1
    }, {
        type: 'Category',
        position: 'bottom',
        fields: ['month'],
        title: 'Month of the Year'
    }],
    series: [{
        type: 'line',
        highlight: {
            size: 7,
            radius: 7
        },
```

```
        axis: 'left',
        smooth: true,
        xField: 'month',
        yField: 'visits2009',
        markerConfig: {
            type: 'cross',
            size: 5,
            radius: 4,
            'stroke-width': 0
        }
    },
    {
        type: 'line',
        highlight: {
            size: 7,
            radius: 7
        },
        axis: 'left',
        smooth: true,
        xField: 'month',
        yField: 'visits2010',
        markerConfig: {
            type: 'circle',
            size: 5,
            radius: 4,
            'stroke-width': 0
        }
    }]
});
```

To display a `Grouped Line Chart`, we do not group the `fields` in the `Line Chart Series` declaration. We have to declare two `Line Series` (or as many as you need to, depending on how many data sets you need to compare). But, we do group the fields in the `Axes` declaration; in this case, in the `Numeric Axis fields` declaration.

We can also customize each line series to look different from each other. In the preceding example, we customized the `markers`; we declared one as `cross` and the other one as `circle`.

 Ext JS 4 also uses different colors for each series. We do not need to manually customize it, but, if we want to, we can. We will learn how to customize a chart later on in this chapter.

The preceding code will output the following chart:

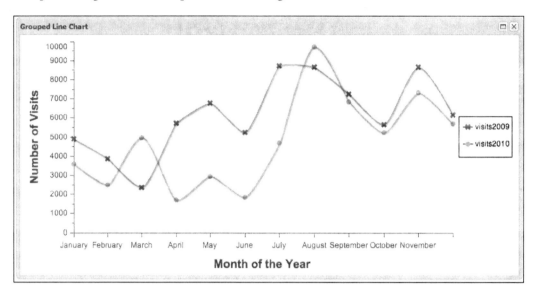

Area Chart

The Area Chart is based on the Line Chart, but the area between the axis and the line is filled with color. It is a chart that displays quantitative data. Generally, the Area Chart compares two or more sets of data. The Area class is a subclass of the Cartesian Chart class.

As the Area Chart is similar than the Line chart, we will use the Store we declared for the Line chart in the Area Chart as well. Let's implement an Area Chart:

```
var areaChart = Ext.create('Ext.chart.Chart', {
    style: 'background:#fff',
    animate: true,
    store: store,
    shadow: true,
    axes: [{
        type: 'Numeric',
        minimum: 0,
        position: 'left',
        fields: ['visits'],
        title: 'Number of Visits',
        minorTickSteps: 1
    }, {
        type: 'Category',
        position: 'bottom',
```

```
        fields: ['month'],
        title: 'Month of the Year'
    }],
    series: [{
        type: 'area',
        highlight: true,
        tips: {
            trackMouse: true,
            width: 140,
            height: 28,
            renderer: function(storeItem, item) {
                this.setTitle(storeItem.get('month') + ': ' + storeItem.
get('visits') + ' visits');
            }
        },
        axis: 'left',
        xField: 'month',
        yField: 'visits'
    }]
});
```

The `Area Chart` does not have any property to configure itself. All the properties used we've discussed already, in previous topics. The only thing we need to do is to set the series `type` as `'area'`. The preceding code will output the following chart:

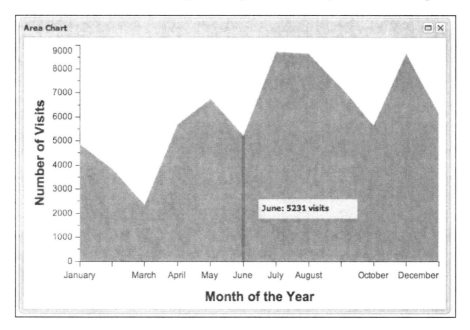

Grouped Area Chart

The most common area charts are used to compare two or more data sets. For the following example, we will use the grouped line chart store:

```
var groupedAreaChart = Ext.create('Ext.chart.Chart', {
    style: 'background:#fff',
    animate: true,
    store: store,
    shadow: true,
    legend: {
        position: 'right'
    },
    axes: [{
        type: 'Numeric',
        minimum: 0,
        position: 'left',
        fields: ['visits2009','visits2010'],
        title: 'Number of Visits',
        minorTickSteps: 1
    }, {
        type: 'Category',
        position: 'bottom',
        fields: ['month'],
        title: 'Month of the Year'
    }],
    series: [{
        type: 'area',
        axis: 'left',
        highlight: true,
        xField: 'month',
        yField: ['visits2009','visits2010'],
        tips: {
            trackMouse: true,
            width: 200,
            height: 28,
            renderer: function(storeItem, item) {
                this.setTitle(item.storeField + ' - '
                    + storeItem.get('month')
                    + ' - ' + storeItem.get(item.storeField));
            }
        },
        style: {
            opacity: 0.93
        }
    }]
});
```

In the preceding code, to implement a `grouped area chart`, we simply need to group the fields. Unlike with the `Line` chart, we do not need to declare a `series` for each data set.

The preceding code will output the following chart:

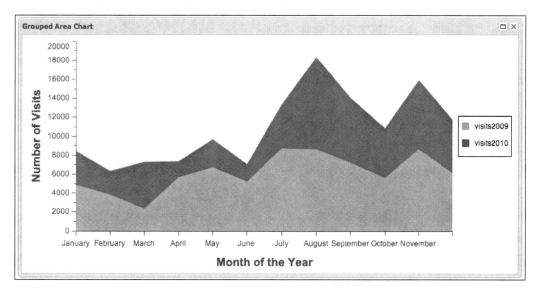

Note that Ext JS 4 will automatically use a different color for each data set. And, if you mouse over the legend items, the chart will highlight the selected area.

Scatter Chart

A `Scatter` Chart is used to display and compare two variables in a `Cartesian` plan. For each variable a point/marker is plotted. The `Scatter` class is a subclass of the `Cartesian Chart` class.

First, we will learn how to implement a scatter chart with a single variable, and then we will learn how to add variables to be displayed in the `Cartesian` plan.

For the following example, we will use the same `Store` we used for the `Line` chart:

```
var scatterChart = Ext.create('Ext.chart.Chart', {
    style: 'background:#fff',
    animate: true,
    store: store,
    shadow: true,
    axes: [{
        type: 'Numeric',
```

```
        minimum: 0,
        position: 'left',
        fields: ['visits'],
        title: 'Number of Visits',
        minorTickSteps: 1
    }, {
        type: 'Category',
        position: 'bottom',
        fields: ['month'],
        title: 'Month of the Year'
    }],
    series: [{
        type: 'scatter',
        highlight: {
            size: 7,
            radius: 7
        },
        axis: 'left',
        xField: 'month',
        yField: 'visits'
    }]
});
```

The preceding code is a sample of how to configure a scatter chart. We have to declare the `type` of the `series` as `'scatter'`, and configure the other series options. As with the `Line` chart, we can also configure a `markerConfig`; but, if we do not, Ext will use the default one, which is `circle`.

If we execute the preceding code snippet, we will have the following output:

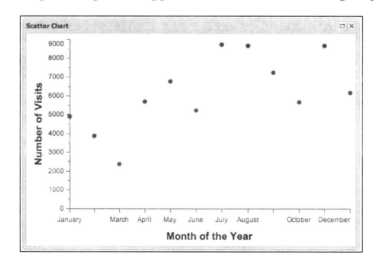

Grouped Scatter Chart

Now we will see how to add a second variable to a `Scatter` chart. You can use as many variables as you need to. For the following example, we will use the `Store` we used for the grouped `Line` chart:

```
var groupedScatterChart = Ext.create('Ext.chart.Chart', {
    style: 'background:#fff',
    animate: true,
    store: store,
    legend: {
        position: 'right'
    },
    axes: [{
        type: 'Numeric',
        minimum: 0,
        position: 'left',
        fields: ['visits2009','visits2010'],
        title: 'Number of Visits',
        minorTickSteps: 1
    }, {
        type: 'Category',
        position: 'bottom',
        fields: ['month'],
        title: 'Month of the Year'
    }],
    series: [{
        type: 'scatter',
        axis: 'left',
        smooth: true,
        xField: 'month',
        yField: 'visits2009',
        markerConfig: {
            radius: 5
        },
        highlight: true
    },
    {
        type: 'scatter',
        axis: 'left',
        smooth: true,
        xField: 'month',
        yField: 'visits2010',
        markerConfig: {
            radius: 5
        },
        highlight: true
    }]
});
```

If you compare the previous code snippet with the Grouped Lined chart, you will see that is very similar.

If we execute the preceding code, it will output the following chart:

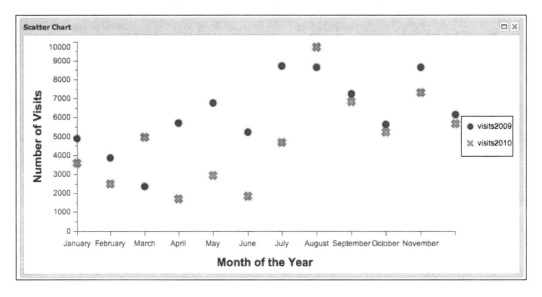

Pie Chart

The Pie Chart is a chart in a shape of a pie (or pizza). It is a circular chart divided into sectors, with each one representing a proportion. The Pie Chart class is a subclass of Series class.

For the Pie Chart example, we will use the Bar Chart Store:

```
var pieChart = Ext.create('Ext.chart.Chart', {
    animate: true,
    shadow: true,
    store: store,
    style: 'background:#fff',
    shadow: true,
    legend: {
        position: 'right'
    },

    series: [{
        type: 'pie',
        showInLegend: true,
        field: ['visits'],
```

```
        label: {
            field: 'os',
            display: 'rotate',
            contrast: true,
            font: '18px Arial'
        },
        highlight: {
            segment: {
                margin: 20
            }
        }
    }
    }]
});
```

To implement a `Pie` chart, we first need to set the `Series type` as `'pie'`. As each sector of the pie will have an angle, we set the `legend` to `rotate` as well, and we also customized the `font` of the `legend`. We also set the `highlight` to have a `margin` of `20 pixels`, when we hover the mouse over a sector.

 An important thing to note is that the `Pie` chart uses the `Radial` axis. As this configuration is applied automatically, we can omit it.

The preceding code snippet will output the following pie chart:

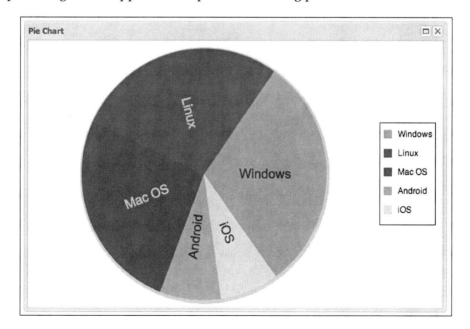

The Pie Chart also has some other properties you can configure:

- colorSet: An array of color values to be used for each sector, in the order they were declared.

- donut: If set to true or a number (radius size), the pie chart will be transformed into a donut chart. The default value is false (zero).

- highlightDuration: The duration of the highlight effect applied to a sector when hovered.

Donut Chart

The Pie chart has a property called donut. When this property is set to true or a number (representing the radius size of the donut), the pie chart is transformed into a Donut chart.

For example, we will add the donut property into the series declaration of the previous example with a value of 30:

```
series: [{
    type: 'pie',
    showInLegend: true,
    field: ['visits'],
    label: {
        field: 'os',
        display: 'rotate',
        contrast: true,
        font: '18px Arial'
    },
    highlight: {
        segment: {
            margin: 20
        }
    },
    donut: 30
}]
```

If we try to execute the preceding code, we will get the following output:

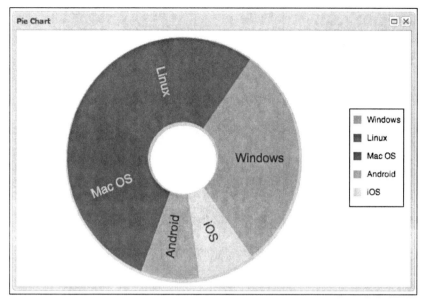

Radar Chart

A `Radar Chart` displays data in the form of a two-dimensional chart, commonly displaying three (or more) data sets starting from the same point. The `Radar Chart` is also known as a spider chart. The `Radar` class is a subclass of `Series` class.

We will use the same `Store` we used for `Line` chart, in the following example:

```
var radarChart = Ext.create('Ext.chart.Chart', {
    style: 'background:#fff',
    animate: true,
    store: store,
    shadow: true,
    axes: [{
        type: 'Radial',
        position: 'radial',
        label: {
            display: true
        }
    }],
    series: [{
        type: 'radar',
        xField: 'month',
```

```
        yField: 'visits',
        showInLegend: true,
        showMarkers: true,
        highlight: true,
        markerConfig: {
            radius: 4
        },
        style: {
            'stroke-width': 2,
            fill: 'none'
        }
    }]
});
```

The Radar chart uses the Radial axis. To declare a radar series, first we need to set the type of the series as 'radar'. The other config options, such as show markerConfig, are very similar to the Line Series configuration. If we execute the preceding code, we will get the following chart as output:

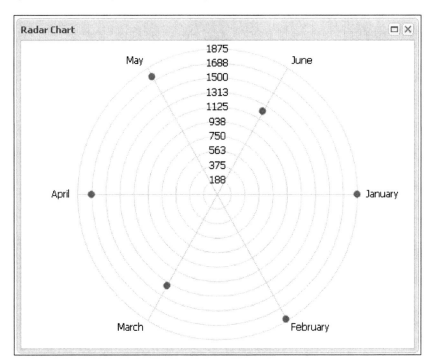

Grouped Radar Chart

To implement a Grouped Radar Chart with multiple data sets, we need to declare a radar series for each data set we want to display on the chart:

```
series: [{
    type: 'radar',
    xField: 'month',
    yField: 'visits2009',
    highlight: true,
    showMarkers: true,
    markerConfig: {
        radius: 4
    },
    style: {
        'stroke-width': 2,
        fill: 'none'
    }
},
{
    type: 'radar',
    xField: 'month',
    yField: 'visits2010',
    highlight: true,
    showMarkers: true,
    markerConfig: {
        radius: 4
    },
    style: {
        'stroke-width': 2,
        fill: 'none'
    }
}]
```

The `Store` we used for the previous example is the same as `Grouped Line Chart`. All the configuration options are very similar to the `Line Chart` as well. The preceding code snippet will output the following chart:

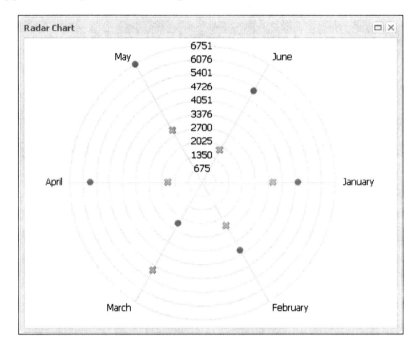

Gauge Chart

The `Gauge` chart is used to show progress. The `Gauge` class is a subclass of the `Series` class and uses a `Gauge Axis` in the `axes` configuration.

To use as an example, let's compare the progress of your reading of this book (supposing you are reading it from cover to cover and reading the chapters in sequence). This is the fourth chapter (from a total of 7). Let's declare a `store` to use in the chart:

```
var store = Ext.create('Ext.data.ArrayStore', {
    fields: [
        {name: 'chapters', type: 'int'}
    ],
    data: [['4']]
});
```

Now let's see how to implement a Gauge chart:

```
var gaugeChart = Ext.create('Ext.chart.Chart', {
    style: 'background:#fff',
    animate: true,
    store: store,
    shadow: true,
    axes: [{
        type: 'gauge',
        position: 'gauge',
        minimum: 0,
        maximum: 7,
        steps: 7,
        margin: -10
    }],
    series: [{
        type: 'gauge',
        field: 'chapters',
        donut: false,
        highlight: true
    }]
});
```

To implement a Gauge series, we first need to set the type of the series as 'gauge'. This series supports only a single field, which is the one we are going to use to display the progress (chapters we already read of this book). When we execute the preceding code, we will see the following output:

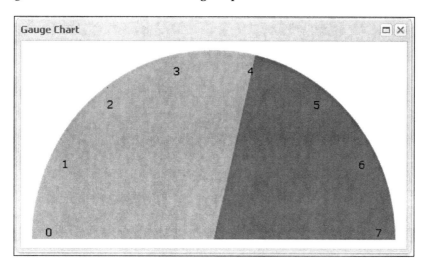

In the preceding chart, two different colors are used to display the progress of the reading. But, if you want to display a needle to point is the exact location of the value the chart is displaying, simply add the `needle:true` property to the `series` declaration. Another change we can make is to set the `donut` property. The `donut` property works similar to the `Pie` chart `donut` property.

```
series: [{
    type: 'gauge',
    field: 'chapters',
    donut: 30,
    needle: true,
    highlight: true
}]
```

If we try to execute the code again, we will have the following output:

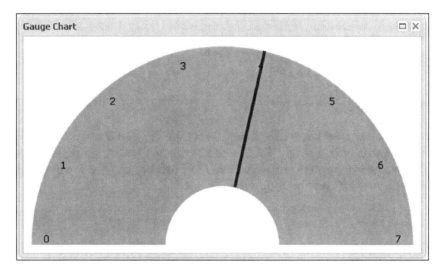

Customizing a Chart

The `Ext.chart` package contains a package called `theme`. Inside this package, we will find there are two classes: `Ext.chart.theme.Base` and `Ext.chart.theme.Theme`.

The `Theme` class is a base class for creating a custom theme in Ext JS 4.

Let's try to create a theme based on blue colors. To do it, we will set base color and use it at the axis and we will declare an array of bluish colors to be used by the series:

```
Ext.define('Ext.chart.theme.Blue', {
    extend: 'Ext.chart.theme.Base',

    baseColor: '#000099',
    colors: ['#3399FF', '#0066CC', '#003366'],

    constructor: function(config) {
        this.callParent([Ext.apply({
            axis: {
                fill: this.baseColor,
                stroke: this.baseColor
            },
            axisLabelLeft: {
                fill: this.baseColor
            },
            axisLabelBottom: {
                fill: this.baseColor
            },
            axisTitleLeft: {
                fill: this.baseColor
            },
            axisTitleBottom: {
                fill: this.baseColor
            },
            colors: this.colors
        }, config)]);
    }
});
```

To use a custom theme in a chart, we simply need to declare it in the theme property (the Theme is a mixin applied to the Chart class):

```
Ext.create('Ext.chart.Chart', {
    theme: 'Blue',

    //other config here
});
```

When we render the chart, we will see it all in blue colors (we applied the theme to the `grouped bar chart`):

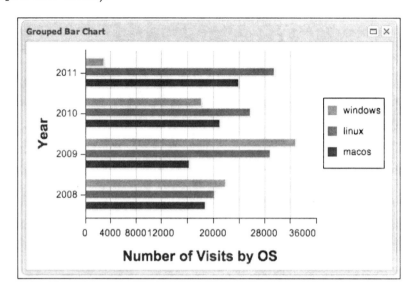

But, which are the options we can set to a custom chart? The configuration can be very complex. You can always use a base theme, consulting the `Base` class configuration:

```
Ext.define('Ext.chart.theme.Custom', {
    extend: 'Ext.chart.theme.Base',

    constructor: function(config) {
        this.callParent([Ext.apply({
            background: false,
            axis: {
                stroke: '#444',
                'stroke-width': 1
            },
            axisLabelTop: {
                fill: '#444',
                font: '12px Arial, Helvetica, sans-serif',
                spacing: 2,
                padding: 5,
                renderer: function(v) { return v; }
            },
            axisLabelRight: {
                fill: '#444',
                font: '12px Arial, Helvetica, sans-serif',
```

```
        spacing: 2,
        padding: 5,
        renderer: function(v) { return v; }
    },
    axisLabelBottom: {
        fill: '#444',
        font: '12px Arial, Helvetica, sans-serif',
        spacing: 2,
        padding: 5,
        renderer: function(v) { return v; }
    },
    axisLabelLeft: {
        fill: '#444',
        font: '12px Arial, Helvetica, sans-serif',
        spacing: 2,
        padding: 5,
        renderer: function(v) { return v; }
    },
    axisTitleTop: {
        font: 'bold 18px Arial',
        fill: '#444'
    },
    axisTitleRight: {
        font: 'bold 18px Arial',
        fill: '#444',
        rotate: {
            x:0, y:0,
            degrees: 270
        }
    },
    axisTitleBottom: {
        font: 'bold 18px Arial',
        fill: '#444'
    },
    axisTitleLeft: {
        font: 'bold 18px Arial',
        fill: '#444',
        rotate: {
            x:0, y:0,
            degrees: 270
        }
    },
    series: {
        'stroke-width': 0
```

```
            },
            seriesLabel: {
                font: '12px Arial',
                fill: '#333'
            },
            marker: {
                stroke: '#555',
                fill: '#000',
                radius: 3,
                size: 3
            },
            colors: [ "#94ae0a", "#115fa6","#a61120", "#ff8809",
   "#ffd13e", "#a61187", "#24ad9a", "#7c7474", "#a66111"],
            seriesThemes: [{
                fill: "#115fa6"
            }, {
                fill: "#94ae0a"
            }, {
                fill: "#a61120"
            }, {
                fill: "#ff8809"
            }, {
                fill: "#ffd13e"
            }, {
                fill: "#a61187"
            }, {
                fill: "#24ad9a"
            }, {
                fill: "#7c7474"
            }, {
                fill: "#a66111"
            }],
            markerThemes: [{
                fill: "#115fa6",
                type: 'circle'
            }, {
                fill: "#94ae0a",
                type: 'cross'
            }, {
                fill: "#a61120",
                type: 'plus'
            }]
        }, config)]);
    }
});
```

The preceding code represents the base theme used in every Ext JS 4 chart. The configuration properties are self-explanatory.

The following chart maps some theme config options:

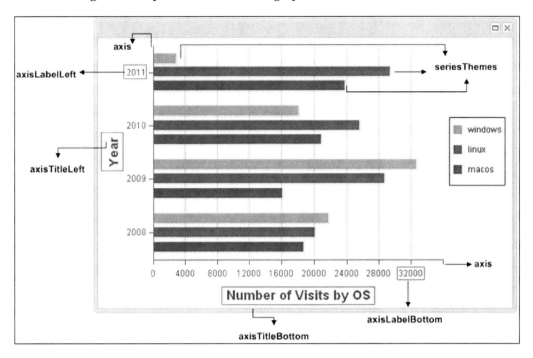

Summary

In this chapter, we covered some basics concepts of the new `draw` package, which is the base for the new `chart` package. We also covered how to configure each part of the chart, such as `axis`, `legend`, and `series`.

We covered every `Series` class with examples, such as, `Bar`, `Stacked Bar`, `Grouped Bar`, `Column` (`Stacked Column` and `Grouped Column`), `Line`, `Grouped Line`, `Area`, `Scatter`, `Pie` (and `Donut`), `Radar`, and `Gauge`. We also covered an example of how to use different series (`mixed`) in the same chart.

We also covered to how create `custom themes` for a chart and how to apply them in a particular chart. We learned that themes can be very useful when you need to change the custom look and feel of a chart, and it can be re-used for other charts as well.

In the next chapter, we will see the new features of some Ext JS 4 components, such as, Grids, Trees, and Forms, and we will also learn the differences between these components using Ext JS 3 and Ext JS 4.

5
Upgraded Grid, Tree, and Form

So far, we have covered new API, system enhancements and changes, the new data package, and layouts; we also introduced the new chart package. But, the main pieces of Ext JS framework we use when we develop an Ext application are the components such as Grid panel, Tree panel, and Forms, because the main goal of an application is to display and manage data.

In this chapter, we will cover some new features and enhancements in the following Components:

- Grid panel
- Tree panel
- Form panel

Grid panel

The **grid panel** is one of the most-used components when developing an application. Ext JS 4 provides some great improvements related to this component.

The Ext JS 4 Grid panel renders a different HTML than Ext JS 3 Grid did. Sencha calls this new feature **Intelligent Rendering**. Ext JS 3 used to create the whole structure, supporting all the features. But, what if someone just wanted to display a simple grid? All the other features not being rendered would just be wasted, because no one was using that structure. Ext JS 4 now renders only the features the grid uses, minimizing and boosting the performance.

Before we examine the grid's new features and enhancements, let's take a look how to implement a simple grid in Ext JS 4:

```
Ext.create('Ext.grid.Panel', {
    store: Ext.create('Ext.data.ArrayStore', {
        fields: [
            {name: 'book'},
            {name: 'author'}
        ],
        data: [['Ext JS 4: First Look','Loiane Groner']]
    }),
    columns: [ {
        text      : 'Book',
        flex      : 1,
        sortable : false,
        dataIndex: 'book'
    },{
        text      : 'Author',
        width     : 100,
        sortable : true,
        dataIndex: 'author'
    }],
    height: 80,
    width: 300,
    title: 'Simple Grid',
    renderTo: Ext.getBody()
});
```

As you can see in the preceding code, the two main parts of the grid are the **store** and the **columns** declarations. Note, as well, names of both `store` and `model fields` always have to match with the column's `dataIndex` (if you want to display the column in the grid).

So far, nothing has changed. The way we used to declare a simple grid in Ext JS 3 is the same way we do for Ext JS 4.

However, there are some changes related to plugins and the new features property. We are going to take a closer look at that in this section.

Let's dive into the changes!

Columns

Ext JS 4 organizes all the column classes into a single package—the `Ext.grid.column` package.

We will explain how to use each column type with an example. But first, we need to declare a `Model` and a `Store` to represent and load the data:

```
Ext.define('Book', {
    extend: 'Ext.data.Model',
    fields: [
        {name: 'book'},
        {name: 'topic', type: 'string'},
        {name: 'version', type: 'string'},
        {name: 'released', type: 'boolean'},
        {name: 'releasedDate', type: 'date'},
        {name: 'value', type: 'number'}
    ]
});

var store = Ext.create('Ext.data.ArrayStore', {
    model: 'Book',
    data: [
        ['Ext JS 4: First Look','Ext JS','4',false,null,0],
        ['Learning Ext JS 3.2','Ext JS','3.2',tr
ue,'2010/10/01',40.49],
        ['Ext JS 3.0 Cookbook','Ext JS','3',true,'2009/10/01',44.99],
        ['Learning Ext JS','Ext JS','2.x',true,'2008/11/01',35.99],
    ]
});
```

Now, we need to declare a grid:

```
Ext.create('Ext.grid.Panel', {
    store: store,
    width: 550,
    title: 'Ext JS Books',
    renderTo: 'grid-example',
    selModel: Ext.create('Ext.selection.CheckboxModel'), //1
    columns: [
        Ext.create('Ext.grid.RowNumberer'), //2
    {
        text: 'Book',//3
        flex: 1,
        dataIndex: 'book'
    },{
```

```
        text: 'Category',  //4
        xtype:'templatecolumn',
        width: 100,
        tpl: '{topic} {version}'
    },{
        text: 'Already Released?', //5
        xtype: 'booleancolumn',
        width: 100,
        dataIndex: 'released',
        trueText: 'Yes',
        falseText: 'No'
    },{
        text: 'Released Date', //6
        xtype:'datecolumn',
        width: 100,
        dataIndex: 'releasedDate',
        format:'m-Y'
    },{
        text: 'Price', //7
        xtype:'numbercolumn',
        width: 80,
        dataIndex: 'value',
        renderer: Ext.util.Format.usMoney
    },{
        xtype:'actioncolumn',   //8
        width:50,
        items: [{
            icon: 'images/edit.png',
            tooltip: 'Edit',
            handler: function(grid, rowIndex, colIndex) {
                var rec = grid.getStore().getAt(rowIndex);
                Ext.MessageBox.alert('Edit',rec.get('book'));
            }
        },{
            icon: 'images/delete.gif',
            tooltip: 'Delete',
            handler: function(grid, rowIndex, colIndex) {
                var rec = grid.getStore().getAt(rowIndex);
                Ext.MessageBox.alert('Delete',rec.get('book'));
            }
        }]
    }]
});
```

The preceding code outputs the following grid:

		Book	Category	Already Released?	Released Date	Price	
☐		**Book**	**Category**	**Already Released?**	**Released Date**	**Price**	
☐	1	Ext JS 4: ...	Ext JS 4	No		0.00	
☐	2	Learning ...	Ext JS 3.2	Yes	10-2010	40.49	
☐	3	Ext JS 3.0...	Ext JS 3	Yes	10-2009	44.99	
☐	4	Learning ...	Ext JS 2.x	Yes	11-2008	35.99	

- The first column is declared as `selModel`, which, in this example, is going to render a checkbox, so we can select some rows from the grid. To add this column into a grid, simply declare the `selModel` (also known as `sm` in Ext JS 3) as `CheckBox` selection model, as highlighted in the code (comment 1 in the code).

- The second column that we declared is the `RowNumberer` column. This column adds a row number automatically into the grid.

- In the third column (with `text:'Book'`), we did not specify a column type; this means the column will display the data itself as a string.

- In the fourth column, we declared a column with `xtype` as `templatecolumn`. This column will display the data from the store, specified by an `XTemplate`, as declared in the `tpl` property. In this example, we are saying we want to display the `topic` (name of the technology) and its `version`.

- The fifth column is declared as `booleancolumn`. This column displays a `true` or `false` value. But, if we do not want to display `true` or `false` in the grid, we can specify the values that we want to get displayed. In this example, we displayed the value as `Yes` (for `true` values) and `No` (for `false` values), as we declared in the `trueText` and `falseText`.

- The sixth column we declared as `datecolumn`, which is used to display dates. We can also declare a date format we want to be displayed. In this example, we want to display only the month and the year. The `format` follows the same rules for `PHP date formats`.

- The seventh column we declared as `numbercolumn`. This column is used to display numbers, such as a quantitative number, money, and so on. If we want to display the number in a particular format, we can use one of the Ext JS `renderers` to create a customized one.

- And the last column we declared is the `actioncolumn`. In this column, we can display icons that are going to execute an action, such as delete or edit. We declare the icons we want to display in the `items` property.

Feature support

In Ext JS 3, when we wanted to add a new functionality to a grid, we used to create a plugin or extend the `GridPanel` class. There was no default way to do it. Ext JS 4 introduces the `Ext.grid.feature.Feature` class that contains common methods and properties to create a plugin.

Inside the `Ext.grid.feature` package, we will find seven classes: `AbstractSummary`, `Chunking`, `Feature`, `Grouping`, `GroupingSummary`, `RowBody`, and `Summary`.

A feature is very simple to use—we need to add the feature inside the `feature` declaration in the grid:

```
features: [{
    groupHeaderTpl: 'Publisher: {name}',
     ftype: 'groupingsummary'
}]
```

Let's take a look at how to use some of these native grid features.

Ext.grid.feature.Grouping

Grouping rows in Ext JS 4 has changed. Now, **Grouping** is a feature and can be applied to a grid through the `features` property.

The following code displays a grid grouped by book topic:

```
Ext.define('Book', {
    extend: 'Ext.data.Model',
    fields: ['name', 'topic']
});

var Books = Ext.create('Ext.data.Store', {
    model: 'Book',
    groupField: 'topic',
    data: [{
        name: 'Learning Ext JS',
        topic: 'Ext JS'
    },{
        name: 'Learning Ext JS 3.2',
        topic: 'Ext JS'
    },{
        name: 'Ext JS 3.0 Cookbook',
        topic: 'Ext JS'
    },{
        name: 'Expert PHP 5 Tools',
```

```
            topic: 'PHP'
    },{
        name: 'NetBeans IDE 7 Cookbook',
        topic: 'Java'
    },{
        name: 'iReport 3.7',
        topic: 'Java'
    },{
        name: 'Python Multimedia',
        topic: 'Python'
    },{
        name: 'NHibernate 3.0 Cookbook',
        topic: '.NET'
    },{
        name: 'ASP.NET MVC 2 Cookbook',
        topic: '.NET'
    }]
});

Ext.create('Ext.grid.Panel', {
    renderTo: Ext.getBody(),
    frame: true,
    store: Books,
    width: 350,
    height: 400,
    title: 'Books',
    features: [Ext.create('Ext.grid.feature.Grouping',{
        groupHeaderTpl: 'topic: {name} ({rows.length}
            Book{[values.rows.length > 1 ? "s" : ""]})'
    })],
    columns: [{
        text: 'Name',
        flex: 1,
        dataIndex: 'name'
    },{
        text: 'Topic',
        flex: 1,
        dataIndex: 'topic'
    }]
});
```

In the `groupHeaderTpl` attribute, we declared a template to be displayed in the grouping row. We are going to display one of the following customized strings, depending on the number of books belonging to the topic:

- `topic: {name}{rows.length} Book`

- `topic: {name}{rows.length} Books`

The string comprises of the topic name (`{name}`) and the count of the book for the topic (`{rows.length}`).

In Ext JS 3, we still had to declare a **grouping field** in the store; but, instead of a `Grouping` feature, we used to declare `GroupingView`, as follows:

```
view: new Ext.grid.GroupingView({
    forceFit:true,
    groupTextTpl: '{text} ({[values.rs.length]} {[values.rs.length > 1
        ? "Books" : "Book"]})'
})
```

If we execute the **grouping grid**, we will get the following output:

Name	Topic ▲
⊟ topic: .NET (2 Books)	
NHibernate 3.0 Cookbook	.NET
ASP.NET MVC 2 Cookbook	.NET
⊟ topic: Ext JS (3 Books)	
Learning Ext JS	Ext JS
Learning Ext JS 3.2	Ext JS
Ext JS 3.0 Cookbook	Ext JS
⊟ topic: Java (2 Books)	
NetBeans IDE 7 Cookbook	Java
iReport 3.7	Java
⊟ topic: PHP (1 Book)	
Expert PHP 5 Tools	PHP
⊟ topic: Python (1 Book)	
Python Multimedia	Python

Books

Ext.grid.feature.GroupingSummary

The **GroupingSummary** feature also groups rows with a field in common, but it also adds a **summary row** at the bottom of each group.

Let's change the preceding example to use the GroupingSummary feature:

```
Ext.create('Ext.grid.Panel', {
    renderTo: Ext.getBody(),
    frame: true,
    store: Books,
    width: 350,
    height: 400,
    title: 'Books',
    features: [{
        groupHeaderTpl: 'Topic: {name}',
        ftype: 'groupingsummary'
    }],
    columns: [{
        text: 'Name',
        flex: 1,
        dataIndex: 'name',
        summaryType: 'count',
        summaryRenderer: function(value){
            return Ext.String.format('{0} book{1}',
                value, value !== 1 ? 's' : '');
        }
    },{
        text: 'Topic',
        flex: 1,
        dataIndex: 'topic'
    }]
});
```

We highlighted two pieces in the preceding code. The first line is the feature declaration: in the previous example (Grouping) we created the feature using the Ext.create declaration. But if we do not want to explicitly create the feature every time we declare, we can use the ftype property, which is groupingsummary in this example.

The groupingsummary that we added to the grid's name column is in the second line of highlighted code. We declared a summaryType property and set its value as count. Declaring the summaryType as count means we want to display the number of books in that particular topic/category; it is going to count how many records we have for a particular category in the grid. It is very similar to the count of the PL/SQL language. Other summary types we can declare are: sum, min, max, average (these are self-explanatory).

In this example, we want to customize the text that will be displayed in the summary, so we are going to use the `summaryRenderer` function. We need to pass a `value` argument to it, and the value is the count of the `name` column. Then, we are going to return a customized string that is going to display the count (token `{0}`) and the string `book` or `books`, depending on the `count` (if it is more than 1 we add `s` at the end of the string `book`).

 `Ext.String.format` is a function that allows you to define a tokenized string and pass an arbitrary number of arguments to replace the tokens. Each token must be unique and must increment in the format {0}, {1}, and so on.

The preceding code will output the following grid:

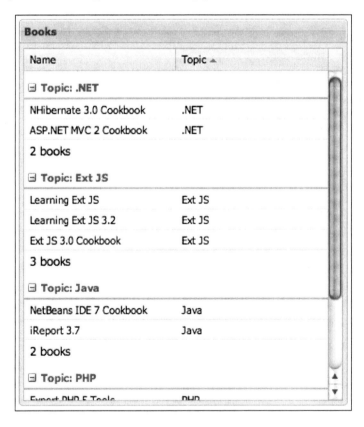

Ext.grid.feature.Summary

The **GroupingSummary** feature adds a row at the bottom of each grouping.
The summary feature adds a row at the bottom of the grid to display summary
information. The property configuration is very similar to that for GroupingSummary,
because both classes are subclasses of AbstractSummary (a class that provides
common properties and methods for summary features).

```
Ext.create('Ext.grid.Panel', {
    renderTo: Ext.getBody(),
    frame: true,
    store: Books,
    width: 350,
    height: 300,
    title: 'Books',
    features: [{
        ftype: 'summary'
    }],
    columns: [{
        text: 'Name',
        flex: 1,
        dataIndex: 'name',
        summaryType: 'count',
        summaryRenderer: function(value){
            return Ext.String.format('{0} book{1}',
                    value, value !== 1 ? 's' : '');
        }
    },{
        text: 'Topic',
        flex: 1,
        dataIndex: 'topic'
    }]
});
```

The only difference from the GroupingSummary feature is the feature declaration
itself. The summayType and summaryRenderer properties work in a similar way.

The preceding code will output the following grid:

Books	
Name	**Topic**
Learning Ext JS	Ext JS
Learning Ext JS 3.2	Ext JS
Ext JS 3.0 Cookbook	Ext JS
Expert PHP 5 Tools	PHP
NetBeans IDE 7 Cookbook	Java
iReport 3.7	Java
Python Multimedia	Python
NHibernate 3.0 Cookbook	.NET
ASP.NET MVC 2 Cookbook	.NET
9 books	

Ext.grid.feature.RowBody

The **rowbody** feature adds a new `tr->td->div` in the bottom of the row that we can use to display additional information.

Here is how to use it:

```
Ext.create('Ext.grid.Panel', {
    renderTo: Ext.getBody(),
    frame: true,
    store: Books,
    width: 350,
    height: 300,
    title: 'Books',
    features: [{
        ftype: 'rowbody',
        getAdditionalData: function(data, idx, record, orig) {
            return {
                rowBody: Ext.String.format(
                    '<div>->topic:<span> {0}</span></div>',
                    data.topic)
            };
        }
    }, {
```

```
    ftype: 'rowwrap'
}],
columns: [{
    text: 'Name',
    flex: 1,
    dataIndex: 'name'
}]
});
```

In the preceding code, we are not only displaying the name of the book; we are using the rowbody to display the topic of the book as well.

The first step is to declare the rowbody feature. One very important thing to be noted is that rowbody will be initially hidden, unless you override the getAdditionalData method.

If we execute the preceding code, we will get the following output:

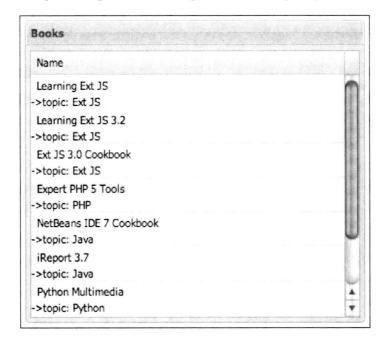

Grid plugins

Ext JS 4 also introduces a plugin package with five classes: `Editing`, `CellEditing`, `RowEditing`, `HeaderResizing`, and `DragDrop`.

The `Editing` class is an abstract class that provides common methods and properties for editing a grid. Its subclasses are `CellEditing` and `RowEditing`.

Ext.grid.plugin.CellEditing

The **CellEditing** plugin enables editing in a particular cell of the grid. When you click on the cell (the cell has to be enabled for editing) the `editor` (field instance or field configuration) will open and we can edit its value.

Before we get to the code for the cell that needs to be edited, we will declare a store:

```
Ext.define('Contact', {
    extend: 'Ext.data.Model',
    fields: ['name', 'email','phone']
});

var Contacts = Ext.create('Ext.data.Store', {
    model: 'Contact',
    data: [
        {name: 'Loiane', email: 'me@loiane.com', phone: '1234-5678'},
        {name: 'Peter', email: 'peter@email.com', phone: '2222-2222'},
        {name: 'Ane', email: 'ane@email.com', phone: '3333-3333'},
        {name: 'Harry', email: 'harry@email.com', phone: '4444-4444'},
        {name: 'Camile', email: 'camile@email.com', phone: '5555-5555'}
    ]
});
```

Now, let's get to the code for the cell that needs to be edited:

```
Ext.create('Ext.grid.Panel', {
    renderTo: Ext.getBody(),
    frame: true,
    store: Contacts,
    width: 350,
    title: 'Contacts',
    selType: 'cellmodel',
    columns: [{
        text: 'Name',
        flex: 1,
        dataIndex: 'name'
    },{
```

```
            text: 'Email',
            flex: 1,
            dataIndex: 'email',
            editor: {
                xtype:'textfield',
                allowBlank:false
            }
        },{
            text: 'Phone',
            flex: 1,
            dataIndex: 'phone',
            editor: {
                xtype:'textfield',
                allowBlank:false
            }
        }],
        plugins: [
            Ext.create('Ext.grid.plugin.CellEditing', {
                clicksToEdit: 1
            })
        ]
    });
```

In the preceding code, we have to pay attention to a few things: the first one is the `plugins` declaration. We declared a `CellEditing` plugin and we also set the `clicksToEdit` property to 1, which means the users have to click on the specific cell to be able to edit it. Declaring only the plugin is not enough in order to make the cell editable. We also have to add the `editor` option to the cell.

We declared, inside the `columns` property, an `editor` property. The `editor` property is an `Ext.form.field.Field` object, which means you can use its properties to configure as if it is a `text field`, a `combobox`, a `checkbox`, or any other component from the field package. The columns are editable only after adding the `editor` property. In the preceding example, we added the `editor` property to the `Email` and `Phone` columns, so these columns become editable when we click on them. We did not add the `editor` property for the `Name` column, thus it will not be editable when we click on it.

Another highlighted line is the `selType` property. We set `cellModel` as the selection model (known as the `sm` property in Ext JS 3), which means that, when we click on a row of the grid, the cell we clicked on will be selected. The default one is `rowModel`, which selects the entire row, including all columns.

If we execute the preceding code, we will have the following output:

Contacts		
Name	Email	Phone
Loiane	me@loiane.com	1234-5678
Peter	peter@email.com	2222-2222
Ane	ane@email.com	3333-3333
Harry	harry@email	4444-4444
Camile	camile@email.com	5555-5555

Ext.grid.plugin.RowEditing

The **RowEditing** plugin enables editing in a particular row of the grid. When you click on the row, the editor (a form) will open and we can edit the row values:

```
Ext.create('Ext.grid.Panel', {
    renderTo: Ext.getBody(),
    frame: true,
    store: Contacts,
    width: 350,
    title: 'Contacts',
    selType: 'rowmodel',
    columns: [{
        text: 'Name',
        flex: 1,
        dataIndex: 'name'
    },{
        text: 'Email',
        flex: 1,
        dataIndex: 'email',
        editor: {
            xtype:'textfield',
            allowBlank:false
        }
    },{
        text: 'Phone',
        flex: 1,
        dataIndex: 'phone',
        editor: {
            xtype:'textfield',
            allowBlank:false
        }
```

```
    }],
    plugins: [
        Ext.create('Ext.grid.plugin.RowEditing', {
            clicksToEdit: 1
        })
    ]
});
```

In the preceding code, we declared the `RowEditing` plugin in the `plugins` declaration. As in the `CellEditing` example, we also set `clicksToEdit` to 1, so the user will have to click only once on the row to open the editor.

We need to add the editor to the `columns/cells`; otherwise the column will not be editable, just like the `CellEditing` plugin.

We also highlighted the `selType` line in the preceding code. We set its value to `rowmodel`, meaning that, when we click on a row in the grid, the entire row will be selected, including all its columns.

When we execute the preceding code, we will have the following output:

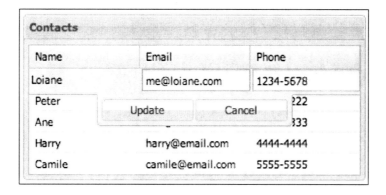

Saving the data to the server

To save the data to the server, we need to change the Store to support the four CRUD (**create, read, update, delete**) actions, as follows:

```
var Contacts = Ext.create('Ext.data.Store', {
    model: 'Contact',
    proxy: {
        type: 'ajax',
        api: {
            read : 'contact/view.php',
            create : 'contact/create.php',
```

```
                update: 'contact/update.php',
                destroy: 'contact/delete.php'
            },
            reader: {
                type: 'json',
                root: 'data',
                successProperty: 'success'
            },
            writer: {
                type: 'json',
                writeAllFields: true,
                encode: false,
                root: 'data'
            }
        }
    }
});
```

We can also add a toolbar with **Add** and **Delete** buttons to the grid, to perform all the four CRUD operations:

```
var rowEditor = Ext.create('Ext.grid.plugin.RowEditing', {
    clicksToEdit: 1
})

var grid = Ext.create('Ext.grid.Panel', {
    //other config options
    plugins: rowEditor,
    dockedItems: [{
        xtype: 'toolbar',
        items: [{
            text: 'Add',
            handler : function() {
                rowEditor.cancelEdit();

                // Create a record instance through the ModelManager
                var r = Ext.ModelManager.create({
                    name: 'New Contact',
                    email: 'newcontact@email.com',
                    phone: '1111-1111'
                }, 'Contact');

                Contacts.insert(0, r);
                rowEditor.startEdit(0, 0);
            }
        },{
```

```
                 text: 'Delete',
                 handler: function() {
                     var sm = grid.getSelectionModel();
                     rowEditor.cancelEdit();
                     Contacts.remove(sm.getSelection());
                     if (store.getCount() > 0) {
                         sm.select(0);
                     }
                 }
            }]
        }]
    });
```

And, if we want to, we can also create another button in the toolbar to save all our actions with the following code in the handler function:

```
Contacts.sync()
```

This way, we will save all the operations we performed on the grid, at once.

 If we want to automatically save the data after every operation, we need to add the config option autoSync to the Store. However, this will generate a request to the server for every update, save, or delete action. If the user is going to perform many CRUD operations in the grid, autoSync may not be the best option; instead, the save handler function would be ideal.

Infinite scrolling

Ext JS 4 also introduces the **infinite scrolling** grid, used for rendering thousands of records without using the **paging** feature. If you worked with Ext JS 3 and tried to display a few thousands records at once, you know it took a big effort to make it work.

To implement an infinite scrolling grid, we just have to configure some properties in the Store and in the Grid. First, let's see how the Store looks:

```
Ext.define('Book', {
    extend: 'Ext.data.Model',
    fields: [
        {name: 'book'},
        {name: 'pages', type: 'int'}
    ]
```

```
});

var store = Ext.create('Ext.data.Store', {
    id: 'store',
    pageSize: 50,
    buffered: true,
    purgePageCount: 0,
    model: 'Book',
    proxy: {
        type: 'ajax',
        url : 'data/infinite.json',
        reader: {
            type: 'json',
            root: 'data'
        }
    }
});
store.guaranteeRange(0, 49);
```

In the preceding code snippet, we have a Model for book. We will display a book and its page number.

Then, we have a variable store and we configured three extra properties. The first one is pageSize (we have to configure this property to use it with paging), where we set how many records we will be buffering at once—we have to set the pageSize even if we are not going to use the paging feature. The second property that we configured is buffered, which is going to buffer and pre-fetch pages of records if we set it as true. The third property we set is the purgePageCount, which represents how many pages we are going to cache before purging more records. When we set its value to zero (0), it indicates that we are never going to purge pre-fetched data.

And finally, we call the guaranteeRange method, passing 0 and 49 (which is a number lower than the value of pageSize). This method will load the variable store with the specific number of records passed as the parameter and then will take care of any additional loading required to display the total number of records.

And finally, we have the grid declaration:

```
var grid = Ext.create('Ext.grid.Panel', {
    width: 400,
    height: 500,
    title: 'Bufffered Grid - 50k records',
    store: store,
    verticalScrollerType: 'paginggridscroller',
    invalidateScrollerOnRefresh: false,
```

```
        disableSelection: true,
        columns:[{
            text: 'Book Name',
            flex:1 ,
            sortable: true,
            dataIndex: 'book'
        },{
            text: 'Pages',
            width: 125,
            sortable: true,
            dataIndex: 'pages'
        }],
        renderTo: Ext.getBody()
    });
```

We need to configure three additional properties to a simple grid to turn it into an infinite scrolling grid.

The first property is `verticalScrollerType`; in this case, we will set it as `paginggridscroller`. The second one is `invalidateScrollerOnRefresh`, which, if set to `false`, will not refresh the scrollbar when we refresh the view. The third one is `disableSelection`, which we have to set as `false`, because the infinite grid does not support selection.

The preceding code will output the following grid:

Bufffered Grid - 50k records	
Book Name	Pages
Book 1	509
Book 2	553
Book 3	953
Book 4	23
Book 5	494
Book 6	161
Book 7	242
Book 8	209
Book 9	19
Book 10	575
Book 11	673
Book 12	512

Tree panel

The **tree** component is much more simplified in Ext JS 4. Like `grid`, it is also a subclass of `Ext.panel.Table`. This means we can add most functionality of the grid in the tree as well.

Let's start declaring a simple tree in Ext JS 3:

```
new Ext.tree.TreePanel({
    renderTo: 'tree-example',
    title: 'Simple Tree',
    width: 200,
    rootVisible: false,

    root: new Ext.tree.AsyncTreeNode({
        expanded: true,
        children: [
            { text: "Menu Option 1", leaf: true },
            { text: "Menu Option 2", expanded: true,
                children: [
                        { text: "Sub Menu Option 2.1", leaf: true },
                        { text: "Sub Menu Option 2.2", leaf: true}
                ] },
            { text: "Menu Option 3", leaf: true }
        ]
    })
});
```

Now, let's see how to declare the same `tree` in Ext JS:

```
Ext.create('Ext.tree.Panel', {
    title: 'Simple Tree',
    width: 200,
    store: Ext.create('Ext.data.TreeStore', {
        root: {
            expanded: true,
            children: [
                { text: "Menu Option 1", leaf: true },
                { text: "Menu Option 2", expanded: true,
                    children: [
                        { text: "Sub Menu Option 2.1", leaf: true },
                        { text: "Sub Menu Option 2.2", leaf: true}
                    ] },
                { text: "Menu Option 3", leaf: true }
```

```
            ]
        }
    }),
    rootVisible: false,
    renderTo: 'tree-example'
});
```

In Ext JS 4, we also have the `title`, `width`, and `div` properties, where the tree is going to be rendered, and a config `store`. The `store` config is a new element for the tree.

If we output both of the codes, we will have the same output, which is the following `tree`:

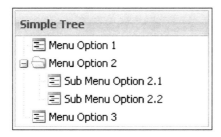

If we take a look at the data package, we will see three files related to `tree`: `NodeInterface`, `Tree`, and `TreeStore`.

`NodeInterface` applies a set of methods to the prototype of a record to decorate it with a **Node API**. The `Tree` class is used as a container of a series of nodes and `TreeStore` is a `store` implementation used by a `Tree`. The good thing about having `TreeStore` is that we can use its features, such as proxy and reader, as we do for any other Store in Ext JS 4.

Drag-and-drop and sorting

The **drag-and-drop** feature is very useful for rearranging the order of the nodes in the `Tree` class.

Adding the drag-and-drop feature is very simple. We need to add the following code into the `tree` declaration:

```
Ext.create('Ext.tree.Panel', {
    store: store,
    viewConfig: {
        plugins: {
            ptype: 'treeviewdragdrop'
```

```
            }
       },
       //other properties
   });
```

And how do we handle drag-and-drop in `store`?

We do it in the same way as we handled the edition plugin on the Grid, using a Writer:

```
var store = Ext.create('Ext.data.TreeStore', {
    proxy: {
        type: 'ajax',
        api: {
            read : '../data/drag-drop.json',
            create : 'create.php'
        }
    },
    writer: {
        type: 'json',
        writeAllFields: true,
        encode: false
    },
    autoSync:true
});
```

> In the earlier versions of Ext JS 4, the `autoSync` config option does work. Another way of synchronizing the `Store` with the server is adding a listener to the `Store` instead of the `autoSync` config option, as follows:
>
> ```
> listeners: {
>     move: function( node, oldParent, newParent, index,
> options ) {
>         this.sync();
>     }
> }
> ```

And, to add the sorting feature to the `Tree` class, we simply need to configure the `sorters` property in the `TreeStore`, as follows:

```
Ext.create('Ext.data.TreeStore', {
    folderSort: true,
    sorters: [{
        property: 'text',
        direction: 'ASC'
    }]
});
```

Check tree

To implement a **check tree**, we simply need to make a few changes in the data that we are going to apply to the Tree. We need to add a property called checked to each node, with a true or false value; true indicates the node is checked, and false, otherwise.

For this example, we will use the following json code:

```
[{
    "text": "Cartesian",
    "cls": "folder",
    "expanded": true,
    "children": [{
        "text": "Bar",
        "leaf": true,
        "checked": true
    }, {
        "text": "Column",
        "leaf": true,
        "checked": true
    }, {
        "text": "Line",
        "leaf": true,
        "checked": false
    }]
}, {
    "text": "Gauge",
    "leaf": true,
    "checked": false
}, {
    "text": "Pie",
    "leaf": true,
    "checked": true
}]
```

And as we can see, the code is the same as that for a simple tree:

```
var store = Ext.create('Ext.data.TreeStore', {
    proxy: {
        type: 'ajax',
        url: 'data/check-nodes.json'
    },
    sorters: [{
        property: 'leaf',
```

```
        direction: 'ASC'
    }, {
        property: 'text',
        direction: 'ASC'
    }]
});

Ext.create('Ext.tree.Panel', {
    store: store,
    rootVisible: false,
    useArrows: true,
    frame: true,
    title: 'Charts I have studied',
    renderTo: 'tree-example',
    width: 200,
    height: 250
});
```

The preceding code will output the following tree:

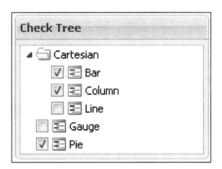

Tree grid

In Ext JS 3, the client JavaScript Component, `Tree Grid`, was an extension part of the ux package. In Ext JS 4, this Component is part of the native API but it is no longer an extension. To implement a `Tree Grid`, we are going to use the `Tree` Component as well; the only difference is that we are going to declare some columns inside the tree. This is the good part of `Tree` being a subclass of `Ext.panel.Table`, the same super class for `Grid` as well.

First, we will declare a `Model` and a `Store`, to represent the data we are going to display in the `Tree Grid`. We will then load the `Tree Grid`:

```
Ext.define('Book', {
    extend: 'Ext.data.Model',
```

```
    fields: [
        {name: 'book',      type: 'string'},
        {name: 'pages',      type: 'string'}
    ]
});

var store = Ext.create('Ext.data.TreeStore', {
    model: 'Book',
    proxy: {
        type: 'ajax',
        url: 'data/treegrid.json'
    },
    folderSort: true
});
```

So far there is no news. We declared the variable store as any other used in a grid, except that this one is a TreeStore.

The code to implement the Component Tree Grid is declared as follows:

```
Ext.create('Ext.tree.Panel', {
    title: 'Books',
    width: 500,
    height: 300,
    renderTo: Ext.getBody(),
    collapsible: true,
    useArrows: true,
    rootVisible: false,
    store: store,
    multiSelect: true,
    singleExpand: true,
    columns: [{
        xtype: 'treecolumn',
        text: 'Task',
        flex: 2,
        sortable: true,
        dataIndex: 'task'
    },{
        text: 'Assigned To',
        flex: 1,
        dataIndex: 'user',
        sortable: true
    }]
});
```

The most important line of code is highlighted—the `columns` declaration. The `columns` property is an array of `Ext.grid.column.Column` objects, as we declare in a grid.

The only thing we have to pay attention to is the column type of the first column, that is, `treecolumn`; this way we know that we have to render the node into the `Tree Grid`.

We also configured some other properties. `collapsible` is a Boolean property; if set to `true` it will allow us to collapse and expand the nodes of the tree. The `useArrows` is also a Boolean property, which indicates whether the arrow icon will be visible in the tree (expand/collapse icons). The property `rootVisible` indicates whether we want to display the root of the tree, which is a simple period (.). The property `singleExpand` indicates whether we want to expand a single node at a time and the `multiSelect` property indicates whether we want to select more than one node at once.

The preceding code will output the following tree grid:

Form

The class `FormPanel` provides a container for forms. We usually use a form for data management. In Ext JS 4, `FormPanel` consists of `Fields`, `FieldContainer`, `FieldSet`, `Label`, and `Actions`. We will start with an example of form fields, explaining each one of them.

Form fields

Ext JS 4 introduces the `Ext.form.field` package, where all the form fields belong. We will look into each one of the classes from the previous diagram, with examples. First, we will declare a form with some fields:

```
Ext.create('Ext.form.Panel', {
    frame: true,
    title: 'Form Fields',
    width: 340,
    bodyPadding: 5,
    renderTo: 'form-example',

    fieldDefaults: {
        labelAlign: 'left',
        labelWidth: 90,
        anchor: '100%'
    },

    items: [{
        xtype: 'hiddenfield', //1
        name: 'hiddenfield1',
        value: 'Hidden field value'
    },{
        xtype: 'displayfield', //2
        name: 'displayfield1',
        fieldLabel: 'Display field',
        value: 'Display field <span style="color:red;">value</span>'
    },{
        xtype: 'textfield', //3
        name: 'textfield1',
        fieldLabel: 'Text field',
        value: 'Text field value'
    },{
        xtype: 'textfield', //4
        name: 'password1',
        inputType: 'password',
        fieldLabel: 'Password field'
    },{
        xtype: 'textareafield', //5
        name: 'textarea1',
        fieldLabel: 'TextArea',
        value: 'Textarea value'
    },{
        xtype: 'filefield', //6
```

```
      name: 'file1',
      fieldLabel: 'File upload'
},{
      xtype: 'timefield', //7
      name: 'time1',
      fieldLabel: 'Time Field',
      minValue: '8:00 AM',
      maxValue: '5:00 PM',
      increment: 30
},{
      xtype: 'datefield', //8
      name: 'date1',
      fieldLabel: 'Date Field',
      value: new Date()
},{
      xtype: 'combobox', //9
      fieldLabel: 'Combobox',
      displayField: 'name',
      store: Ext.create('Ext.data.Store', {
         fields: [
             {type: 'string', name: 'name'}
         ],
         data: [
             {"name":"Alabama"},
             {"name":"Alaska"},
             {"name":"Arizona"},
             {"name":"Arkansas"},
             {"name":"California"}
         ]
      }),
      queryMode: 'local',
      typeAhead: true
},{
      xtype: 'numberfield',
      name: 'numberfield1', //10
      fieldLabel: 'Number field',
      value: 20,
      minValue: 0,
      maxValue: 50
},{
      xtype: 'checkboxfield', //11
      name: 'checkbox1',
      fieldLabel: 'Checkbox',
      boxLabel: 'box label'
```

```
        },{
           xtype: 'radiofield', //12
           name: 'radio1',
           value: 'radiovalue1',
           fieldLabel: 'Radio buttons',
           boxLabel: 'radio 1'
        },{
           xtype: 'radiofield', //13
           name: 'radio1',
           value: 'radiovalue2',
           fieldLabel: '',
           labelSeparator: '',
           hideEmptyLabel: false,
           boxLabel: 'radio 2'
        },{
           xtype: 'multislider', //14
           fieldLabel: 'Multi Slider',
           values: [25, 50, 75],
           increment: 5,
           minValue: 0,
           maxValue: 100
        },{
           xtype: 'sliderfield', //15
           fieldLabel: 'Single Slider',
           value: 50,
           increment: 10,
           minValue: 0,
           maxValue: 100
        }]
    });
```

In the preceding code, after we set the width and height of the form, we declared the fieldDefaults property. This property contains the configuration applied to all label instance fields (subclasses of Ext.form.field.Base or Ext.fom. FieldContainer). As all fields in the preceding form are subclasses of Ext.form. field.Base, the default config applies to all fields. In the previous example, we said that the alignment of the label should be at the left of the form; the labelWidth should be 90 pixels and all fields are going to use 100% of the available width (anchor: '100%').

The previous form will have the following output:

Now, we will look into the `fields`/`items` declarations:

- The first field we declared is a **hidden field** (`xtype:'hiddenfield'`). This field stores hidden values, which we do not want to show to the user but want to submit to the server. We can use a hidden field to store the ID information; we do not want to display the ID in the form, but we want to send it back to the server, say to perform updates.

- The second field we declared is a **display field** (`xtype:'displayfield'`). This field is useful when we want to display read-only information in the form.

- The third field we declared is a **text field** (`type:'textfield'`). The text field is a simple input field, where the user can enter any information.

- The fourth field is a **text field** as well (`type 'password'`), which means this field is going to mask the input value.

- The fifth field is a **textarea** (`xtype 'textareafield'`). It is a multiline text input field, where the user can enter multiple lines of information. `TextArea` is a subclass of the `Text` field.

- The sixth field is a **file upload field** (xtype:'filefield'), also known as **File Uploader**. This field contains a button used to browse for a file at the user's machine end, and the text field will display the path of the file. This field is also a subclass of the Text field.

Next, we have some fields from the Trigger class, which also have Text as a super class. The trigger fields contain a trigger button. The Trigger fields are Picker or Spinner. Picker contains a button, which opens a picker popup to select the value, such as the combobox, date picker, and time picker. The Spinner fields contain a spinner with up and down buttons, such as the number field.

- The seventh field we declared is a **time field** (xtype: 'timefield'), which is a trigger field. In the time field, we can also configure minValue and maxValue, which are the minimum time and maximum time, set in this example as 8:00 AM and 5:00 PM, respectively. We can also set the increment interval (set to 30 minutes in this example), which means the field is going to display 8 AM, 8:30 AM, 9 AM, and so on.

- The eighth field is a **date field** (xtype: 'datefield'). The date field is also a trigger field used to handle dates. In the preceding example, it is set to a default value — the current date.

- The ninth field is a combo box, which is also a **trigger field**: (xtype:'combobox' or 'combo'). The combo box needs a Store to load the information that is going to populate it. In this example, we declared the config, store that loads the data from the memory. displayField is the field we are going to display in the combo box.

- The tenth field is a **number field** (xtype:'numberfield'). numberfield is a spinner field with up and down buttons, used to increase and decrease the value. In the previous example, the default value is 20, the minimum value is 0, and the maximum value is 50. If we want to remove the spinner button and leave it as a number text field, we have to add the following config:

```
hideTrigger: true,
keyNavEnabled: false,
mouseWheelEnabled: false
```

- The eleventh field we declared is a **checkbox** (xtype: 'checkboxfield' or 'checkbox'). We have also set a value for the label.

- The next two fields are **radio fields** (xtype:'radiofield' or 'radio'). The Radio class is a subclass of Checkbox, which is why the config is very similar.

- The fourteenth field is a **multi-slider field** (xtype:'multislider'). To configure this field, we can set an array of default, minimum, and maximum values, and also the increment interval.

- The same applies to the **single slider field** (xtype:'slider' or 'sliderfield'), but instead of multiple values, we have a single one.

Validation

Having only a form to load and update information is not useful without validating the data the user has input, correct?

Ext JS 4 also provides a validation mechanism. Let's see an example of how to validate some fields:

```
Ext.create('Ext.form.Panel', {
    frame: true,
    title: 'Form Fields Validation',
    width: 340,
    bodyPadding: 5,
    renderTo: 'form-example',

    fieldDefaults: {
        labelAlign: 'left',
        labelWidth: 90,
        anchor: '100%',
        msgTarget: 'under'
    },

    items: [{
        xtype: 'textfield',
        name: 'textfield1',
        fieldLabel: 'Required',
        allowBlank: false //1
    }, {
        xtype: 'textfield',
        name: 'textfield2',
        fieldLabel: 'Min 2',
        minLength: 2 //2
    }, {
        xtype: 'textfield',
        name: 'textfield3',
        fieldLabel: 'Max 5',
        maxLength: 5 //3
    }, {
```

```
        xtype: 'textfield',
        name: 'textfield7',
        fieldLabel: 'Regex - Phone',
        regex: /^\d{3}-\d{3}-\d{4}$/, //4
        regexText: 'Must be in the format xxx-xxx-xxxx'
    },{
        xtype: 'textfield',
        name: 'textfield4',
        fieldLabel: 'Email',
        vtype: 'email' //5
    },{
        xtype: 'textfield',
        name: 'textfield5',
        fieldLabel: 'Alpha',
        vtype: 'alpha' //6
    },{
        xtype: 'textfield',

        name: 'textfield6',

        fieldLabel: 'AlphaNum',

        vtype: 'alphanum' //7
    },{
        xtype: 'textfield',
        name: 'textfield6',
        fieldLabel: 'Url',
        vtype: 'url' //8
    },{
        xtype: 'textfield',
        name: 'textfield8',
        fieldLabel: 'Custom: IP Address',
        vtype: 'IPAddress' //9
    }]
});
```

First, if we need to validate the information, we have to display something to the user if the data is not valid. To do so, we can configure msgTarget (message target location). It can take the following values: side, under, or top. In the preceding example, we configure it to be displayed under the field for all fields, but we can also configure each field separately.

The first validation (comment 1) is the `allowBlank` form field. This is a Boolean property, which, if set to `true`, will allow the user to leave the field blank. If it is set to `false`, the user will have to enter a value—it cannot be left blank—otherwise, the form will display an error message.

Then, we have the `minLength` and `maxLength` validations (comment 2 and comment 3), through which we can set a value for the minimum number of characters and the maximum number of characters. In the preceding example, the `minLength` is set to 2 and the `maxLength` to 5. Therefore, if the user inputs only one character or more than five characters, the form will display an error message.

We can perform another validation by creating a regular expression for the field (comment 4). In the previous example, we set a `regex` property. The input field value must have the following format: xxx-xxx-xxxx, where x can be any number from zero to nine. We can also configure the error message that the form will display to the user, in case the field does not match the regular expression.

The form package provides some validation types, also known as `vtype`. There are validations that are available, such as `email`, `alpha`, `alphanum`, and `url`.

A field with a validation type `email` (comment 5) must have a value in the format of an e-mail address, such as `email@something.com`.

A field with a validation type `url` (comment 6) must have a value in the format of a URL, such as `http://something.com`.

A field with validation type `alpha` (comment 7) allows the user to enter alphabetic values only, that is, from *A* to *Z* (lowercase and uppercase), and underscore (_).

A field with validation type `alphanum` (comment 8) allows the user to enter alphabetic and numeric values, that is, from *A* to *Z* (lowercase and uppercase), *0* to *9*, and underscore (_).

We can also create a customized validation type and reuse it. Let's create a validation type, `vtype`, to validate an IP address:

```
Ext.apply(Ext.form.field.VTypes, {
    IPAddress:  function(v) {
        return /^\d{1,3}\.\d{1,3}\.\d{1,3}\.\d{1,3}$/.test(v););
    },
    IPAddressText: 'Must be a numeric IP address',
    IPAddressMask: /[\d\.]/i
});
```

On the `IPAddress` function, we applied a regular expression that validates an IP address. The regular expression is only valid when the user enters an IP address with the format *xxx.xxx.xxx.xxx*, where *x* must be a digit (number), and the user can enter one, two, or three digits. The IPs *1.1.1.1*, or *1.11.111.111*, or *111.111.111.111* are valid examples.

The preceding validation type is named as `IPAddress` (comment 9), and we used it on the last field declared in the previous form.

If we try to execute the preceding code and enter some invalid values in the form fields, we will get some errors, as shown in the following screenshot:

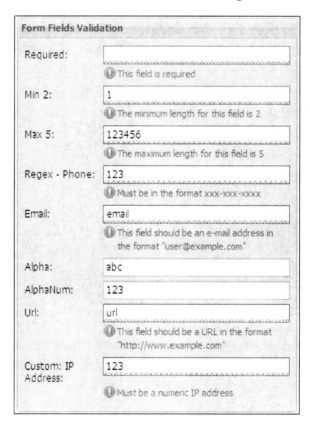

Form label

A **label** is simply text that can be displayed inside a form. We can use the following code to display a label:

```
Ext.create('Ext.form.Panel', {
    title: 'Form with Label',
    width: 100,
    bodyPadding: 10,
    renderTo: 'form-example',
    items: [{
        xtype: 'label',
        forId: 'myFieldId',
        text: 'Just a Label',
        margins: '0 0 0 10'
    }]
});
```

We can add a label in the `items` property of a form and use it with other form fields as well. The preceding code will output the following form:

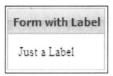

Actions

We can handle two kinds of actions within forms: loading the data and submitting the data. We will implement an example where we have two buttons: one to load the data from the server and another to send the data to the server:

```
Ext.create('Ext.form.Panel', {
    title: 'Book Info',
    renderTo: 'form-example',
    width: 300,
    bodyPadding: 5,
    fieldDefaults: {
        labelAlign: 'left',
        labelWidth: 90,
        anchor: '100%'
    },
    items: [{
        xtype: 'hiddenfield',
        name: 'bookId'
```

```
        },{
            xtype: 'textfield',
            name: 'bookName',
            fieldLabel: 'Title'
        },{
            xtype: 'textfield',
            name: 'bookAuthor',
            fieldLabel: 'Author'
        }],
        buttons: [{
            text: 'Load',
            handler: function() {
                var form = this.up('form').getForm();
                form.load({
                    url: 'data/form.json',
                    failure: function(form, action) {
                        Ext.Msg.alert("Load failed", action.result.
errorMessage);
                    }
                });
            }
        },{
            text: 'Submit',
            handler: function() {
                var form = this.up('form').getForm();
                form.submit({
                    url: 'form-submit.php',
                    waitMsg: 'Sending the info...',
                    success: function(fp, o) {
                        Ext.Msg.alert('Success', 'Form submitted.');
                    }
                });
            }
        }]
    });
```

To load data for populating the form, we need to call the `load` action. To do so, we need to specify the `url` config to load the data from; we can pass any additional parameter and we can also handle any error message.

When we load data to populate the previous form, the data should have the following format:

```
{
    success: true,
    data: {
        bookId: 10,
        bookName: "Ext JS 4 First Look",
        bookAuthor: "Loiane Groner"
    }
}
```

 We have to match the name of the field with the name of the data that we are loading.

And to submit the data, we simply need to call the `submit` action and pass a `url` to send the data to. We can also handle any error message and add a 'waiting' message to be displayed while the form is being submitted.

The previous form will have the following output:

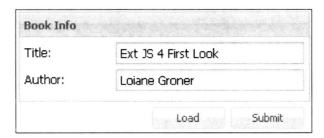

Summary

This chapter covered some really important changes made to the grid, tree, and form package. Related to these components, we covered some new features, plugins, and API changes, using hands-on examples.

In the next chapter, we will learn step-by-step how to create a new Ext JS 4 theme with Sass and Compass.

6
Ext JS 4 Themes

Ext JS 4 provides a new engine to create new themes. It is now much easier to create and customize themes than it was in Ext JS 3.

In this chapter, we will cover how to create a new theme using the CSS3 features:

- Install Sass and Compass
- Create a new Ext JS 4 theme
- Create new UI Components
- Support legacy browsers

Getting started with Ext JS 4 themes

If you have already tried to customize an Ext JS 3 theme, you know that it was a complicated task— and a bit annoying, too. You had to open Firebug, inspect every single element, go to the CSS file, and then change it to a new color/background, and so on. Some Components of Ext JS 3 were composed of some images, such as the Button Component. If we wanted to change the button color, we had to create new images and then apply them to the Ext JS 3 button.

All of these complications are no longer present in Ext JS 4. Version 4 introduces a new way to customize and create new themes, using CSS3 features.

Ext JS 4 uses Sass and Compass to create themes. If you take a look at the Ext JS 4 `resources` folder, you will see that there are folders and files that will help us to create and customize a theme (Ext JS 3 does not contain these files):

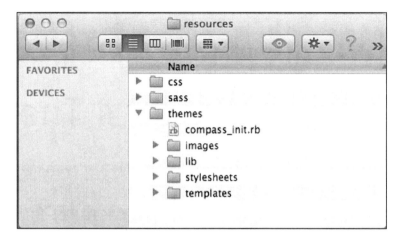

Installing Ruby

Sass and Compass are Ruby gems, which are Ruby package managers. Prior to the installation of these gems, we need to install Ruby.

Windows and Mac OS

If you use Windows, go to `http://rubyinstaller.org/` and download the latest version.

If you use Mac OS, you do not need to worry, because Ruby comes installed on Mac OS. However, on the Sencha website, they recommend that you install XCode (it installs all required dependencies); to install XCode, please go to `http://developer.apple.com/xcode/`.

Linux

If you use Linux, well, there are several Linux distributions available today, and the best way to install Ruby is to use the default package manager for the particular distribution that you use.

Ubuntu and Debian

Debian, Ubuntu, and other Debian-derived Linux distributions use the *apt-get* tool to manage package installation. If you are running Ubuntu Linux and get the following output from the Ruby command, you need to install Ruby:

```
$ ruby

The program 'ruby' is currently not installed.  You can install it by
typing:
sudo apt-get install ruby

-bash: ruby: command not found
```

To install Ruby, simply run the *apt-get* command, as follows:

```
sudo apt-get install ruby
```

Red Hat Enterprise and Fedora

Red Hat Enterprise Linux and Fedora Linux both use the **YUM** installation manager and the Red Hat Package Manager (**RPM**). The first step is to verify if Ruby is already installed. This can be achieved using the following rpm command:

```
rpm -q ruby

package ruby is not installed
```

If Ruby is not installed, it can be installed using the YUM Update Manager. This needs to be performed as root, so the superuser password will be required:

```
su -

yum install ruby
```

Installing Sass and Compass

Sass is a CSS 3 extension and Compass is an open source CSS3 framework. To learn more about them and how they work, please visit http://sass-lang.com/ and http://compass-style.org/.

After installing Ruby, we need to install Sass and Compass gems. If you are using Windows, go to **Start Command Prompt with Ruby** from the **Start** menu and type the following command:

```
gem install compass
```

You should get something like the following:

```
Start Command Prompt with Ruby
ruby 1.9.2p290 (2011-07-09) [i386-mingw32]

C:\Users\Loiane>gem install compass
Fetching: sass-3.1.7.gem (100%)
Fetching: chunky_png-1.2.0.gem (100%)
Fetching: fssm-0.2.7.gem (100%)
Fetching: compass-0.11.5.gem (100%)
Successfully installed sass-3.1.7
Successfully installed chunky_png-1.2.0
Successfully installed fssm-0.2.7
Successfully installed compass-0.11.5
4 gems installed
Installing ri documentation for sass-3.1.7...
Installing ri documentation for chunky_png-1.2.0...
Installing ri documentation for fssm-0.2.7...
Installing ri documentation for compass-0.11.5...
Installing RDoc documentation for sass-3.1.7...
Installing RDoc documentation for chunky_png-1.2.0...
Installing RDoc documentation for fssm-0.2.7...
Installing RDoc documentation for compass-0.11.5...

C:\Users\Loiane>
```

After the gem installation, type `compass -v` and `sass -v` to verify if everything is ok on your computer:

```
Start Command Prompt with Ruby
C:\Users\Loiane>compass -v
Compass 0.11.5 (Antares)
Copyright (c) 2008-2011 Chris Eppstein
Released under the MIT License.
Compass is charityware.
Please make a tax deductable donation for a worthy cause: h
s

C:\Users\Loiane>sass -v
Sass 3.1.7 (Brainy Betty)

C:\Users\Loiane>_
```

If you are using Mac OS (or Linux), please open the terminal application
(/Applications/Utilities/Terminal.app on Mac OS) and type:

```
sudo gem intall compass
```

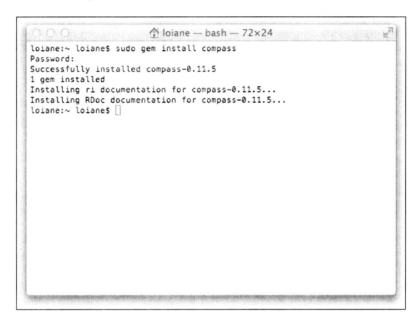

After the installation, please check if everything is ok by typing compass -v and
sass -v:

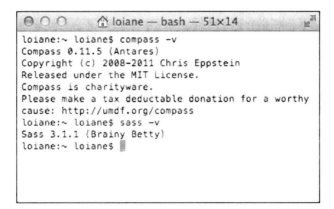

Now we are ready to create Ext JS 4 themes!

Setting up an Ext project

Before we get started with Ext JS 4 theming, we need to make couple of adjustments. First, let's create a new Ext application named `appName`; inside this application, we will paste the `extjs` folder (that you downloaded from the Sencha website). The folder structure should look like the following:

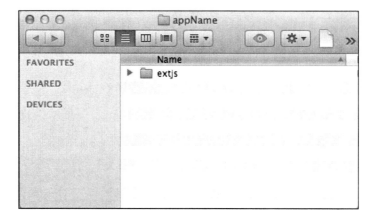

Now, let's copy the `index.html` and `themes.js` file from the `extjs/examples/themes` folder and paste them into the `appName` folder:

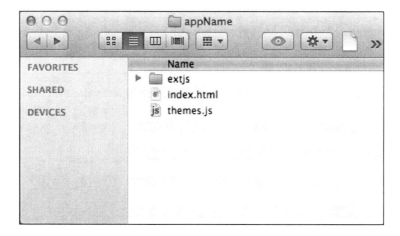

Open the `index.html` file and make the required changes so that the file can contain the following code:

```
<html>
    <head>
        <meta http-equiv="Content-Type" content="text/html;
charset=utf-8" />
```

```
        <title>Ext JS 4 Themes</title>

        <link rel="stylesheet" type="text/css" href="extjs/resources/
css/ext-all.css" />

        <script type="text/javascript" src="extjs/bootstrap.js"></
script>

        <script type="text/javascript" src="themes.js"></script>
    </head>
    <body>
    </body>
</html>
```

Open the `index.html` page and you should see something like the following (and other Components as well):

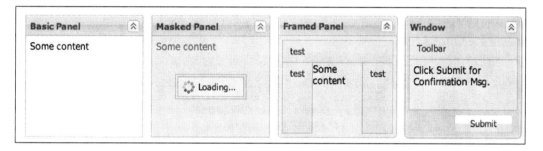

Now, we will set up the custom theme files. Open the folder `extjs/resources/themes/templates` and copy the folder `resources` to the root of the `appName` folder. Also copy the `images` folder from `extjs/resources/themes` and paste it into the `appName/resources` folder. The `appName` folder structure should look like the following:

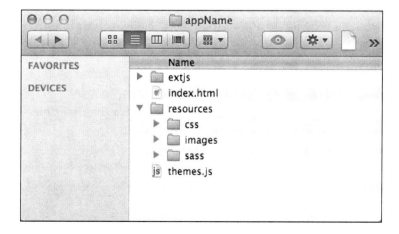

Open the file located at `appName/resources/sass/config.rb` and change the line 4 to:

```
$ext_path = "../../extjs"
```

Save the file and close it.

The project setup is now completed. Let's create a new theme!

Creating a new theme

Before we get started, we will compile the `my-ext-theme.scss` file with no changes, just to make sure everything is working correctly. Delete the file `appName/resources/css/my-ext-theme.css`.

Now, open the terminal application and change the folder to `appName/resources/sass`, and then type the command `compass compile`, as displayed in the following image:

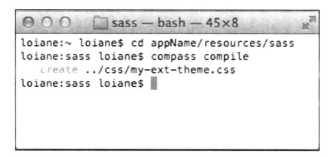

Since the file `appName/resources/css/my-ext-theme.css` does not exist, it will be created.

Open the `index.html` file again and change the CSS file import to the following and reload the page:

```
<link rel="stylesheet" type="text/css" href="resources/css/my-ext-
theme.css" />
```

The page should look just as it did when we opened it for the first time.

Open the file `appName/resources/sass/my-ext-theme.scss`; let's take a look at it:

```
$include-default: false; //1

// Insert your custom variables here. //3
```

```
// $base-color: #aa0000; //4

@import 'compass'; //6
@import 'ext4/default/all'; //7

@include extjs-boundlist; //9
@include extjs-button;
@include extjs-btn-group;
@include extjs-datepicker;
@include extjs-colorpicker;
@include extjs-menu;
@include extjs-grid;
@include extjs-form;
    @include extjs-form-field;
    @include extjs-form-fieldset;
    @include extjs-form-checkboxfield;
    @include extjs-form-checkboxgroup;
    @include extjs-form-triggerfield;
    @include extjs-form-htmleditor;
@include extjs-panel;
@include extjs-qtip;
@include extjs-slider;
@include extjs-progress;
@include extjs-toolbar;
@include extjs-window;
@include extjs-messagebox;
@include extjs-tabbar;
@include extjs-tab;
@include extjs-tree;
@include extjs-drawcomponent;
@include extjs-viewport; //34

$relative-image-path-for-uis: true;
```

At line 1, we have the variable `$include-default` set to `false`. This means we want to create a compact CSS file that does not include all the Components. This is very useful when your application uses only a few Components, not all the available Components that are provided by Ext JS. This way you can create a compact CSS file with only the Components you need to use.

The lines 6 and 7 contain the library and file imports. First, we import the compass library and then we import all the SCSS files that are within the `appName/extjs/resources/themes/stylesheets/ext4/default` folder This folder contains all file SCSS files with Ext JS default styles. When we execute the compass command, the new theme will be generated according to the default Ext theme, but with the changes that we applied. Throughout this chapter, we will dive into more details about these concepts.

The lines 9 to 34 contain *includes* of the Components; this means that we are importing all the Ext JS themes. You can edit it and include only the Components you are going to use (if you set `$include-default` to `false`).

However, if you want to customize all the Components, you can remove the lines 9 to 34 and change `$include-default` to `true`. This way, the CSS file will contain styles for every Ext Component.

The lines 3 and 4 are with comments. In this section, we will add our custom variables. If we want to change the default color scheme to any other color, we simply need to declare the `$base-color` variable and set it to the color we want.

And, in the last line (line 36), we have `$relative-image-path-for-uis` set to `true`. If this variable is set to `true`, it will change the location of the theme images to be relative instead of within the Ext JS folder. If the value is `true`, the path will be `appName/resources/images/`. If we set it to `false`, it is going to use the images within the Ext JS folder. It is very important to set this variable to `true` if we want to create a new theme and support legacy browsers. We have to manually generate the images to support legacy browsers. We will talk about this issue later on, but, for now, we will keep this variable set as `true`. If you want to change the image's paths to other values, you can set a string value with the image's path instead of the value `true`.

In this chapter, we will create a custom theme for all Components, so we will change the previous file a little bit to reflect the following:

```
$include-default: true;

@import 'compass';
@import 'ext4/default/all';

$relative-image-path-for-uis: true;
```

Compile the file again with compass (the `compass compile` command) and reload the `index.html` page:

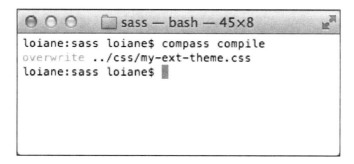

We should get a message that `my-ext-theme.css` has been overwritten.

Now the fun begins! We will insert a `$base-color` variable. When we compile the SCSS again, it will change the bluish default text theme color to a greenish color:

```
$include-default: true;
$base-color: #bbe4b6; //green-ish
@import 'compass';
@import 'ext4/default/all';
$relative-image-path-for-uis: true;
```

Type `compass compile` on the terminal again (we should get a `the overwrite ../css/my-ext-theme.css` message) and reload the `index` page:

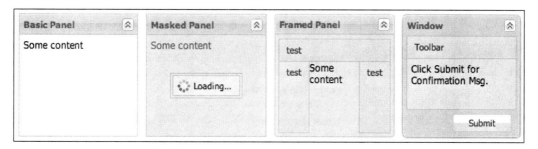

Now, all the Components have this green color. It is much easier than customizing a theme in Ext JS 3 and we spent less than 10 minutes doing it.

Another thing that is very important to pay attention to is that, for every single change that we make in the SCSS file, we have to compile it again. To see the changes on our Ext application, we simply need to reload the page—we do not need to redeploy the app or do anything complex. This is also a big accomplishment for the Ext JS 4 framework.

Variables

What are the options that we have to customize an Ext JS 4 theme using Sass and Compass? If we want to change the background color of the panel, how do we do it?

All the defined variables for each Ext JS 4 Component are located in the `appName/extjs/resources/themes/stylesheets/ext4/default/variables` folder:

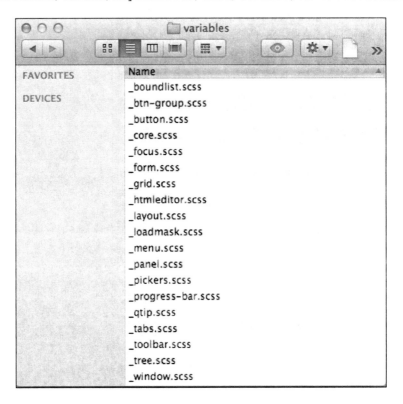

Let's open the _panel.scss file and see the contents and take a look at some variables:

```
$panel-border-radius: null !default;
$panel-border-width: 1px !default;
$panel-border-color: adjust-color($base-color, $hue: 0.844deg,
$saturation: 7.644%, $lightness: -8.627%) !default;
```

If we compare the CSS properties with the declared variables, we will have the following comparison:

CSS Property	Variable
border-radius	panel-border-radius
border-width	panel-border-width
border-color	panel-border-color

The variable for the background color of the panel body is `panel-body-background-color`, and, for the window body background color, is `window-body-background-color`. It is very intuitive.

Now, let's change some variables in our `my-ext-theme.scss` file. Add the following variables to it:

```
$include-default: true;

$base-color: #bbe4b6; //green-ish

$panel-border-radius: 3px;
$panel-header-font-size: 16px;

@import 'compass';
@import 'ext4/default/all';

$relative-image-path-for-uis: true;
```

Type the `compass compile` command again and reload the `index.html` page. You will see the differences in the panel border radius and the panel header font size (it will be bigger):

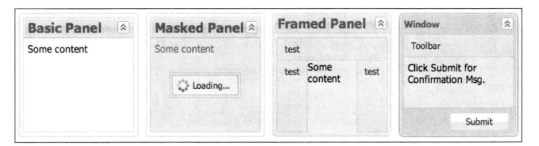

Note that we only change the panel header font size. The window header font size is still the same.

And, we can keep playing with variables and changing them as we like.

Bugs in earlier versions of Ext JS 4.1

If you are using an earlier version of Ext JS 4.1, when you customize a theme by changing the `base-color`, you will note that some Components do not have their color changed—they still show the bluish Ext JS default color scheme. To fix this, add the following variables in the `my-ext-theme.scss` file to change it—after Ext JS 4.1, everything works as expected:

```
//grid
$grid-header-over-border-color: adjust-color($base-color, $hue:
-0.175deg, $saturation: 25.296%, $lightness: -2.549%) !default;

//accordion
$accordion-header-background-color: adjust-color($base-color, $hue:
-1.333deg, $saturation: -3.831%, $lightness: 4.51%) !default;

//toolbar
$toolbar-separator-color: adjust-color($base-color, $hue: 0deg,
$saturation: 0.542%, $lightness: 7.843%) !default;

//buttons
$btn-group-background-color: adjust-color($base-color, $hue:
-1.333deg, $saturation: -3.831%, $lightness: 4.51%) !default;
$btn-group-border-color: adjust-color($base-color, $hue: 0deg,
$saturation: 7.644%, $lightness: -8.627%) !default;
$btn-group-inner-border-color: lighten($base-color, 20%) !default;
```

```
$btn-group-header-color: #000 !default;
$btn-group-header-background-color: $btn-group-background-color;


//menus
$menu-item-active-background-color: lighten($base-color, 20%)
!default;
$menu-item-active-border-color: darken($base-color, 40%) !default;
```

Creating new Ext JS Component UIs

Sometimes we want to change the theme of a single Component to use it in a very specific case, without changing the default theme of the Component. For example, in the application, we have greenish windows as part of the default theme, yet we want to display a red window in a particular situation. In other words, we want to use both windows in the application, but with a different theme.

Some Ext JS 4 Components have Sass mixins, which allow us to create new UIs. Some of these Components are panel, button, and window.

For example, we will create a new UI for the Window Component. The first step is to take a look at the file appName/extjs/resources/themes/stylesheets/ext4/default/widgets/_window.scss. Open it and go to the lines 68-82. Copy this block of code and paste it into the my-ext-theme.scss file. Make the required changes, so it looks like this:

```
@include extjs-window-ui(
    'custom',

    $ui-border-radius: 10px,
    $ui-border-color: darken($base-color, 40%),
    $ui-inner-border-color:darken($base-color, 30%),

    $ui-header-color: darken($base-color, 60%),

    $ui-body-border-color: darken($base-color, 30%),
    $ui-body-background-color: $window-body-background-color,
    $ui-body-color: darken($base-color, 30%),

    $ui-background-color: $base-color
);
```

We can change it as we like, but the most important point to note is that we changed the second line from default to custom. This change will allow us to use both UIs in a project.

To apply the changes, use the `compass compile` command on the file `my-ext-theme.scss` again.

Now, we will create a new file to see how the UI that we created looks.

Create a new file named `index2.html` and paste the following content into it:

```
<html>
<head>
<title>Ext JS 4 Themes</title>
<link rel="stylesheet" type="text/css" href="resources/css/my-ext-theme.css" />

<script type="text/javascript" src="extjs/bootstrap.js"></script>

<script type="text/javascript" src="custom-window.js"></script>

</head>
<body>

    <div id="defaultUIWindow" style="padding:100px;"></div>
    <div id="customUIWindow" style="padding:150px;"></div>
</body>
</html>
```

We also need a file named `custom-window.js`. The content will be as follows:

```
Ext.require([
    'Ext.window.*'
]);

Ext.onReady(function() {

    Ext.createWidget('window', {

        renderTo: 'defaultUIWindow',
            width   : 150,
            height  : 150,

            title: 'Window',

            bodyPadding: 5,
            html         : 'Some text here',

            collapsible: false,
```

```
            closable:false

    }).show();

    Ext.createWidget('window', {
        ui:'custom',

        renderTo: 'customUIWindow',
          width   : 150,
          height  : 150,

          title: 'Window',

          bodyPadding: 5,
          html        : 'Some text here',

          collapsible: false,
          closable:false

    }).show();
});
```

In the previous code, we created two windows. Both contain the same configuration, which means they look the same, except for a small detail—in the second window, we also declared a property called `ui`. This means the first window will use the default UI, and in the second one, we apply the UI we just created.

When we execute the preceding code, we will get the following output:

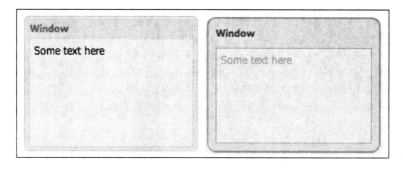

We can use different UIs for a Component in the same application, without needing to create a new theme.

Complete my-ext-theme.scss file

We are now done editing the `my-ext-theme.scss` file. This is how it should look:

```scss
@import 'compass';
@import 'ext4/default/all';

$include-default: true;

$base-color: #bbe4b6; //green-ish

$panel-border-radius: 3px;
$panel-header-font-size: 16px;

//---To fix bug on Ext JS 4.1 previous versions: BEGIN

//grid
$grid-header-over-border-color: adjust-color($base-color, $hue:
-0.175deg, $saturation: 25.296%, $lightness: -2.549%) !default;

//accordion
$accordion-header-background-color: adjust-color($base-color, $hue:
-1.333deg, $saturation: -3.831%, $lightness: 4.51%) !default;

//toolbar
$toolbar-separator-color: adjust-color($base-color, $hue: 0deg,
$saturation: 0.542%, $lightness: 7.843%) !default;

//buttons
$btn-group-background-color: adjust-color($base-color, $hue:
-1.333deg, $saturation: -3.831%, $lightness: 4.51%) !default;
$btn-group-border-color: adjust-color($base-color, $hue: 0deg,
$saturation: 7.644%, $lightness: -8.627%) !default;
$btn-group-inner-border-color: lighten($base-color, 20%) !default;
$btn-group-header-color: #000 !default;
$btn-group-header-background-color: $btn-group-background-color;

//menus
$menu-item-active-background-color: lighten($base-color, 20%)
!default;
$menu-item-active-border-color: darken($base-color, 40%) !default;

//---To fix bug on Ext JS 4.1 previous versions: END
```

```
@include extjs-window-ui(
    'custom',

    $ui-border-radius: 10px,
    $ui-border-color: darken($base-color, 40%),
    $ui-inner-border-color:darken($base-color, 30%),

    $ui-header-color: darken($base-color, 60%),

    $ui-body-border-color: darken($base-color, 30%),
    $ui-body-background-color: $window-body-background-color,
    $ui-body-color: darken($base-color, 30%),

    $ui-background-color: $base-color
);

$relative-image-path-for-uis: true;
```

Supporting legacy browsers

This new theme engine is very nice, but there is an issue. Web applications run in a browser. Sometimes we do not know which browser the user is going to use in order to access the application, and we have to make the application work in every browser. Legacy browsers do not support these CSS3 features, and we have to use images to be able to render the corners, background gradients, and so on.

If we open the index.html file, which we are using for testing on the latest versions of Chrome, Firefox, and Internet Explorer, you will not note any issue. The browser will render the Components exactly as presented in the screenshots of this chapter. Now, let's try to open index.html in Explorer 6 or 7 and see what happens:

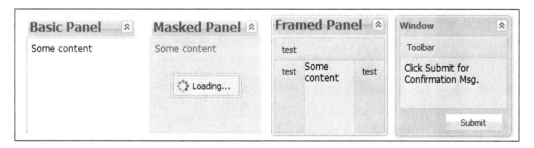

Note that the corners, the background, and the header are still bluish (the default color of the default Ext theme). That is because legacy browsers need images to render these resources.

Fortunately, Sencha has **Slice Tool**, which allows us to create images that are going to be used for legacy browsers. The Slice Tool is part of the **SDK Tools** package. To download it, go to http://www.sencha.com/products/sdk-tools/. SDK Tools are available for Window, Mac, and Linux.

After downloading and installing the Sencha SDK Tools software, let's go back to our sample application and fix the issues related to legacy browsers. Open the terminal and change the folder to appName. Then, execute the following command:

```
sencha slice theme -d extjs -c resources/css/my-ext-theme.css -o
resources/images -v
```

Let's take a look at each option of this command:

- --ext-dir[=]value, -d[=]value (required): This represents the path to the root of Ext JS 4 folder.

- --css[=]value, -c[=]value: This represents the path to the CSS file that we created with Sass/Compass. It is optional; if we do not provide any CSS file, it is going to use the Ext JS default one.

- --output-dir[=]value, -o[=]value: This represents the path to generate all the custom theme images. The default path is to the root folder.

- --verbose, -v: This displays a message for every image that is generated.

So, as we are in the appName folder, the Ext folder is extjs and the CSS folder is resources/css/my-ext-theme.css; we want to generate the images in the resources/images folder and we also want to display a message for each image generated.

This is what you should get when you execute the previous command:

When the Sencha Slice Tool is done generating the custom images, it is going to display a **Done!** message with the same content as the previous screenshot:

```
sencha slice theme -d extjs -c resources/css/my-ext-theme.css -o
resources/images -v

Sencha Theme Generator

Copyright (c) 2011 Sencha Inc.

Generating theme images, please wait...

Saving sprite resources/images/menu/menu-item-active-bg

Saving sprite resources/images/btn/btn-default-small-corners

Saving sprite resources/images/btn/btn-default-small-sides

Saving sprite resources/images/btn/btn-default-small-bg

Saving sprite resources/images/btn/btn-default-small-over-corners

Saving sprite resources/images/btn/btn-default-small-over-sides

Saving sprite resources/images/btn/btn-default-small-over-bg

Saving sprite resources/images/btn/btn-default-small-focus-corners

Saving sprite resources/images/btn/btn-default-small-focus-sides

Saving sprite resources/images/btn/btn-default-small-focus-bg

Saving sprite resources/images/btn/btn-default-small-pressed-corners

Saving sprite resources/images/btn/btn-default-small-pressed-sides

//more saving sprite messages…

Done!
```

When we try to open the index.html page in a legacy browser again, it should work fine.

There is another issue—if we try to open the index2.html page in a legacy browser, we will see a black-and-white window, as follows:

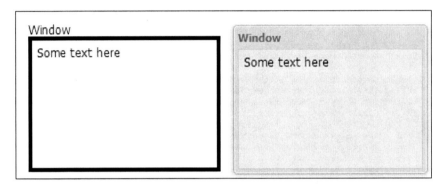

This is because we also have to generate images for this custom mixin. We will execute the Sencha slice theme command again, with an extra option:

- --manifest [=] value, -m[=] value: This is the path to your Theme Generator JSON manifest file, for example, manifest.js. This option will use the default packaged manifest, if not provided.

The manifest.js file will tell the slicing tool which custom widget we want, to generate the custom images. For example, we want to generate images for legacy browsers, for this we created custom Window Component. Our manifest.js file will look like this:

```
Ext.onReady(function() {
    Ext.manifest = {
        widgets: [
            {
                xtype: 'widget.window',
                ui   : 'custom'
            }
        ]
    };
});
```

The widget.window is the Component we created—a custom UI. You can list all the UIs you created in this file. It is very important for the Ext.manifest to be inside the Ext.onReady function. We will create this file inside the appName/resources folder.

Now, we will execute the slice command again:

```
sencha slice theme -d extjs -c resources/css/my-ext-theme.css -o
resources/images -m resources/manifest.js -v
```

The terminal will look something like this:

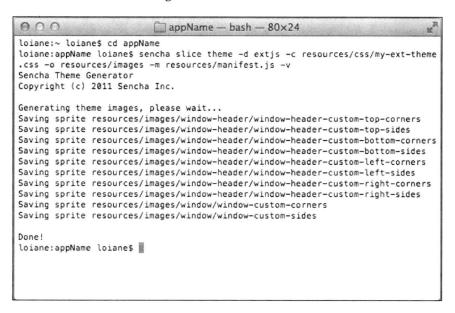

Open the `index2.html` file in a legacy browser again. Now, it will look like it should!

Remember, you will execute the Sencha Slice tool with the `manifest` option only if you create custom UIs. If you do not create custom UIs, you do not need to execute it.

Missing custom images

Let's open the index.html file again (in any browser). Note that there are still some icons that are not customized:

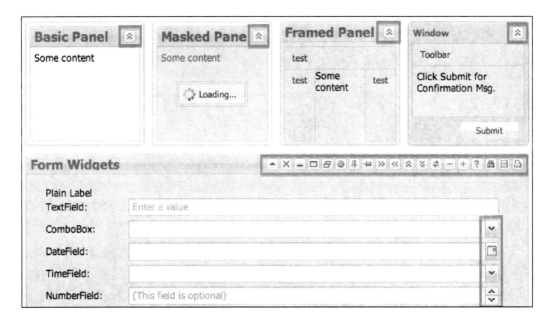

These icons are not in the slice tool yet and, unfortunately, you will have to customize these manually (if you do not mind using the default ones). To create these new icons, you can use GIMP, Fireworks, Photoshop, or any other graphics edition software.

These icons are the only things not yet customized. But as you can see, creating custom themes in Ext JS 4 is much easier than creating them in Ext JS 3, where you had to do everything manually.

Summary

In this chapter, we covered how to customize an Ext JS 4 theme from scratch. To do so, we covered how to install Sass/Compass and how to create and compile an SCSS file. We also covered how to solve issues while using legacy browsers, creating the required images using Sencha SDK tools.

In the next chapter, we will learn more about the new Ext JS MVC architecture and will create an application using this new way of developing Ext JS applications.

7

MVC Application Architecture

Ext JS 4 introduces a new way of building Ext JS applications.

In this chapter, we will discuss how to create an application by using the new MVC architecture. We'll cover:

- The new MVC application architecture
- The Ext.ComponentQuery and Ext.container.Container queries
- Creating an application the old-fashioned way
- Migrating or creating an application in the new MVC architecture
- Useful tips to develop an MVC application
- Building the application for production

The new MVC application architecture

When we develop an example application, we usually write only one JavaScript file that contains all our code. However, real-world applications are larger than a simple data grid or form. Usually, we have layout combinations, panels, forms, trees, data grids, and other Components. And, if we are managing data, we need to use **Models** (**Records**, in previous Ext versions) and **Stores**. There are a lot of Components; how do we organize all these Components? Do we have to put them in a single JavaScript file? Do we create a couple of JavaScript files and try to organize these components in these two files? Do we create a JavaScript file for every piece of the application?

The development phase is over; the application is in production already, but the work is not over yet—you also need to maintain the application. But, if the application is written in a single JavaScript file, it must be a really big file. You can get confused or get lost. Maybe it is not the best option.

Each developer will have his/her own way to organize an Ext JS application. Until Ext JS 4, there was no pattern to organize an Ext JS application. That is why, in Ext JS4, Sencha introduces us to the new MVC architecture, already used by Sencha Touch applications.

The new Ext JS 4 MVC architecture introduces a new way to organize the code (and, as a result, reduces the amount of code you will have to write). The application structure follows an MVC-like pattern. **MVC** is the **Model-view-controller** pattern (if you do not know what MVC is or how it works, please go to `http://en.wikipedia.org/wiki/Model-view-controller`, for further reading).

There are a few MVC architecture definitions. The Ext JS 4 MVC architecture work is defined by:

- **Model**: This is a collection of fields and their data. It is defined by the `Model` class (called `Record` in Ext's earlier versions). We also use the `Store` class to present/persist the data.
- **View**: This is a Component. It can be a data grid, tree, panel, form, and so on.
- **Controllers**: This is where the action happens, say, what happens when the user clicks on a button.

We will create an application the old-fashioned way (in a single file), and then we will learn how to migrate/create the same application using the MVC architecture.

Creating a sample application the old-fashioned way

Before we get our hands on the MVC architecture, we will create a sample application. As this application is a simple sample (and as it is small), we will declare everything in a single JavaScript file. Then, we will learn how to migrate this app to the Ext MVC pattern.

Our sample application looks like the following:

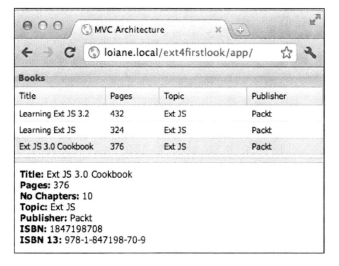

It is a data grid with some book information, and when we click on a grid row, we will see more information about the book in the **details panel** below the grid.

Let's try to list everything we need to build this sample app:

- First, we need a model where we will declare all the book fields
- Then, we need a store to load the book information and populate the grid
- As we need to populate a data grid, we also need to implement one
- For the details panel, we need to implement a panel
- And to display the book details, we need a template
- We need to implement the listener, so that when the user clicks on a row of the grid, the app will update the book details on the template
- And at last, we need a viewport/container to hold the grid and the details panel

This is how the application's directory structure is going to look:

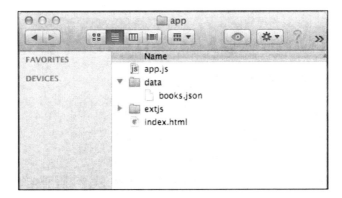

All the Components we listed previously are part of the file app.js. Let's take a look at their implementation:

1. Implement a Model:

```
Ext.define('Book',{
    extend: 'Ext.data.Model',
    fields: ['id','title','pages','numChapters',
            'topic','publisher','isbn','isbn13']
});
```

It is a simple Model, with a few fields. There is nothing special about it.

2. Implement a Store:

```
var store = Ext.create('Ext.data.Store', {
    model: 'Book',
    proxy: {
        type: 'ajax',
        url: 'data/books.json'
    }
});
```

This variable store is going to load the books.json file that is inside the data folder, as you can check in the project's directory structure, displayed in the previous screenshot.

The books.json file contains an array of book models, as follows:

```
[
    {
        "id": 11,
```

```
        "title": 'Learning Ext JS 3.2',
        "pages": 432,
        "numChapters": 17,
        "topic": 'Ext JS',
        "publisher": 'Packt',
        "isbn": '1849511209',
        "isbn13": '978-1-849511-20-9'
    },
    {
        "id": 12,
        "title": 'Learning Ext JS',
        "pages": 324,
        "numChapters": 14,
        "topic":'Ext JS',
        "publisher":'Packt',
        "isbn": '1847195148',
        "isbn13": '978-1-847195-14-2'
    },
    {
        "id": 13,
        "title": 'Ext JS 3.0 Cookbook',
        "pages": 376,
        "numChapters": 10,
        "topic":'Ext JS',
        "publisher":'Packt',
        "isbn": '1847198708',
        "isbn13": '978-1-847198-70-9'
    }
]
```

3. Create a variable grid, where we are going to display some book information:

```
var grid = Ext.create('Ext.grid.Panel', {
    store: store,
    title: 'Books',
    columns: [
        {text: "Title", width: 120, dataIndex: 'title', sortable:
true},
        {text: "Pages", flex: 1, dataIndex: 'pages', sortable:
true},
        {text: "Topic", width: 115, dataIndex: 'topic', sortable:
true},
        {text: "Publisher", width: 100, dataIndex: 'publisher',
sortable: true}
    ],
    viewConfig: {
        forceFit: true
    },
    region: 'center'
});
```

This `grid` is also a simple grid; there's nothing advanced about it. We simply:

- ° Declared the `store` config
- ° Gave a `title` to the grid, declared some columns

We are not displaying all the columns that are in the Book model. We want the columns to fit in the grid width, so we are forcing the fit

- ° Declared the `region` as `center`, because we are going to render this grid in a viewport later.

4. Create the details panel to display the book details:

```
var details = Ext.create('Ext.panel.Panel',{
    id: 'bookDetail',
    bodyPadding: 7,
    bodyStyle: "background: #ffffff;",
    html: 'Please select a book to see additional details.',
    height: 150,
    split: true,
    region: 'south'
});
```

This panel is also very simple. We are going to specify the config `id` for this panel, so we can get its reference later. We also declared a `bodyPadding` config, so the text is not very close to the border and the body of the panel will have a white background. We declared an initial message/phrase to be displayed when we render the panel; the region in the viewport where this panel is going to be rendered is `south`, and because of this, we have to declare a `height`. We also want to resize the panel, so we'll declare the `split` attribute as `true`.

5. Declare a template to format the book details in the way we want to display them in the details panel:

```
var bookTplMarkup = [
        '<b>Title:</b> {title}<br/>',
        '<b>Pages:</b> {pages}<br/>',
        '<b>No Chapters:</b> {numChapters}<br/>',
        '<b>Topic:</b> {topic}<br/>',
        '<b>Publisher:</b> {publisher}<br/>',
        '<b>ISBN:</b> {isbn}<br/>',
        '<b>ISBN 13:</b> {isbn13}<br/>'
    ];
var bookTpl = Ext.create('Ext.Template', bookTplMarkup);
```

In the variable `bookTplMarkup`, we created an HTML template to display the book details. All the description labels are in bold, followed by the respective detail, and each detail is in a single line. Then, we created an instance of the class `Ext.Template` and applied the markup as template.

6. Now that we have the grid, the panel, and the template, let's create a listener, so when the user clicks on a row of the grid, we update the template in the details panel:

```
grid.getSelectionModel().on('selectionchange', function(sm,
selectedRecord) {
        if (selectedRecord.length) {
            var detailPanel = Ext.getCmp('bookDetail');
            bookTpl.overwrite(detailPanel.body, selectedRecord[0].
data);
        }
    });
```

When the user changes the selected row, it is going to fire the `selectionchange` event. Then, we check if there is any selected row, and if positive, we get a reference of the details panel (by its `id`) and we overwrite (update) the body of the panel with the book detail information, according to the template we defined.

7. Create a **viewport** to hold these two components, as follows:

```
Ext.create('Ext.container.Viewport', {
    frame: true,
    layout: 'border',
    items: [grid,details]
});
```

The **viewport** is going to be rendered in the HTML body of the page. This viewport has a frame and we are using the Border Layout. We will only use the center (required) and south regions, because the two Components: the **grid** (in the **center** region) and the **book details panel** in the **south**.

8. We simply need to load the `Store` Component to populate the grid, thus:

```
store.load();
```

And we are done implementing the `app.js` file. The only file missing is the `index.html`:

```
<html>
  <head>
    <title>MVC Architecture</title>

      <link rel="stylesheet" type="text/css"
        href="extjs/resources/css/ext-all.css" />
    <script type="text/javascript" src="extjs/ext-all.js"></
script>

    <script type="text/javascript" src="app.js"></script>
    </head>
    <body>
    </body>
  </html>
```

It is a very small HTML page. We have a `title`, the link to the Ext JS CSS file, the import of the Ext file, and the import of the `app.js`. The body is empty, because the viewport will be rendered automatically in it.

Migrating/creating an app using the MVC architecture

Now that we are done implementing a sample app in the old way, we will implement the same application, using the MVC architecture.

One of the benefits of using the MVC architecture is the re-use of code; you will have to learn how to create an app using MVC only once, because all the other projects will follow the same steps.

Project directory structure

First, let's see how the project's directory structure looks, when we finish
implementing it:

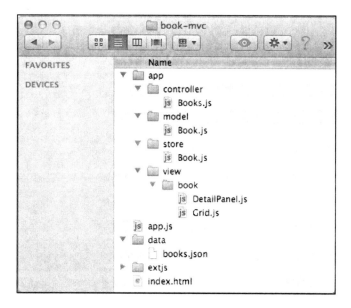

Every project you create, using the MVC architecture, will have this same structure.
So, this is how MVC projects are organized:

- `index.html`: This is the HTML page of your application.

- `app.js`: This is the JS file that will wrap the application code.

- `extjs sdk`: We need the Ext JS SDK folder because we are implementing a
  project with Ext JS.

- `data` folder: As we are not doing any integration with the server-side
  language/framework, we are loading JSON files from this folder. However,
  this is not a standard Ext JS application directory— we will use it only
  because we are not integrating our Ext JS code with server-side technology.

- `app` folder: In this folder, we will create all the Ext application files.

Before we get started with development, we will take a closer look at some of the
topics we mentioned previously.

When we start with the development of an Ext application, the first thing we add to the project is the Ext JS 4 SDK. When we download the SDK, there are a lot of files that come with it (as we discussed in *Chapter 1, What's is New in Ext JS 4?*). We do not need all of them to develop a MVC application. We need the `resources` folder, because it contains the CSS files (if you want to, you can also clear it up and leave only the files needed). We need the `ext-debug.js` or `ext.js` files, depending on the environment we are working on. If it is development, we will use `ext-debug.js`, and if it is production we will use `ext.js`. And we will need the `src` folder, which contains the source code for the Ext JS framework. Why only these files? The MVC application will load only the files it needs to execute the application; that is why we are using the `src` folder. For example, if the application uses a data grid, it will load the `Grid` Component's source code and its dependencies; if the application is not using a `Tree` Component, there is no need to load it, correct?

The **app** folder will contain all the files related to the application, and we have to organize it into four folders/packages:

- `model`: This package contains all the `Model` classes.
- `store`: This package contains all the `Store` classes.
- `view`: This package contains all the `View` Components, such as, `grid`, `panel`, `tree`, `form`, and so on—one Component per file.
- `controller`: This package contains all the Controllers related to the project.

Ext.ComponentQuery

Before we look into the creation or migration of our application, we need to learn how to use the `Ext.ComponentQuery` class.

This class is very useful when we need to control the views in the `Controller` class, and we are going to learn how to use it properly.

This class provides searching of Components within `Ext.ComponentManager` (globally) or within a specific `Ext.container.Container` in the document, with syntax similar to a CSS selector.

 For more information about the CSS selector syntax, please go to
http://www.w3schools.com/cssref/css_selectors.asp

For the next examples, we are going to use the following code:

```
var panel1 = Ext.create('Ext.panel.Panel', {
    title: 'Panel 1',
    html: 'Body 1',
    id: 'panel1Id',
    columnWidth: .25, //means 25%
    height: 120
});

var panel2 = Ext.create('Ext.panel.Panel', {
    title: 'Panel 2',
    html: 'Body 2',
    columnWidth: .25,   //means 25%
    height: 120
});

var panel3_1 = Ext.create('Ext.panel.Panel', {
    title: 'Panel 4',
    html: 'Panel 4 within Panel 3',
    height: 60
});

var panel3 = Ext.create('Ext.panel.Panel', {
    title: 'Panel 3',
    columnWidth: 1/2, //means 50%
    items:[panel3_1],
    height: 120
});

var column = Ext.create('Ext.window.Window', {
    title: 'My Window',
    id: 'myWindow',
    width: 400,
    height: 170,
    layout:'column',
    defaults: {
        bodyStyle: 'padding:10px'
    },
    items: [panel1, panel2, panel3]
});
column.show();
```

The preceding code will output a window with four panels, as displayed in the following screenshot:

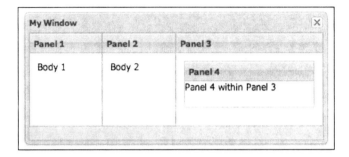

The most important function of the Ext.ComponentQuery class is **query**, which we are going to use in the next examples. This function returns an array of the matched Components from the selector string.

For example, let's say we want to know all the panels that are in the application. We can do it using two selectors:

- Ext.ComponentQuery.query('panel');
- Ext.ComponentQuery.query('.panel');

If it is a panel, we can use it, or we can use the xtype with the . prefix.

To visualize the matched panels from the selector string, we will highlight the result:

```
var resultQuery = Ext.ComponentQuery.query('panel');

var colors = ['#ACFA8A','#F4FA8A','#FAB38A','#8AE9FA','#CA8AFA',];
   for (var i = 0; i < resultQuery.length; i++) {
      resultQuery[i].body.highlight(colors[i], {duration: 10000});
}
```

The output will be as follows:

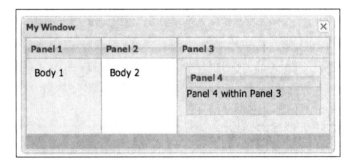

Since the `Window` class is a subclass of `Panel`, it will also be highlighted.

Now, let's try to highlight the panels that match the following selectors:

- Ext.ComponentQuery.query('panel[title="Panel 1"]'); //1
- Ext.ComponentQuery.query('#panel1Id'); //2

In the first query, we are trying to find all the panels with the title `Panel 1`. This means that we can also retrieve Components using their attributes.

In the second query, we are trying to retrieve the panel with the ID `panel1Id`. This means that we can retrieve Components using their IDs, with the # prefix.

Both these queries output the following result—only `Panel 1` is highlighted:

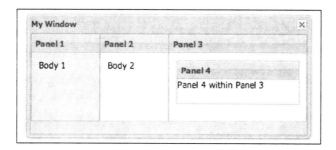

The following line of code retrieves all the panels that are children of the `column` variable (of the `Window` class):

```
Ext.ComponentQuery.query('#myWindow panel');
```

We can pass the Window's id config (`myWindow`) to make sure we will only retrieve its children (in case we have more than one `Window` Component in the application, which is not the case in this example), and we add a space with the child Component's `xtype` we are looking for (`panel`).

If we try to highlight the result of the preceding selector, we will get the following output:

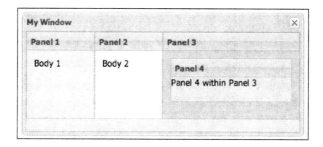

All the panels were highlighted, even the `Panel 4`, which is a child of `Panel 3`.

If we want to retrieve only the direct children of the `Window` class, we have to use the following selector:

```
Ext.ComponentQuery.query('#myWindow > panel');
```

The difference is the greater-than (>) symbol between the Window's `id` config and the Component's `xtype`. When we run the previous query, we will get the following output:

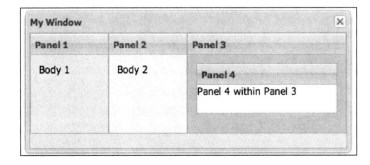

The only highlighted panels are `Panel 1`, `Panel 2`, and `Panel 3`. `Panel 4` was not highlighted, because it is not a direct child from the `Window` class in this example.

Ext.container.Container functions: query, child, down, and up

We can also use the Component itself to retrieve the Components.

Query function

The `query` function retrieves all the descendent Components that match the passed selector and executes the `Ext.ComponentQuery.query` method using the container itself as its root.

In this example, we have a variable called `column`, which is a reference to the `Window` Component. If we want to retrieve all its direct children, we can use the following code:

```
column.query('> panel');
```

The preceding code will have the same result as the `#myWindow > panel` selector.

Child function

The `child` function retrieves the first direct child of the Container that matches the passed selector. The passed-in selector must comply with an `Ext.ComponentQuery` selector.

For example, we want to retrieve the first child of the `Window` whose `title` is `Panel 2`:

```
column.child('panel[title="Panel 2"]');
```

If we highlight the result, the output will be as follows:

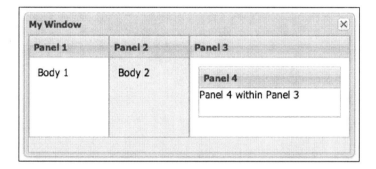

 For the `child`, `up`, and `down` functions, if the result has more than one `Component`, the functions will return the first one, not an array. That is why it is very important to specify the selector in a way that the matched `Component` is unique.

Down function competency

The `down` function retrieves the first descendant of the Container that matches the passed selector. The passed-in selector must comply with an `Ext.ComponentQuery` selector.

For example, we want to retrieve the panel with title `Panel 2`:

```
column.down('panel[title="Panel 2"]');
```

Up function

The up function walks up to the owner container, looking for an ancestor `Container` that matches the passed simple selector.

For example, let's say that we want to retrieve the parent `Panel` from `Panel 4`:

```
panel3_1.up('panel');
```

The highlighted output will be:

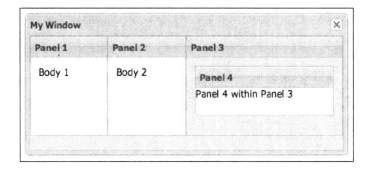

It is very important to play with selectors, because they are very helpful when we develop an Ext JS 4 application by using the new MVC architecture, as we are going to learn in the next topic.

Creating the MVC application

We will build/migrate our application step-by-step. At each step, we will explain what we have to do, present the code, and present the current application's directory structure and the current output.

Creating the book-mvc application

So, the first step is to create an application (we will call it book-mvc) and add the Ext JS 4 SDK to it. We have to do it manually.

The second step it to create an HTML page with the following content:

```
<html>
<head>
    <title>MVC Architecture</title>

    <link rel="stylesheet" type="text/css" href="exts/resources/css/
ext-all.css" />
```

```
        <script type="text/javascript" src="extjs/ext-debug.js"></script>

        <script type="text/javascript" src="app.js"></script>
    </head>
    <body>
    </body>
    </html>
```

We will not make any changes to the HTML file in further steps.

Then, we will create a JavaScript file named `app.js`, and we will implement the following:

```
Ext.require('Ext.container.Viewport');

Ext.application({
    name: 'App',

    appFolder: 'app',

    launch: function() {
        Ext.create('Ext.container.Viewport', {
            layout: 'fit',
            items: [
                {
                    xtype: 'panel',
                    title: 'Books',
                    html : 'List of books will be displayed here'
                }
            ]
        });
    }
});
```

Let's look into this file content.

The class `Ext.app.Application` represents an Ext JS 4 application, which uses a single page; this page contains a viewport with all the application's Components in it.

In the second line of code, we have `name: 'App'`, which is the name of our application. This option `name` is the name of the application, but it will also create a global variable with the app name, and it will be used as namespace for all the Models, Stores, Views, and Controllers. As the name is a string, you should use alphanumeric values; do not use spaces or special characters.

The next config option we set is `appFolder`. `appFolder` is the path to the application folder directory; in this example, we created the folder `app` to hold all our application files (Models, Stores, Views, and Controllers). We can change the name of the folder `app`, but we have to remember to change it in the `Ext.application` code as well. The default value is `app`; as we are using `app` in this example as well, we do not need to declare it.

The next declaration is the `launch` function. This function is called automatically when the application is created, so we need to implement the code to get the application running; therefore, we created a `Viewport` Component. This function also needs to be overridden by every application, because it has no implementation in its super class.

In this example, we are creating a viewport with: a panel, the `title` config as `Books`, and HTML content. So far, this is everything that our application is doing:

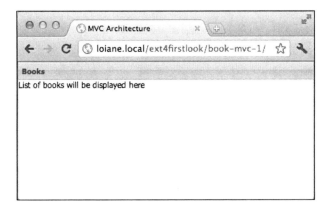

We cannot forget to create the `app` folder and its subdirectories as well. At the end of this step, we will have the following directory structure:

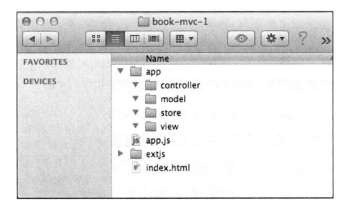

Creating the controller class

In this step, we will create a `Controller` and will integrate it with `Ext.application`.

In the `book_mvc/app/controller` folder, create the `Books.js` file with the following content:

```
Ext.define('App.controller.Books', {
    extend: 'Ext.app.Controller',

    init: function() {
        console.log('Initialized Books Controller');
    }
});
```

> We are defining the class name as `App.controller.Books`.
> This means the file that the application will be looking for is called
> `Books.js` and it is located in the `app/controller` folder. Also
> note that the class name starts with the app name we defined in
> the application `app.js` file.

The `App.controller.Books` class extends the `Ext.app.Controller` class. The `Controller` is what binds the application; it is going to communicate with `store` and `view`, and will take a specific action when a particular event is fired.

Next, we have declared the `init` function. This function will be executed before the application's `launch` function, and, in this function, we will implement all the code that will be executed before the application boots and before the creation of the viewport.

In this example, for now, we are only logging the phrase `Initialized Books Controller`. In the next step, we will implement more meaningful code, related to the application we developed in the previous topic.

We have to make some changes to the `app.js` file, as follows:

```
Ext.require('Ext.container.Viewport');

Ext.application({
    name: 'App',

    appFolder: 'app',

    controllers: ['Books'],
```

```
launch: function() {

    console.log('called function launch - application');

    Ext.create('Ext.container.Viewport', {
        layout: 'fit',
        items: [
            {
                xtype: 'panel',
                title: 'Books',
                html : 'List of books will be displayed here'
            }
        ]
    });
}
});
```

In the preceding code, we added the `controllers` declaration, and, inside the controller's array list, we listed the controller we created – `Books`. The application will try to load the `Books` controller, according to the MVC application's structure. In other words, it will look for the class `App.controller.Books` (`App` is the namespace, `controller` is the folder inside the `app` folder, and `Books` is the name of the file).

Then, we added a `log` function, which means that, when the application is launched, the log message will be showed in the JavaScript console.

The controller's `init` function will be called first, then the `launch` function, as we can see in the following screenshot:

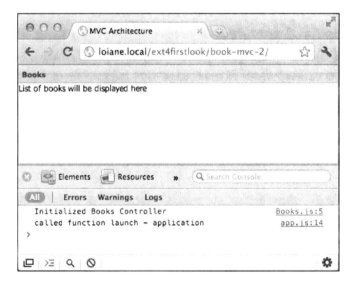

In this step, we introduced the `Controller` class, and we also integrated the controller we created with the `Ext.application` class.

In the next step, we will learn how to control a view in the `Controller` class.

The current application's directory structure for this step looks like this:

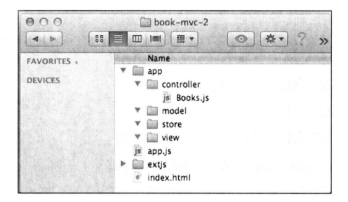

Controlling a view in the controller class

In this step, we will make a small change on the `Controller` class to see how the controller can control the events fired by the `View` Components.

This is how the `Controller` class looks:

```
Ext.define('App.controller.Books', {
    extend: 'Ext.app.Controller',

    init: function() {
        this.control({
            'viewport > panel': {
                render: this.onPanelRendered
            }
        });
    },

    onPanelRendered: function() {
        console.log('The panel was rendered');
    }
});
```

The init function is a great place to implement how the controller will interact with the view, and we usually do it using the control function. The control function listens to the events on the View classes and takes some action using the handler function. The control function uses the new ComponentQuery engine to get references from the components on the page.

In the preceding example, we will listen to the render event fired by the panel we have on the viewport. We will get all the panels that are children of the Viewport class. As we only have one, we will listen to this one. Once the panel is rendered, it will fire the render event, and we will handle it using the function onPanelRendered, which will only log a message on the console.

When we execute the application again, we will get the following output:

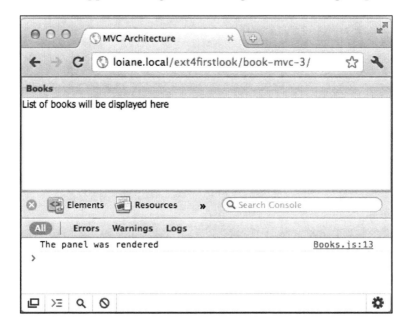

And the screenshot of the application's directory structure will be as follows:

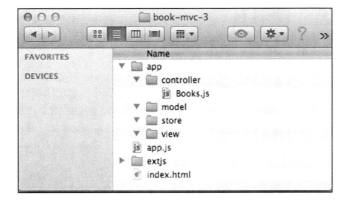

Creating the model and store classes

In the next step, we will implement every step we need to, to display the `Books` grid and list all the books in the grid.

To display the grid, we need a **Book Model**, a `Store` to load the data, and the **Books Grid**.

So, we will start declaring the **Book Model** inside the `app/model` folder. The file we will create will be named `Book.js`:

```
Ext.define('App.model.Book',{
    extend: 'Ext.data.Model',
    fields: ['id','title','pages','numChapters',
            'topic','publisher','isbn','isbn13']
});
```

The **Book Model** we declared just now is exactly the same as we declared in the application that we implemented previously, except for the name. Now, we are calling the model `App.model.Book` because of the MVC architecture. `App` is the name of the namespace we gave to the application; `model` is the folder in which we put all the models; and `Book` is the name of the file and the model we created.

The next step is to create a `Store` to load the data. We will create the file `Book.js` inside the `store` folder (because we have to put all the Stores inside the `store` folder):

```
Ext.define('App.store.Book', {
    extend: 'Ext.data.Store',
    model: 'App.model.Book',
```

```
      proxy: {
         type: 'ajax',
         url: 'data/books.json'
      }
  });
```

The code inside the Store is the same for the application we implemented previously, except for some details. The differences are located in the first three lines of the code. Earlier, we were creating a Store and assigning it to a variable called store. Now, we are defining a Store so we can instantiate it later. The model declaration is a little bit different, too. Now, we have to declare the complete name of the Model class (App.model.Book), instead of simply Book.

Next, we have to create the grid. We will create a file named Grid.js, inside the view/book folder, as follows:

```
Ext.define('App.view.book.Grid' ,{
    extend: 'Ext.grid.Panel',
    alias : 'widget.bookList',

    title: 'Books',

    initComponent: function() {

        this.store = 'Book';

        this.columns = [
            {text: "Title", width: 120, dataIndex: 'title', sortable:
    true},
            {text: "Pages", flex: 1, dataIndex: 'pages', sortable:
    true},
            {text: "Topic", width: 115, dataIndex: 'topic', sortable:
    true},
            {text: "Publisher", width: 100, dataIndex: 'publisher',
    sortable: true}
        ];

        this.viewConfig = {
            forceFit: true
          };

        this.callParent(arguments);
    }
});
```

In the preceding code, we defined a class called App.view.book.Grid; this class extends the class Grid from Ext JS 4. We also created an alias so we can instantiate this class using xtype. Then, we declared a title for the grid and, inside the initComponent, we will declare all the config options to initialize the grid. The store, columns, and viewconfig configuration options are the same as we declared in the previous application.

Now, we have to modify the controller class:

```
Ext.define('App.controller.Books', {
    extend: 'Ext.app.Controller',

    stores: ['Book'],

    models: ['Book'],

    views: ['book.Grid'],

    init: function() {

        this.getBookStore().load();
    }
});
```

We added three new configurations to the controller — stores, models, and views. In the stores config, we will list all the Stores the controller cares about. It is the same for models, where we will list all the Models important to the controller and also for views, where we will declare the list of Components the controller cares about.

We do not need to declare the complete path for these classes. The controller will try to find them by their default path — [namespace] + [name of the folder] + [name of the declared class]. In case of Book stores, it will try to find the the App.store.Book class in the app/store/Book.js file; it will try to find the App.model.Book model in the app/model/Book.js file, and it will try to find the the book.Grid class in the app/view/book.Grid.js path.

When we declare stores and models, the controller will automatically create getter functions for them. In this example, the controller will create the getBookStore and getBookModel get functions. The getter function follows the following naming convention for stores: get + [name of your store] + Store and get + [name of your model] + Model.

Next, we have the init function, where we are loading the Book store.

We also have to change the `app.js` file:

```
Ext.require('Ext.container.Viewport');

Ext.application({
    name: 'App',

    appFolder: 'app',

    controllers: ['Books'],

    launch: function() {
        Ext.create('Ext.container.Viewport', {
            layout: 'fit',
            items: [
                {
                    xtype: 'bookList'
                }
            ]
        });
    }
});
```

We removed the temporary panel and replaced it with the `bookList` grid we created in this step.

 The `xtype` in `Viewport` is the `alias` that we declared in the `Grid.js` file.

After we finish implementing this step, the following is the current application's directory structure:

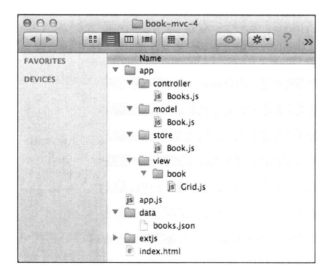

Remember to make a copy of the `data` folder, because we are now loading the book's data from it.

If we try to execute the application, we will get the following output:

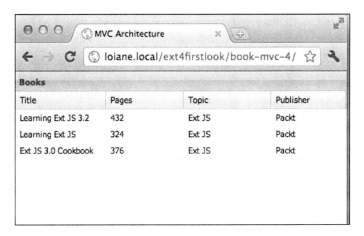

Adding the book details panel

This is our last step before we have the previous application migrated to the MVC architecture.

In this step, we will add the **details panel**.

We will create a file named `DetailPanel.js`, inside the `app/view/book` folder. According to the naming convention, this class will be defined as `App.view.book.DetailPanel`:

```
Ext.define('App.view.book.DetailPanel', {
    extend: 'Ext.Panel',

    alias: 'widget.detailPanel',

    bookTplMarkup: [
        '<b>Title:</b> {title}<br/>',
        '<b>Pages:</b> {pages}<br/>',
        '<b>No Chapters:</b> {numChapters}<br/>',
        '<b>Topic:</b> {topic}<br/>',
        '<b>Publisher:</b> {publisher}<br/>',
        '<b>ISBN:</b> {isbn}<br/>',
        '<b>ISBN 13:</b> {isbn13}<br/>'
```

```
    ],

    startingMarkup: 'Please select a book to see additional details.',

    bodyPadding: 7,

    initComponent: function() {
        this.tpl = Ext.create('Ext.Template', this.bookTplMarkup);
        this.html = this.startingMarkup;

        this.bodyStyle = {
            background: '#ffffff'
        };

        this.callParent(arguments);
    },

    updateDetail: function(data) {
        this.tpl.overwrite(this.body, data);
    }
});
```

We defined a `DetailPanel` class We also created an alias, so that we can instantiate this class using an `xtype` config later.

In the previous application, we declared a variable called `bookTplMarkup`; now, we are declaring the same variable, but as a property of this class.

We are also creating a new property called `startingMarkup`, so that we can apply it to the panel's HTML property.

We declared a `bodyPadding` config, as we had declared on the `details` variable from the previous application.

Then, we have the `initComponent` function. First, we will create a template using the class `Ext.Template`, with the property `bookTplMarkup`, and apply it to the `tpl` property of the panel. We also assigned the property `startingMarkup` to the initial `html` property of the panel. We also set the `bodyStyle` config. Next, we will call the `initComponent` function from the superclass.

We will also create a new method called `updateDetail`, so the controller can call it later, to update the book details on the template.

This is everything we need to declare in this file.

We removed direct control over the grid and the panel communication. This task will be assigned to the controller. We only have to create a method to be called from the controller; we are going to take a look at this in the next topic.

The following code is for the controller with all the changes we need in order to make the application work like the previous one, which we developed without using the MVC architecture.

```
Ext.define('App.controller.Books', {
    extend: 'Ext.app.Controller',

    stores: ['Book'],

    models: ['Book'],

    views: ['book.Grid','book.DetailPanel'],

    refs: [
            {
                ref: 'panel',
                selector: 'detailPanel'
            }
        ],


    init: function() {

        this.getBookStore().load();

        this.control({
                'viewport>bookList dataview': {
                    itemclick: this.bindGridToPanel
                }
            });
    },

    bindGridToPanel : function(grid, record) {
        this.getPanel().updateDetail(record.data);
    }
});
```

We added the `book.DetailPanel` class as a view of the controller, which means it will have control over the book details panel.

We also added a new config on the controller, the `refs` config. The `ref` system is very useful when we need to make a reference of a view inside the `Controller`. The `ref` system uses the new class `Ext.ComponentQuery` to get the reference of a view. In this example, we want to get a reference of `detailPanel` (xtype of the instance of `Panel` we created) — we named this reference `panel`; to get a reference of this panel, we simply need to call the `getPanel` function, as declared in the `bindGridToPanel` function, in the previous code.

Then, we have the `init` function, and we added a new method `control` to the controller. The line of code `'viewport > booklist dataview'` is a reference to the `dataview` of the `Grid` class that we created to display the list of all books. We are listening to the event `itemclik`, which means that, when the user clicks on a row of the grid, it will fire the `itemclick` event, and then we will call the function `bindGridToPanel`, declared below the `init` function.

Remember the `Ext.ComponentQuery` selector? The line of code `'viewport > booklist dataview'` means that we want to retrieve the first `booklist` Component of the `viewport`; this `booklist` has a `dataview` Component, which is the one that we want to get to.

The `bindGridToPanel` function simply calls the method `updateDetail`, of the book detail Panel, passing the selected record of the grid.

We are now done with our MVC application. When we execute the code, we will get the following output:

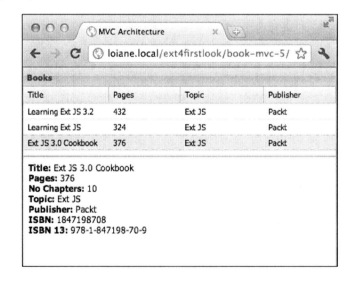

The application's directory structure is shown in the following screenshot:

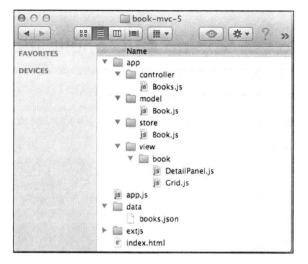

Controller getter methods

The `Controller` also has some useful methods you can use in case you have some issues using the generated getter methods:

- `getModel(name)`: This method returns a reference of the given Model name;
- `getStore(name)`: This method returns a reference of the given Store name;
- `getView(name)`: This method returns a reference of the given View name;

 The Model has to be declared properly through the `model/ store/view` JavaScript file, or those methods will never work.

For an example, we will use the same instance of `Controller` that we used, to develop the MVC application:

```
init: function() {

    this.getStore('Book').load();

    this.control({
        'viewport>bookList dataview': {
            itemclick: this.bindGridToPanel
        }
    });

}
```

As you can see, we called the method `getStore('Book')`, to get the reference of the `App.store.Book` store (alternative to `getBookStore()`).

Useful tips to develop an MVC application

Here is what we need to do when we are implementing an MVC application:

- Create the `Model`, `Store`, and `View` classes.
- We do not take any action on the `View` class; we can create *functions* that will be called by the controller.
- On the controller, we have to list the `models`, `stores`, and `views` the controller will care about.
- The controller automatically generates the *getter functions* for `Models` and `Stores`.
- To easily get a reference of a `View` on the `Controller`, we can *declare references* using the `ref` system, which uses the instance of `Ext.ComponentQuery`; the controller will create getter functions for the references.
- As Ext JS is event-driven, we have to listen to the events fired by the Views/ Components using the `control` config; we can *declare functions to handle the events.*
- The `init` function on the `Controller` is called *before* the `launch` application function.

MVC architecture can be a little difficult to learn in the beginning, but you will have to learn how it works. Once you have learned it, you can apply it to every single application you develop.

Nested models and MVC

Another issue you may find while developing with MVC is while declaring `Model` classes with *associations*.

Let's take a closer look when we declare the `Store` in a `Grid`:

```
this.store = 'Book';
```

Take a look at the following code:

```
Ext.define('App.controller.Books', {
    extend: 'Ext.app.Controller',

    stores: ['Book'],

        models: ['Book'],

    views: ['book.Grid','book.DetailPanel'],
```

We did not have to specify the complete name of the class, correct? The controller knows that it will find the Model classes inside the App[namespace]/model folder, the Store classes in the [namespace]/store folder, and the View classes in the [namespace]/view folder.

Now, let's declare a nested association using the MVC architecture. We have the class Author; an author can have many (hasMany association) books, and a book can have many chapters:

```
Ext.define('App.model.Author',{
    extend: 'Ext.data.Model',

    fields: [
        {name: 'id', type: 'int'},
        {name: 'name', type: 'string'},
    ],

    hasMany: {
        model: 'Book',
        foreignKey: 'authorId',
        name: 'books'
    },

    proxy: {
      type: 'ajax',
      url : 'data/authors/1.json',
      reader: {
          type: 'json',
          root: 'authors'
      }
    }
});
```

```
Ext.define('App.model.Book',{
    extend: 'Ext.data.Model',

    fields: [
        {name: 'id', type: 'int'},
        {name: 'title', type: 'string'},
        {name: 'pages', type: 'int'},
        {name: 'numChapters', type: 'int'},
        {name: 'authorId', type: 'int'}
    ],

    hasMany: {
        model: 'Chapter',
        foreignKey: 'bookId',
        name: 'chapters'
    }
});

Ext.define('App.model.Chapter',{
    extend: 'Ext.data.Model',

    fields: [
        {name: 'id', type: 'int'},
        {name: 'number', type: 'int'},
        {name: 'title', type: 'string'},
        {name: 'bookId', type: 'int'}
    ]
});
```

By instinct, we only declared the name of the associated model.

In the controller, we will declare the models config and will try to load an Author model and log some information about it:

```
Ext.define('App.controller.Books', {
    extend: 'Ext.app.Controller',

    models: ['Author', 'Book', 'Chapter'],

    init: function() {

        this.getAuthorModel().load(1, {

            success: function(author) {
```

```
            var books = author.books();

            console.log("Author "+ author.get('name') + " has
written " + books.getCount() + " books");

            books.each(function(book) {

                var title = book.get('title');
                var chapters = book.chapters();

                console.log("Book " + title + " has " +  chapters.
getCount() + " chapters");

                chapters.each(function(chapter) {
                    console.log(chapter.get('number') + " " +
chapter.get('title'));
                });
            });
        }
    });

    }

});
```

When we try to execute the preceding code, we will get the following error:

This is because we did not declare the complete class name on the association. Even while using the MVC architecture, we have to declare the complete path of the associated model so that Ext JS can find it:

```
Ext.define('App.model.Author',{
    extend: 'Ext.data.Model',

    fields: [
        {name: 'id', type: 'int'},
        {name: 'name', type: 'string'},
    ],

    hasMany: {
        model: 'App.model.Book',
        foreignKey: 'authorId',
        name: 'books'
    },

    proxy: {
        type: 'ajax',
        url : 'data/authors/1.json',
        reader: {
            type: 'json',
            root: 'authors'
        }
    }
});

Ext.define('App.model.Book',{
    extend: 'Ext.data.Model',

    fields: [
        {name: 'id', type: 'int'},
        {name: 'title', type: 'string'},
        {name: 'pages', type: 'int'},
        {name: 'numChapters', type: 'int'},
        {name: 'authorId', type: 'int'}
    ],

    hasMany: {
        model: 'App.model.Chapter',
        foreignKey: 'bookId',
        name: 'chapters'
    }
```

```
    });

    Ext.define('App.model.Chapter',{
        extend: 'Ext.data.Model',

        fields: [
            {name: 'id', type: 'int'},
            {name: 'number', type: 'int'},
            {name: 'title', type: 'string'},
            {name: 'bookId', type: 'int'}
        ]
    });
```

If we try to execute the application now, we will be able to read the author information from the console successfully:

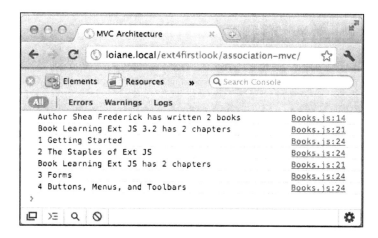

Always remember: for `Controller`, `Store`, `View`, and so on, we do not need to declare the complete class name; but, for nested associations, we do.

Building your application for production

Now that you are done with development, it is time to deploy your application for production. Sencha developed the Sencha SDK tools that we used for customizing the Ext JS 4 theme; they help us to easily generate a manifest of all Javascript dependencies in the JSB3 format (JSBuilder file format) and customize it with only the files that the application needs.

If you do not have SDK tools installed on your machine yet, please go to `http://www.sencha.com/products/sdk-tools/` and download and install it.

Now that we have the Sencha SDK tools installed, open the terminal and change the directory to where your app is located.

We will need to execute two commands. The first one is:

```
sencha create jsb -a index.html -p app.js
```

You can also point the `index` file of you local server:

```
sencha create jsb -a http://local.loiane/books-mvc/index.html -p app.jsb3
```

After executing one of the commands, a file named `app.jsb3` will be created and should look something like this:

```
{
    "projectName": "Project Name",
    "licenseText": "Copyright(c) 2011 Company Name",
    "builds": [
        {
            "name": "All Classes",
            "target": "all-classes.js",
            "options": {
                "debug": true
            },
            "files": [
                {
                    "path": "extjs/src/util/",
                    "name": "Observable.js"
                },
                {
                    "path": "extjs/src/data/",
                    "name": "Association.js"
                },
                {
                    "path": "extjs/src/data/",
                    "name": "Operation.js"
                },
                //more
            ]
        },
        {
            "name": "Application - Production",
            "target": "app-all.js",
            "compress": true,
            "files": [
                {
                    "path": "",
```

```
                    "name": "all-classes.js"
                },
                {
                    "path": "",
                    "name": "app.js"
                }
            ]
        }
    ],
    "resources": []
}
```

We can customize some information before making the build.

Then, we need to execute one more command:

`sencha build -p app.jsb3 -d .`

This command will create two files:

- `all-classes.js`: This file contains all of our application's classes. It is not minified so is very useful for debugging problems with your built application.

- `app-all.js`: This file is a minimized build of our application and contains all the Ext JS classes required to run it. It is the minified and production-ready version of all classes `.js` and `app.js` files combined.

After running the two previous commands, you should have something like the following screenshot on your terminal:

```
loiane:book-mvc loiane$ sencha create jsb -a index.html -p app.jsb3
loiane:book-mvc loiane$ sencha build -p app.jsb3 -d .
Loading the Project Name Project
Loaded 0 Packages
Loaded 2 Builds
  * Parse all-classes.js with options:
    - debug: true
    - debugLevel: 1
  * Parse app-all.js with options:
    - debug: false
    - debugLevel: 1
  * Compress and obfuscate app-all.js...
Copy resources...
Done building!

loiane:book-mvc loiane$
```

The application's directory structure should look like this:

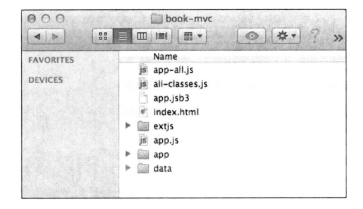

Now, we need to make a small change to the `index.html`:

```html
<html>
  <head>
    <title>MVC Architecture</title>

    <link rel="stylesheet" type="text/css" href="extjs/resources/css/
ext-all.css" />
    <script type="text/javascript" src="extjs/ext-debug.js"></script>

    <script type="text/javascript" src="app-all.js"></script>
  </head>
  <body>
  </body>
</html>
```

If you open `app-all.js`, you will see that the file is obfuscated, so it is much harder to read.

The application is now ready to be deployed!

Summary

Throughout this book, we have learned about Ext JS API and Component features. In this chapter, we covered how to put together everything that we have learned, into an application, using the new MVC architecture.

We covered what to do in each step of the process of building an application with Ext JS 4. We also demonstrated how to use the Sencha SDK tools to build the application and make it ready to be deployed in production.

Ext JS 4 Versus Ext JS 3 Class Names

Ext JS 4 introduces a new package organization and that is why some class names are not the same as they were in Ext JS 3.

When we start migrating an application from Ext JS 3 to Ext JS 4, it can get a little confusing, because some class names are different. The classes in Ext JS 4 that have changed from Ext JS 3 contain a property called `alternateClassName`, which indicates that the Ext JS 3 class names are compatible with Ext JS 4. You can still use Ext JS 3 class names when implementing an Ext JS 4 application, but it is recommended that you use the new class names.

This appendix lists all the Ext JS 4 classes that have a name compatible with Ext JS 3 classes.

Some of Ext JS 4 classes can have more than one compatible Ext JS 3 class name, so this class will appear twice (or more times) in the list:

 You can also check this list online at `http://loianegroner.com/extjs/examples/ext4-ext3-class-names/`.

Ext JS 4 Class	Alternate Class Name
Ext.button.Button	Ext.Button
Ext.button.Cycle	Ext.CycleButton
Ext.button.Split	Ext.SplitButton
Ext.chart.axis.Axis	Ext.chart.Axis
Ext.chart.axis.Category	Ext.chart.CategoryAxis

Ext JS 4 Class	Alternate Class Name
Ext.chart.axis.Numeric	Ext.chart.NumericAxis
Ext.chart.axis.Time	Ext.chart.TimeAxis
Ext.chart.series.Bar	Ext.chart.BarSeries
Ext.chart.series.Bar	Ext.chart.BarChart
Ext.chart.series.Bar	Ext.chart.StackedBarChart
Ext.chart.series.Cartesian	Ext.chart.CartesianSeries
Ext.chart.series.Cartesian	Ext.chart.CartesianChart
Ext.chart.series.Column	Ext.chart.ColumnSeries
Ext.chart.series.Column	Ext.chart.ColumnChart
Ext.chart.series.Column	Ext.chart.StackedColumnChart
Ext.chart.series.Line	Ext.chart.LineSeries
Ext.chart.series.Line	Ext.chart.LineChart
Ext.chart.series.Pie	Ext.chart.PieSeries
Ext.chart.series.Pie	Ext.chart.PieChart
Ext.ComponentManager	Ext.ComponentMgr
Ext.container.ButtonGroup	Ext.ButtonGroup
Ext.container.Container	Ext.Container
Ext.container.Viewport	Ext.Viewport
Ext.data.Model	Ext.data.Record
Ext.data.proxy.Ajax	Ext.data.HttpProxy
Ext.data.proxy.Ajax	Ext.data.AjaxProxy
Ext.data.proxy.Client	Ext.data.ClientProxy
Ext.data.proxy.Direct	Ext.data.DirectProxy
Ext.data.proxy.JsonP	Ext.data.ScriptTagProxy
Ext.data.proxy.LocalStorage	Ext.data.LocalStorageProxy
Ext.data.proxy.Memory	Ext.data.MemoryProxy
Ext.data.proxy.Proxy	Ext.data.DataProxy
Ext.data.proxy.Proxy	Ext.data.Proxy
Ext.data.proxy.Rest	Ext.data.RestProxy
Ext.data.proxy.Server	Ext.data.ServerProxy
Ext.data.proxy.SessionStorage	Ext.data.SessionStorageProxy
Ext.data.proxy.WebStorage	Ext.data.WebStorageProxy
Ext.data.reader.Array	Ext.data.ArrayReader
Ext.data.reader.Json	Ext.data.JsonReader
Ext.data.reader.Reader	Ext.data.Reader

Ext JS 4 Class	Alternate Class Name
Ext.data.reader.Reader	Ext.data.DataReader
Ext.data.reader.Xml	Ext.data.XmlReader
Ext.data.StoreManager	Ext.StoreMgr
Ext.data.StoreManager	Ext.data.StoreMgr
Ext.data.StoreManager	Ext.StoreManager
Ext.data.writer.Json	Ext.data.JsonWriter
Ext.data.writer.Writer	Ext.data.DataWriter
Ext.data.writer.Writer	Ext.data.Writer
Ext.data.writer.Xml	Ext.data.XmlWriter
Ext.dd.DragDropManager	Ext.dd.DragDropMgr
Ext.dd.DragDropManager	Ext.dd.DDM
Ext.direct.Transaction	Ext.Direct.Transaction
Ext.flash.Component	Ext.FlashComponent
Ext.FocusManager	Ext.FocusMgr
Ext.form.action.Action	Ext.form.Action
Ext.form.action.DirectLoad	Ext.form.Action.DirectLoad
Ext.form.action.DirectSubmit	Ext.form.Action.DirectSubmit
Ext.form.action.Load	Ext.form.Action.Load
Ext.form.action.Submit	Ext.form.Action.Submit
Ext.form.Basic	Ext.form.BasicForm
Ext.form.field.Base	Ext.form.Field
Ext.form.field.Base	Ext.form.BaseField
Ext.form.field.Checkbox	Ext.form.Checkbox
Ext.form.field.ComboBox	Ext.form.ComboBox
Ext.form.field.Date	Ext.form.DateField
Ext.form.field.Date	Ext.form.Date
Ext.form.field.Display	Ext.form.DisplayField
Ext.form.field.Display	Ext.form.Display
Ext.form.field.File	Ext.form.FileUploadField
Ext.form.field.File	Ext.ux.form.FileUploadField
Ext.form.field.File	Ext.form.File
Ext.form.field.Hidden	Ext.form.Hidden
Ext.form.field.HtmlEditor	Ext.form.HtmlEditor
Ext.form.field.Number	Ext.form.NumberField
Ext.form.field.Number	Ext.form.Number

Ext JS 4 Class	Alternate Class Name
Ext.form.field.Picker	Ext.form.Picker
Ext.form.field.Radio	Ext.form.Radio
Ext.form.field.Spinner	Ext.form.Spinner
Ext.form.field.Text	Ext.form.TextField
Ext.form.field.Text	Ext.form.Text
Ext.form.field.TextArea	Ext.form.TextArea
Ext.form.field.Time	Ext.form.TimeField
Ext.form.field.Time	Ext.form.Time
Ext.form.field.Trigger	Ext.form.TriggerField
Ext.form.field.Trigger	Ext.form.TwinTriggerField
Ext.form.field.Trigger	Ext.form.Trigger
Ext.form.Panel	Ext.FormPanel
Ext.form.Panel	Ext.form.FormPanel
Ext.grid.column.Action	Ext.grid.ActionColumn
Ext.grid.column.Boolean	Ext.grid.BooleanColumn
Ext.grid.column.Column	Ext.grid.Column
Ext.grid.column.Date	Ext.grid.DateColumn
Ext.grid.column.Number	Ext.grid.NumberColumn
Ext.grid.column.Template	Ext.grid.TemplateColumn
Ext.grid.Panel	Ext.list.ListView
Ext.grid.Panel	Ext.ListView
Ext.grid.Panel	Ext.grid.GridPanel
Ext.grid.property.Grid	Ext.grid.PropertyGrid
Ext.grid.property.HeaderContainer	Ext.grid.PropertyColumnModel
Ext.grid.property.Property	Ext.PropGridProperty
Ext.grid.property.Store	Ext.grid.PropertyStore
Ext.layout.container.Absolute	Ext.layout.AbsoluteLayout
Ext.layout.container.Accordion	Ext.layout.AccordionLayout
Ext.layout.container.Anchor	Ext.layout.AnchorLayout
Ext.layout.container.Border	Ext.layout.BorderLayout
Ext.layout.container.Box	Ext.layout.BoxLayout
Ext.layout.container.Card	Ext.layout.CardLayout
Ext.layout.container.Column	Ext.layout.ColumnLayout
Ext.layout.container.Container	Ext.layout.ContainerLayout
Ext.layout.container.Fit	Ext.layout.FitLayout

Ext JS 4 Class	Alternate Class Name
Ext.layout.container.HBox	Ext.layout.HBoxLayout
Ext.layout.container.Table	Ext.layout.TableLayout
Ext.layout.container.VBox	Ext.layout.VBoxLayout
Ext.menu.Item	Ext.menu.TextItem
Ext.menu.Manager	Ext.menu.MenuMgr
Ext.ModelManager	Ext.ModelMgr
Ext.panel.Panel	Ext.Panel
Ext.panel.Proxy	Ext.dd.PanelProxy
Ext.picker.Color	Ext.ColorPalette
Ext.picker.Date	Ext.DatePicker
Ext.PluginManager	Ext.PluginMgr
Ext.resizer.Resizer	Ext.Resizable
Ext.selection.Model	Ext.AbstractSelectionModel
Ext.slider.Multi	Ext.slider.MultiSlider
Ext.slider.Single	Ext.Slider
Ext.slider.Single	Ext.form.SliderField
Ext.slider.Single	Ext.slider.SingleSlider
Ext.slider.Single	Ext.slider.Slider
Ext.tab.Panel	Ext.TabPanel
Ext.tip.QuickTip	Ext.QuickTip
Ext.tip.Tip	Ext.Tip
Ext.tip.ToolTip	Ext.ToolTip
Ext.toolbar.Fill	Ext.Toolbar.Fill
Ext.toolbar.Item	Ext.Toolbar.Item
Ext.toolbar.Paging	Ext.PagingToolbar
Ext.toolbar.Separator	Ext.Toolbar.Separator
Ext.toolbar.Spacer	Ext.Toolbar.Spacer
Ext.toolbar.TextItem	Ext.Toolbar.TextItem
Ext.toolbar.Toolbar	Ext.Toolbar
Ext.tree.Panel	Ext.tree.TreePanel
Ext.tree.Panel	Ext.TreePanel
Ext.util.History	Ext.History
Ext.util.KeyMap	Ext.KeyMap
Ext.util.KeyNav	Ext.KeyNav
Ext.view.AbstractView	Ext.view.AbstractView

Ext JS 4 Class	Alternate Class Name
Ext.view.BoundList	Ext.BoundList
Ext.view.View	Ext.DataView
Ext.window.MessageBox	Ext.MessageBox
Ext.window.Window	Ext.Window
Ext.ZIndexManager	Ext.WindowGroup

Index

Q

query function 278

R

Radar Chart
  about 189, 190
  Grouped Radar Chart 191, 192
Radial axis 163
Reader class
  property 83
Record class 45
  differentiating, with Model class 42
Red Hat Enterprise 243
Red Hat Package Manager (RPM) 243
remoteSort store option 93
render event 286
resetTitle method 19
RESTful URLs
  principle 78
root config option 86
rotate property 150
rotation transformation 150
rowbody feature 213
RowEditing plugin 217
Ruby
  installing 242
Ruby installation
  Debian 243
  Linux 242
  Mac OS 242
  Ubuntu 243
  Windows 242

S

Sass
  about 243-245
  installing 243-245
Scalable Vector Graphics. *See* SVG
scale transformation 151
Scatter Chart
  about 183, 184
  Grouped Scatter Chart 185, 186
SDK Tools 260
Search box 10
selectionchange event 271

selType property 215
Sencha Touch 36
Series
  about 163
  Area Chart 180, 181
  Bar chart 164-166
  Gauge Chart 192-194
  Line Chart 173-175
  Pie Chart 186-188
  Radar Chart 189, 190
  Scatter Chart 183, 184
Series class 164
series property 156
server proxies, Ext JS 4
  about 70
  AjaxProxy 63, 71-77
  DirectProxy 63
  Ext.data.proxy.Ajax 70
  Ext.data.proxy.Direct 70
  Ext.data.proxy.JsonP 70
  Ext.data.proxy.Rest 70
  Ext.data.proxy.Server 70
  JsonP proxy 80, 82
  Rest proxy 63, 78, 79
  ScriptTagProxy 63
setTitle method 19
showMarkers property 177
Slice Tool 260
smooth property 176
sortParam 73
source codes, Ext JS 4 SDK
  builds 12
  docs 12
  examples 12
  jsbuilder 12
  overview 12
  pkgs 12
  welcome 12
Sprite 144
Sprites
  MVC diagram, drawing 152, 154
  types 146-149
Stacked Bar Chart 169, 171
startParam 73
Store class 82
store class, creating 287-291
Stores
  about 82

Thank you for buying
Ext JS 4 First Look

About Packt Publishing

Packt, pronounced 'packed', published its first book "*Mastering phpMyAdmin for Effective MySQL Management*" in April 2004 and subsequently continued to specialize in publishing highly focused books on specific technologies and solutions.

Our books and publications share the experiences of your fellow IT professionals in adapting and customizing today's systems, applications, and frameworks. Our solution based books give you the knowledge and power to customize the software and technologies you're using to get the job done. Packt books are more specific and less general than the IT books you have seen in the past. Our unique business model allows us to bring you more focused information, giving you more of what you need to know, and less of what you don't.

Packt is a modern, yet unique publishing company, which focuses on producing quality, cutting-edge books for communities of developers, administrators, and newbies alike. For more information, please visit our website: www.packtpub.com.

About Packt Open Source

In 2010, Packt launched two new brands, Packt Open Source and Packt Enterprise, in order to continue its focus on specialization. This book is part of the Packt Open Source brand, home to books published on software built around Open Source licences, and offering information to anybody from advanced developers to budding web designers. The Open Source brand also runs Packt's Open Source Royalty Scheme, by which Packt gives a royalty to each Open Source project about whose software a book is sold.

Writing for Packt

We welcome all inquiries from people who are interested in authoring. Book proposals should be sent to author@packtpub.com. If your book idea is still at an early stage and you would like to discuss it first before writing a formal book proposal, contact us; one of our commissioning editors will get in touch with you.

We're not just looking for published authors; if you have strong technical skills but no writing experience, our experienced editors can help you develop a writing career, or simply get some additional reward for your expertise.

Learning Ext JS 3.2

ISBN: 978-1-849511-20-9   Paperback: 432 pages

Build dynamic, desktop-style user interfaces for your data-driven web applications using Ext JS

1. Learn to build consistent, attractive web interfaces with the framework components

2. Integrate your existing data and web services with Ext JS data support

3. Enhance your JavaScript skills by using Ext's DOM and AJAX helpers

4. Extend Ext JS through custom components

5. An interactive tutorial packed with loads of example code and illustrative screenshots

Oracle Application Express 4.0 with Ext JS

ISBN: 978-1-84968-106-3   Paperback: 392 pages

Deliver rich desktop-styled Oracle APEX applications using the powerful Ext JS JavaScript library

1. Build robust, feature-rich web applications using Oracle APEX and Ext JS

2. Add more sophisticated components and functionality to an Oracle APEX application using Ext JS

3. Build your own themes based on Ext JS into APEX - developing templates for regions, labels, and lists

Please check **www.PacktPub.com** for information on our titles

Ext JS 3.0 Cookbook

ISBN: 978-1-847198-70-9   Paperback: 376 pages

Clear step-by-step recipes for building impressive rich internet applications using the Ext JS JavaScript library

1. Master the Ext JS widgets and learn to create custom components to suit your needs

2. Build striking native and custom layouts, forms, grids, listviews, treeviews, charts, tab panels, menus, toolbars and much more for your real-world user interfaces

3. Packed with easy-to-follow examples to exercise all of the features of the Ext JS library

4. Part of Packt's Cookbook series: Each recipe is a carefully organized sequence of instructions to complete the task as efficiently as possible

Learning jQuery, Third Edition

ISBN: 978-1-84951-654-9   Paperback: 428 pages

Create better interaction, design, and web development with simple JavaScript techniques

1. An introduction to jQuery that requires minimal programming experience

2. Detailed solutions to specific client-side problems

3. Revised and updated version of this popular jQuery book

Please check **www.PacktPub.com** for information on our titles

CPSIA information can be obtained at www.ICGtesting.com
Printed in the USA
LVOW052357050312

271690LV00003B/28/P